P9-DMC-382

UNITED STATES DIPLOMATS AND THEIR MISSIONS

UNITED STATES DIPLOMATS AND THEIR MISSIONS

A Profile of American Diplomatic Emissaries since 1778

Elmer Plischke

American Enterprise Institute for Public Policy Research
Washington, D. C.

Elmer Plischke is professor of government and politics at the University of Maryland.

ISBN 0-8447-3153-6

Foreign Affairs Study No. 16, March 1975

Library of Congress Catalog Card No. 75-709

Printed in the United States of America

CONTENTS

War, it was said, was the extension of diplomacy by other means. Modern weapons make recourse to war suicidal. It is thus not a question of giving diplomacy a chance. Diplomacy is the only chance we have.

Drew Middleton

Nations, it has frequently been observed, are judged by their representatives abroad. For this if for no other reasons governments should take special pains in selecting their envoys.

Charles W. Thayer

FOREWORD

Matthew Arnold once portrayed man as "Wandering between two worlds, / one dead, / The other powerless to be born." There is a certain relevance to these words a century later as we go through one of history's great transition periods, moving from the postwar era into the challenging and complex new world of the 1970s and 1980s. What the precise contours of that new world will be, and whether we get there safely, remain to be seen.

It is obvious that the nature of American involvement in international affairs and the conduct of our foreign policy are undergoing profound change. Two factors alone would have brought this about: (1) the development of instant communications, and (2) the introduction of nuclear weapons. But there are a dozen other developments that are now contributing to the transformation, including, among others, the population explosion, the growing shortage of food, the liquidation of the old colonial system, the energy crisis, the worldwide inflationary spiral, the great increase in the number of sovereign states, the pollution of the environment, the near collapse of the international monetary system, the increasing importance of science and technology in world affairs, the widening gap between the rich and the poor nations, the proliferation of nuclear weapons, the constantly growing interdependence of nations, and the increased resort to parliamentary diplomacy for the solution of world problems. Clearly diplomacy is not what it used to be.

If modern diplomacy differs from that of former years, so tomorrow's diplomats will differ from those who went before. Thus it is important to understand where we have been in order that we may see a little better where we are going. Studies like this one—which, in effect, is a profile of American diplomatic missions since 1778—are very valuable additions to the literature, for they shed helpful light upon the conduct of our foreign policy in an extremely difficult transition period.

The topics dealt with in this book are of such great interest to me that I cannot resist the temptation to comment briefly on three of them. They are: (1) the great expansion of the American diplomatic establishment, (2) political appointments to ambassadorial posts, and (3) the role of women ambassadors. I would also like to say a few words about the challenge diplomacy offers to young blacks in the United States.

One thing that must impress the reader of this volume is the fantastic growth of the American diplomatic establishment over the years. In the early days of the republic—when Thomas Jefferson ran the State Department with a staff of half-a-dozen people and an annual budget of something over $6,000—the United States had diplomatic relations with only a few countries in Europe: England, France, the Netherlands, Russia, and Spain, and a little later Portugal, Prussia, and Sweden. For all intents and purposes these were the states that made up the international community.

The growth was relatively slow during the nineteenth century. At the outbreak of World War I we were sending diplomatic emissaries to forty-nine countries, mainly in Europe and the Western Hemisphere. Then the process began to accelerate. By the time of the attack on Pearl Harbor the United States was exchanging diplomatic representatives with sixty nations, and in the years since 1941 we have more than doubled the size of our diplomatic representation abroad. By March 1973, we were appointing resident emissaries to 132 different countries—counting Cuba, Congo (Brazzaville), and those Arab countries with which we temporarily did not have diplomatic relations.

And the end is not yet in sight. Potential additions to the U.S. diplomatic community include such entities as North Korea, North Vietnam, Nauru, Mongolia, Mainland China, Southern Yemen (Aden), Albania, Angola, Bhutan, Mozambique, Rhodesia, and Namibia—to mention only a few of the most likely prospects. Moreover, there are thirty or forty additional territories in the world, some of which will undoubtedly aspire to statehood as the move for self-determination continues. In the next twenty years it is not unlikely that the United States will have full diplomatic relations with 160 or more nations.

In some ways this proliferation of new nations has been unfortunate, for it has brought on to the world stage a number of very small states that are neither politically stable nor economically viable. Indeed, some of them may not be strong enough to maintain their independence over the long pull. In restrospect, it would have been far better to bring a number of them into the United Nations as regional groups of states rather than as independent entities. But they all wanted independence, and they all looked upon membership in the United Nations as the symbol of their sovereign status. Under the circumstances, with the Soviet Union and certain other countries posing as the great champions of self-determination, independence, and sovereign equality, it was simply not possible for the United States to oppose the admission of these small states to the United Nations once they had gained their independence.

The proliferation has also brought in its wake many tough problems for those who conduct American foreign policy. It means, among other things, making thirty-five to forty ambassadorial appointments each year. It means a heavy burden for our diplomatic representatives in maintaining relations with all these countries. It means a great deal of extra effort in maintaining liaison and lining up support for our policies and programs in the United Nations and other international agencies. It means increased difficulties in coordinating the activities of our diplomats and our ambassadors in their posts abroad. It means many more official visits from foreign dignitaries, many of whom are anxious to come to the United States.

Diplomacy, which was once a relatively simple process, has now become vastly complicated, not only because of the growing number of complex problems we face in the world, but also because of the constantly increasing number of states with which we have to deal.

Given the growing complexity of our international relations, it is encouraging to note that the relative number of political appointments to ambassadorial posts has been declining over the years. Since World War I, Foreign Service career officers have been given some 60 percent of the appointments as chief of mission. The ratio, though it fluctuates, appears to be leveling off somewhere between 65 and 75 percent. In applauding this trend, however, one should keep in mind that the *total* number of ambassadorial posts available has increased considerably since 1945, with over thirty-five new posts in Africa alone. This obviously means a substantial increase in the number of political appointees.

From the early days of the republic, lame duck congressmen and party hacks have been rewarded with ambassadorial appointments. This is part and parcel of our political system. I certainly do not object to the appointment of a loyal party worker or a person who makes a substantial contribution to the party's campaign fund, provided always that he or she is qualified for the job. But those responsible for the conduct of our foreign policy have to contend with enough built-in handicaps without being saddled with incompetent ambassadors who are unable to represent the United States with the dignity, experience, and wisdom it deserves.

Most Foreign Service Officers of my acquaintance would agree that the appointment of a reasonable number of noncareer people to ambassadorial posts can do much to bring added strength to the Foreign Service and new vitality to our diplomatic efforts. One needs only to mention the names of David Bruce, Ellsworth Bunker, Douglas Dillon, and George McGhee—to pick a few of the most illustrious—to make the argument a convincing one. To most Americans, however, the idea of "buying" an ambassadorial appointment with a huge contribution to a political party's campaign fund is not only highly unethical but is most unbecoming to a great power like the United States.

The Senate Foreign Relations Committee, which has reasserted its authority with respect to presidential nominations in recent years, is probably the best guarantor we have for quality appointments to ambassadorial posts. The State Department, of course, is anxious to have able ambassadors represent us abroad, but it must yield from time to time to the political pressures of the White House and the major parties. The Foreign Relations Committee has relatively little to do with the nominating process, and therefore cannot assure that the President will nominate capable people. But it does have the right to say "no," and in that capacity it can prevent the appointment of poorly qualified candidates.

I recall one incident during the Eisenhower administration when the President, over the course of a year or so, sent three very weak political appointees to the Senate for confirmation. The Foreign Relations Committee, after a good deal of grumbling, approved the nominations. At the time I was serving as chief of staff of the committee, and I warned the Department of State that the committee was in a rebellious mood and that any further nominations of that type would be flatly rejected. The State Department, secretly pleased at the attitude of the committee, passed the warning on to the White House and the Republican National Committee. For many months thereafter the quality of ambassadorial candidates was markedly improved.

Statistics on the duration of ambassadorial appointments reveal yet another serious shortcoming in our diplomatic system. As Plischke shows here, in practice the turnover has been much too rapid to assure optimum results. The sad fact is that the majority of our ambassadors are not staying at their posts long enough to be fully effective. Obviously there are justifiable reasons for some of these rapid turnovers. Some missions are shortened by death or the severance of diplomatic relations. In some hardship posts where the climate is poor and living conditions unusually bad, the tour of duty is shorter than most. Nevertheless, it must be apparent to even the casual student of world affairs that it takes a considerable period of time for an ambassador to establish his credentials as a diplomat in a new country, to get acquainted with its leaders, its people, its geography, its culture and its economic and political systems. While I realize we cannot be too rigid about this, it has always seemed to me that we should expect our ambassadors going to a new post to serve from three to five years. As former Ambassador Ellis Briggs has reminded us in his *Administration of National Security:* "The most important as well as the easiest way to improve the conduct of foreign affairs would be to leave each ambassador at his post long enough for him to become fully effective."

In going over the data Plischke has compiled, one of the first figures that catches the eye is the abysmally low number of women ambassadors who have served our country abroad. It is true, of course, that diplomacy has always been considered a man's profession. It is true, too, that "women's lib" did not really get under way until a few years ago. In any event, it is a sad fact that during the last forty years only fifteen women (about 1.5 percent of the posts available) have been named to head United States missions abroad.

This has not been due to any lack of available talent. Certainly some of the noncareer women ambassadors—such as Eugenie Anderson and Clare Boothe Luce—have served ably and well. Similarly, the few who have been chosen from the career service—notably Frances Willis and Carol Laise—have carried out their responsibilities with distinction. They have clearly demonstrated that diplomacy is no longer dependent on masculine talents.

Fortunately, the trend is in the right direction. During the 1960s some new avenues emerged when our government appointed more women to important posts with various international organizations and designated others as ambassadors to several non-European countries. At this writing (November 1974) we have four women ambassadors in the field. For me it would be a sign of real progress if we could double that figure before the decade is out.

Equality of opportunity for women in the Foreign Service leads quite naturally to a consideration of equality of opportunity for our black citizens. Plischke does not give us the statistics on the number of black ambassadors serving in U.S. missions abroad, but the figure remains discouragingly low. As of 1 July 1974, there were five. (There were also two ambassadors with a Spanish-American background.) I am not suggesting that we fill our embassy posts in accordance with the principle of proportional representation; our first emphasis must always be on ability rather than such factors as geography, religion, racial background, and school ties. But when one considers the number of embassies we have and the size of our black population, it is obvious that the record is not as good as it ought to be.

One way to remedy the situation would be to appoint more ambassadors from among the leaders of the black community in America. I have no objection to this as a short-run expedient, but it is not a satisfactory long-range answer to the problem. A more acceptable approach would be to put forth more vigorous efforts to recruit young blacks into the Foreign Service from our colleges and universities. Here, at long last, we have begun to make some progress. According to State Department figures, there are ninety-three blacks in the Foreign Service as compared to seventeen in 1961 and nineteen in 1967. In addition there are ninety-three blacks in the Foreign Service Reserve.

Until very recently, many able black students simply have not realized the fine career potential available to them in the field of diplomacy. Now that the door is open, what we need to encourage the process is federal support for a well-planned and carefully organized scholarship and training program to help black students who might wish to make the Foreign Service a career. It is understandable that many young blacks are anxious to stay at home and tackle the tough problems of the ghetto. But the opportunities in diplomacy are now so great that an able young black who enters the Foreign Service might well aspire to an ambassadorial post within fifteen or twenty years.

November 1974

FRANCIS O. WILCOX
Dean Emeritus,
Johns Hopkins School of
Advanced International
Studies

PREFACE

A remarkable profusion of books, monographs, articles, documentary collections, and other published materials on contemporary American diplomacy is streaming into the marketplace. Much of this literature focuses primarily on the substance, sagacity, and propriety of the foreign policy of the United States, on the progression of its expanding participation in world affairs, and on its external relations as they affect particular countries, geographic areas, institutions, issues, and international crises.

Far less research is done on and literary attention paid to diplomacy as the fundamental ingredient of pragmatic state practice for managing American relations with other countries, or, more precisely, to the conduct of foreign affairs—except for certain aspects of the Washington policy-making mechanism and the status and reform of the diplomatic career system. Since World War II, dozens of volumes, as well as many shorter essays, have been devoted to such components of the foreign policy complex as the political, institutional, and bureaucratic roles of the President, Congress, the secretary and the Department of State, the Foreign Service, and the military, together with central interdepartmental coordination and decision making, including the operation of the National Security Council and the President's personal foreign relations staff.

However, little of this literature concentrates on top-level diplomatic emissaries in an integrated, inclusive, and penetrating manner, or systematically probes the methods of implementing foreign affairs in the field by accredited diplomats. On the other hand, limited and usually fragmentary contributions are contained in the hundreds of autobiographies, biographies, personal memoirs, reflections, and collations of addresses, letters, and public papers, published by and about American statesmen, diplomatic and consular practitioners, and other officials concerned with foreign relations. Often these are revealing and useful resources for the study of United States diplomacy, but generally the memoir literature, which most directly reveals the capacities and activities of the emissary in the field, evokes the interest only of the professional contemporary or the historian.

On rare occasions, fundamental and comprehensive treatments of diplomats and their profession are published. These may be broad in scope, such as E. Wilder Spaulding's *Ambassadors Ordinary and Extraordinary* (1961)—which surveys seven categories of American emissaries, varying from the old masters to recent careerists, and from men of letters and learning to would-be diplomats indebted to the spoils system—and Charles W. Thayer's *Diplomat* (1959)—which deals with various topical features of diplomatic practice and personnel, including diplomatic missions, ambassadorial appointees, and members of the Foreign Service. Some of the literature endeavors to treat the conduct of diplomacy in panoramic perspective, concentrating more on organization, institutionalization, and process than on ranking envoys, although some attention is paid to diplomatic officers. By way of illustration, this reservoir of commentary includes: John M. Mathews, *The Conduct of American Foreign Relations* (1922) and *American Foreign Relations: Conduct and Policies* (revised edition, 1938); Graham H. Stuart, *American Diplomatic and Consular Practice* (second edition, 1952); Benjamin H. Williams, *American Diplomacy: Policies and Practice* (1936); Quincy Wright, *The Control of American Foreign Relations* (1922); and this author's *Conduct of American Diplomacy* (third edition, 1967).

Other publications are more narrowly circumscribed, the majority of which are functionally delimited. They deal with such aspects of diplomatic practice as treaty and agreement making, international conferences, negotiating style, privileges and immunities, protocol, the influence of pressure groups and public opinion, and various specific types of diplomatic activities. The growing emphasis is on the peaceful settlement of disputes, conflict resolution, and crisis management. A few studies concentrate on particular categories of diplomats. For example: Lee H. Burke, *Ambassador at Large: Diplomat Extraordinary* (1972); Alfred Vagts, *The Military Attaché* (1967); Maurice Waters, *The Ad Hoc Diplomat* (1963); Henry M. Wriston, *Executive Agents in American Foreign Relations* (1929); and several dissertations on political advisers (POLADs) attached to military commands. The authors of a good many other volumes address themselves specifically to the career service and its members. These contributions are represented by William Barnes and John Heath

Morgan, *The Foreign Service of the United States* (1961); John Ensor Harr, *The Professional Diplomat* (1969); a series of monographs by Harr, Arthur G. Jones, and Regis Walther published by the Carnegie Endowment for International Peace; and the writings of James Rives Childs, Warren F. Ilchman, David Lavine, Tracy H. Lay, Peter Lisagor and Marguerite Higgins, Smith Simpson, and others mentioned in chapter 8 of this study.

The paucity of broad-scope literature on senior diplomats—both careerist and noncareerist—is readily apparent and somewhat disappointing. This volume—a statistical and analytical survey of the spectrum of top-level United States diplomats since the 1770s—is intended to help fill this void. It focuses primarily on ambassadors, ministers, and other chiefs of mission accredited to foreign governments, but also pertains to ambassadors at large, mission chiefs to international organizations, and senior officers of the Department of State (who are appointed by the President with Senate confirmation). It encompasses more than 1,800 such senior diplomatic appointees named to nearly 3,000 assignments, including more than 350 appointments to top-level Department of State offices and nearly 2,500 to posts as chiefs of mission to American embassies and legations in foreign capitals. This study is not concerned, however, with such other specialized groups of diplomats as the corps of Foreign Service Officers (FSOs) and staff members below the level of mission chief, consular officials, presidential special emissaries, or delegates appointed to represent the United States at international conferences or in sessions of the various international organizations (except for resident chiefs of mission to such forums).

Attention is devoted here to three main subjects—diplomatic appointments per se, the ranking diplomatic officers commissioned and accredited to these appointments, and certain aspects of their diplomatic missions—covering a span of nearly two centuries, from the revolutionary period to 1973. Reviewed are: the historical extension of United States diplomatic representation since the 1770s, the numerical and geographic growth and identifiable categories of diplomatic appointments, the quantity and types of both sequential and simultaneous multiple accreditation, the commencement and duration of diplomatic missions, and the prevalence and reasons for the nonconsummation and termination of appointments. The study classifies and extrapolates statistical information concerning the geographic origin (or state of legal residence), sex, and age of diplomatic appointees, and investigates the evolution of American practice respecting the use of diplomatic ranks and titles. It examines the career and professional status of diplomats, their presidential and vice-presidential aspirations, their prior congressional service, and their literary interests and publishing endeavors.

These and related matters are surveyed historically and functionally, and are analyzed statistically. Sixteen comprehensive tabulations, which present largely aggregate quantitative data, are provided in the appendix, supplemented by four summary tables in the text. Refined and detailed statistical information is embodied in the commentary. The primary purposes of this study are to establish and convey salient facts concerning the entire corps of senior United States diplomats and their missions and to define established practices and trace evolving trends based on these facts. It is not the objective of the author to assess either the quality or the performance of specific individuals or groups of diplomats, or to evaluate the motives or efficaciousness of American diplomatic performance, although, at times, general conclusions can scarcely be avoided.

This study is based substantially upon information contained in the comprehensive, pioneering compilation entitled *United States Chiefs of Mission, 1778-1973,* produced by Richardson Dougall and Mary Patricia Chapman of the Historical Office, Bureau of Public Affairs, of the Department of State, and published by the Government Printing Office in 1973; without this carefully prepared listing, this treatise would not have been possible. The author has relied upon the work of Dougall and Chapman for much of the data utilized in his statistical tabulations and analysis. Other compilations, used in preparing some of the materials contained in sections concerned with congressmen-diplomats and diplomats as authors, are cited in the documentation of chapters 6 and 7. The author acknowledges his appreciation for the availability of these resources, but assumes responsibility for the tabulation, explication, and interpretation of the data contained in this volume.

March 1975

ELMER PLISCHKE
College Park, Maryland

1

DEVELOPMENT OF UNITED STATES DIPLOMATIC REPRESENTATION

During and immediately following the revoluntionary period and prior to the establishment of the federal union in 1789, the first American diplomats were dispatched to Europe as secret agents, joint commissioners, chargés d'affaires and, for major treaty negotiations, as ministers plenipotentiary. Some fifteen to twenty such emissaries —either elected, appointed, or otherwise commissioned by the Continental Congress—represented the interests of the emergent United States primarily in England, France, the Netherlands, Prussia, Russia, and Spain.[1]

Prior to 1789, however, only five regular diplomatic appointments were made: Benjamin Franklin to France, John Adams to the Netherlands and later to Great Britain, Francis Dana to Russia, and John Jay to Spain.[2] Franklin was also accredited to Sweden in 1782,[3] and three years later Thomas Jefferson replaced him in Paris. After

---

[1] These included John Adams, Thomas Barclay, William Carmichael, Francis Dana, Silas Deane, Charles W. F. Dumas, Benjamin Franklin, David Humphreys, Ralph Izard, John Jay, Thomas Jefferson, Henry Laurens, John Laurens, Arthur Lee, William Lee, and William Smith. In addition to emissaries sent to European countries, perhaps somewhat surprisingly in this early period John Lamb served as an agent to Algiers, Oliver Pollock was appointed commercial representative to Havana, and Thomas Randal and Samuel Shaw exercised consular functions at Canton. For a brief description of these officials and their assignments, see U.S. Department of State, *Register of the Department of State, October 1, 1937* (Washington, D. C.: Government Printing Office, 1937), pp. 335–337.

[2] Benjamin Franklin was appointed minister plenipotentiary to France, presented his credentials on 23 March 1779, and served until 1785. John Adams, commissioned minister plenipotentiary to the Netherlands, was formally recognized by the Dutch government on 19 April 1782; he also was appointed to Great Britain and served in London from 1785 to 1788. Francis Dana, named minister to Russia in 1780, was not formally received, and John Jay, appointed minister plenipotentiary to Spain in 1779, arrived there in January of the following year, but was not formally acknowledged.

[3] Franklin negotiated a treaty with Sweden in Paris, signed in April 1783.

the Constitution went into effect, the United States also named regular resident emissaries to Portugal (1791), Prussia (1797), and Sweden (1814). From 1809 to 1820, while the court of Portugal was established in Brazil, American emissaries accredited to the Portuguese government temporarily resided in Rio de Janeiro.

Growth of the American Diplomatic Community

Since this initial period when the United States commenced diplomatic relations with eight major European countries, its diplomacy has been extended to encompass the entire world, and this expansion of its representation has taken place in a series of recognizable waves. The first of these occurred between 1823 and 1838. In keeping with its basic de facto recognition policy launched at the time of the French Revolution, the United States readily acknowledged as independent states a group of Latin American colonies which revolted against Spain and Portugal early in the nineteenth century. Between 1823 and 1827 it appointed resident emissaries to Argentina, Brazil, Chile, Colombia, Mexico, Peru, and the combined Central American countries.[4] Venezuela was added in 1835 and, when Texas became independent, a chargé d'affaires was appointed to Houston in 1837. Seeking to enhance its international credibility in Europe, Washington also appointed resident representatives to Denmark (1827), the two Sicilies (1831), Belgium (1832), and Austria (1838), and opened its first regular mission in the Middle East in Turkey (1831).

With this early nineteenth century expansion the United States nearly tripled its diplomatic representation to a total of twenty-two countries—twelve in Europe, nine in the Western Hemisphere, and one in the Middle East. In the 1840s Ecuador (1848) and Bolivia (1849) in Latin America, as well as Italy (1840)[5] and the Papal States or Vatican City (1848)[6] in Europe, and Egypt (1849) in the Middle East were added, and the United States also established its first regularized diplomatic mission in the Orient when Caleb Cushing was accredited to China (1843).[7] Diplomatic relations with Texas were

---

[4] Diplomatic representatives to Central America were variously accredited to the Republic of Central America, the Federation of Central America, Central America, or the Central American States, and generally they were resident in Guatemala.

[5] Representatives were commissioned to Sardinia (capital at Turin) from 1840 to 1861, and thereafter to Italy.

[6] Representatives were appointed to the Papal States, the Pontifical States, the Holy See, or the State of Vatican City.

[7] Although appointed in May 1843, he was not officially accepted until June of the following year.

terminated when it was annexed to the United States in 1845, so that by mid-century Washington was maintaining resident diplomatic missions in twenty-seven countries.[8]

A second major wave of American diplomatic expansion started after the Mexican War, when a dozen states were added to the American diplomatic community. These embraced two European countries, namely Switzerland (1853) and Greece (1868), Hawaii (1853) and Japan (1859) in the Pacific area, and Liberia (1864), the first mission to sub-Saharan Africa. During this period separate relations were established with each of the five Central American republics [9] as well as with Paraguay (1861), Haiti (1862), and Uruguay (1867). Six more states were added in the 1880s—Romania (1881), Serbia (1882), Siam (1882), Korea (1883), Persia (1883), and the Dominican Republic (1884). Missions to the Two Sicilies and Vatican City terminated in the 1860s, and diplomatic relations with Hawaii ended when it was annexed in 1898, fixing United States representation at forty-two by 1900.[10]

Another wave of expansion occurred in the early twentieth century, to a large extent as a result of the Spanish-American and Balkan wars. The United States augmented its diplomatic roster by nearly a dozen and a half more countries. Between 1903 and 1909, missions were established in four European, two African and, following the war in the Caribbean, the remaining two Latin American states.[11] When it was annexed by Japan in 1905, diplomatic relations with Korea were terminated, so that, by the time of World War I, the United States was appointing diplomatic emissaries to the governments of forty-nine countries, covering all of the Western Hemisphere and Europe and including the principal independent powers of Asia, the Middle East, and Africa.

As a consequence of World War I, Montenegro, recognized in 1905, was absorbed into emerging Yugoslavia late in 1918, and resident missions of the United States were established in eight Baltic and other Eastern European countries between 1919 and 1922,[12]

[8] See Table A-1, column C. Note that Texas, to which the United States sent emissaries from 1837 to 1845, does not show in column C. For information on representatives to Texas, see Table A-5.

[9] Representation was continued in Guatemala, but individual missions also were accredited to Nicaragua (1852), Costa Rica (1858), Honduras (1858), and El Salvador (1863). Also see chapter 2 for a discussion of multiple diplomacy.

[10] See Table A-1, column C.

[11] These included Bulgaria (1903), Luxembourg (1903), Norway (1905), and Montenegro (1905); Morocco (1906) and Ethiopia (1909); and Cuba (1902) and Panama (1903).

[12] Czechoslovakia (1919), Poland (1919), Finland (1920), Albania (1922), Hungary (1922), and the three Baltic states of Estonia, Latvia, and Lithuania (1922).

increasing representation to fifty-six missions. During the 1920s and 1930s three former British dominions, Canada (1927), Ireland (1927), and South Africa (1930), together with Iraq (1931) and Afghanistan (1935), were added. After the outbreak of war in Europe, emissaries were commissioned to Australia and Saudi Arabia (1940), and to Iceland (1941). In the meantime, Italian forces occupied Albania in 1939 [13] and the Soviet Union took over the three Baltic states in June 1940. Following these events, United States diplomats were withdrawn from the capitals of the occupied states.[14] By the time of Pearl Harbor, therefore, the United States had established resident diplomatic missions to seventy countries, terminated representation to ten of them,[15] and was maintaining diplomatic relations with sixty.[16]

By far the most extensive independence boom took place during and after World War II when, in little more than a quarter century, some seventy-five new states joined the family of nations, primarily in the Arab world, Africa, Asia, and the Pacific. As a result, the United States more than doubled the size of its diplomatic representation. Between the attack at Pearl Harbor and 1973, Washington accredited emissaries to seventy-two of these new countries (including its missions to Lebanon, New Zealand, and Syria which were opened in 1942). At the conclusion of the war, the United States led the way in launching the massive independence movement by granting the Philippines independence on 4 July 1946. And diplomatic relations were established with four former British territories in the Caribbean area,[17] two Mediterranean island states which had formerly belonged to Britain,[18] twelve nations in the Mideast and North

---

[13] Diplomatic relations have not been revived with Albania since World War II.

[14] Nevertheless, Estonian, Latvian, and Lithuanian legations continue to handle residual diplomatic and consular functions in Washington; see U.S. Department of State, current issue of the *Diplomatic List*.

[15] States with whom relations had been terminated include Albania, Estonia, Hawaii, Korea, Latvia, Lithuania, Montenegro, Texas, the Two Sicilies, and Vatican City.

[16] See Table A-1, column C. In addition representation to Vatican City was temporarily revived late in 1941: See U.S. Department of State, *United States Chiefs of Mission, 1778–1973* (Washington, D. C.: Government Printing Office, 1973), p. 165. However, the extraordinary resident mission of Myron Taylor to the Vatican for more than a decade during and immediately after World War II is not included in the statistics of this survey because he is regarded as having been a presidential special agent, appointed without senatorial confirmation. Also see notes 32 and 34 below.

[17] Jamaica (1962), Trinidad and Tobago (1962), Guyana (1966), and Barbados (1967).

[18] Cyprus (1960) and Malta (1965).

Africa,[19] seventeen in Asia and the Pacific, and an impressive thirty-three in sub-Saharan Africa—totalling sixty-nine.[20]

The late 1940s and the 1950s, while six Middle Eastern and two African states were involved, was primarily a period of expansion of diplomatic relations with Asia and the South Pacific. Emissaries were accredited to a dozen new countries—including such major countries as India (1947), Pakistan (1948), and Indonesia (1949), as well as the Southeast Asian states of Cambodia (Khmer Republic), Laos, and Vietnam (1950)—and diplomatic relations were renewed with Korea (1949). During the 1960s and early 1970s the United States initiated diplomatic relations with an additional forty-nine states—equalling its total diplomatic commitment as of the time of World War I. This period was the era of sub-Saharan African emergence, in which American resident emissaries were accredited to thirty-one newly independent countries in this area.

As of 31 March 1973 the United States had established regularized diplomatic relations with 141 countries since 1778, terminated representation to nine of them,[21] and was currently appointing resident emissaries to 132 states. These figures do not reflect the temporary discontinuance of normal diplomatic relations with Cuba,[22] the Congo (Brazzaville),[23] and those Arab countries which broke relations with the United States at the time of the 1967 Arab-Israeli War.[24]

Table A-1 shows the commencement, continuity, and, where applicable, discontinuance, of United States diplomatic representation to these 141 countries during a period of nearly two centuries, together with their membership in the League of Nations and the United Nations. It depicts representation by half century to 1900 and by decades thereafter, tracing the progression of American diplomatic relations with each foreign country and aggregating totals for each period. Table A-2 groups these 141 countries by major geographic areas—the Western Hemisphere, Europe, the Middle East and North

---

[19] Yemen (1946), Israel (1949), Jordan (1950), Libya (1952), Sudan (1956), Tunisia (1956), Kuwait (1961), Algeria (1962), Bahrain (1972), Oman (1972), Qatar (1972), and the United Arab Emirates (1972).

[20] See Tables A-1 and A-2.

[21] For list, see footnote 15 above; relations with Korea were revived after World War II.

[22] The United States severed relations with Cuba on 3 January 1961.

[23] The United States withdrew all diplomatic personnel from Brazzaville on 15 August 1965.

[24] Algeria, Egypt, Iraq, and Syria severed relations on 6 June 1967; Mauritania, the Sudan, and Yemen took similar action on the following day. Relations with all but Iraq have since been revived.

Africa, sub-Saharan Africa, and Asia and the Pacific. In addition to providing area and population figures for each country, it specifies the commencement, suspension, termination where applicable, and duration of diplomatic relations, together with the number of years of American representation, the number of United States representatives appointed, and the average length of their service as chiefs of mission.

Table 1 summarizes United States diplomatic representation since 1778.

Table 1

U.S. DIPLOMATIC REPRESENTATION BY GEOGRAPHIC AREA

(As of 31 March 1973)

Area	Diplomatic Relations Established	Termination of Relations[a]	Suspension of Relations[a]	Diplomatic Relations (31 March 1973)
Western Hemisphere	26	1	1	24
Europe	34	7	0	27
Mideast and North Africa	20	0	4	16
Sub-Saharan Africa	36	0	1	35
Asia and Pacific	25	1	0	24
Total	141	9	6	126[b]

[a] The cases of discontinuance and temporary suspension of diplomatic relations are identified in column E of Table A-2.

[b] With the revival of relations with Algeria, Egypt, and Syria, and the establishment of relations with the Bahamas, East Germany, Grenada, Guinea-Bissau, and the Chinese People's Republic, as of January 1975, this total rose to 134.

Source: Geographic distribution based on Table A-2.

Temporary Suspension of Diplomatic Relations

Over two centuries the United States has endured a fairly substantial number of suspensions of diplomatic relations, especially in recent decades. Excluding the many deferrals of appointment of an American chief of mission for a few weeks or months pending local political stabilization and United States recognition of a new government, and a number of temporary suspensions of representation in time of hostilities when the governments of occupied countries fled into exile,[25] the United States has experienced nearly thirty cases of severed diplomatic relations, most lasting for periods of several years.[26]

Many of these occur as a consequence of wars such as those with Great Britain, Mexico, and Spain in the nineteenth century,[27] World War I—involving Austria-Hungary (1917–1921), Germany (1917–1921), and Turkey (1917–1927)—and World War II, which resulted in the severance of relations with ten countries. Between 1941 and 1955 relations were severed with six enemy belligerents: Bulgaria (1941–1947), Germany (1941–1955), Hungary (1941–1946), Italy (1941–1945), Japan (1941–1952), and Romania (1941–1947)—all of which either declared war on, or otherwise took the initiative in breaking relations with, the United States. In addition, relations were severed with three countries annexed to or occupied by Axis powers, including Austria (1938–1946), France (1942–1944), and Thailand (1941–1946), as well as with Finland (1944–1946). Similarly, diplomacy with Ethiopia was suspended during the Italian occupation (1937–1943) following the Abyssinian War, and seven Arab countries broke relations with the United States at the time of the Arab-Israeli War of 1967. While Mauritania revived normal diplomatic representation in 1971, and the Sudan and the Yemen Arab Republic (San'a) followed suit a year later, Algeria, Egypt, Iraq, and Syria continued the suspension, with Algeria, Egypt, and Syria reviving normal relations in 1974.

For political reasons, diplomacy with the Communist government of the Soviet Union remained in abeyance for sixteen years (1917–1933), and with the People's Republic of China after 1949. When Ambassador Donald R. Heath, accredited to Sofia, was declared *persona non grata* during the cold war period, the United States broke relations with Bulgaria (1950-1960). Of a more exceptional nature, when Syria joined Egypt in forming the United Arab Republic (U.A.R.) in 1958, the American embassy was converted into a consulate general, but a few years later the U.A.R. foundered and the American mission was reestablished at embassy level with a new mission chief accredited in January 1962. When the Republic of the Congo (Brazzaville), which proclaimed its independence in 1960,

---

25 This was the plight of Belgium, Czechoslovakia, Denmark, Greece, Luxembourg, the Netherlands, Norway, Poland, and Yugoslavia during World War II. American representation to the exile governments is discussed later.

26 Such suspension of diplomatic relations is indicated in column E of Table A-2.

27 War of 1812 with Great Britain (relations severed 1812–1815), Mexican War (relations severed for several months in 1845), and Spanish-American War (relations severed 1898–1899).

harassed American officials, the United States withdrew its diplomatic staff in 1965—a step regarded as somewhat short of formal severance of diplomatic relations. Similarly, in November 1973, the American embassy in Uganda was closed (although, relations not being severed, the Uganda embassy in Washington continued to function).

Future Expansion of United States Diplomatic Representation

A number of developments are bound to affect the future expansion of United States diplomacy. As in the past, temporary breaches of diplomatic relations will probably be mended, so that such interruptions will have little long-range influence on the size and nature of the American diplomatic community. Second, occasionally states amalgamate with others,[28] or they split up,[29] but these changes are relatively infrequent, and therefore will have little effect on the quantity of United States diplomatic representation abroad.

Third, certain currently independent and semi-autonomous countries are being accepted into the society of nations, some of which are bound to be added to the American diplomatic roster, as was the case with the Bahamas in 1973 and Grenada, Guinea-Bissau, and the East German Democratic Republic in 1974. One group consists of those which have already been recognized by other states and are admitted to United Nations membership. The probability of establishing regularized United States diplomacy with some of them is considerable. On the one hand, although Byelorussia and the Ukraine enjoy original membership in the United Nations, in the absence of any attempt to gain independence from the Soviet Union, the United States is not apt to seek separate diplomatic exchanges with them. On the other hand, the establishment or revival of diplomatic relations are not inconceivable with such members of the United Nations as Albania, Bhutan, the Congo (Brazzaville), Cuba, Iraq, the Mongolian People's Republic, Southern Yemen (Aden), and Uganda. In the course of time the same may well apply to Rhodesia, and to independent Nauru in the Pacific (with which the United States deals through its embassy in Australia). However, the Chinese People's Republic, though seated in the United Nations in 1971, has posed special problems, but in 1973 liaison missions were exchanged, and may eventually be con-

---

[28] Illustrated recently by the abortive United Arab Republic (Egypt and Syria, 1958–1961), the attempted union of Libya and Tunisia (1974), and the West Indies Federation (Jamaica, Tobago, and Trinidad, 1957–1962).

[29] The two Chinas, Germanies, Koreas, and Vietnams, as well as Bangladesh.

verted into normal embassies. North Korea and North Vietnam, in view of past hostilities with them, also present unique difficulties. While grave problems inhibit the creation of normal diplomatic relations with some of these countries, theoretically all of them—except Byelorussia and the Ukraine—may eventually be added to the American diplomatic community.

Another group comprises four miniature quasi-independent European principalities and republics—Andorra, Liechtenstein, Monaco, and San Marino—whose foreign affairs are administered by neighboring states.[30] Unless they should seek full independent national status, gain recognition from other states, and be admitted to United Nations membership,[31] the United States is unlikely to initiate the regularization of diplomatic representation to them. Similarly, unless Congress changes its mind on the matter, the Department of State is not apt to establish normal diplomatic relations with the state of Vatican City.[32]

Fourth, there are the remaining dependent and quasi-dependent territories—a few in the Western Hemisphere and Asia, but located primarily in Africa and the Pacific. On the matters of their independence and United States diplomatic relations, these fall into two main groups—those which are relatively substantial in size and

---

[30] Nevertheless, both Liechtenstein and San Marino are separate members of the International Court of Justice; Liechtenstein also is a member of the European Free Trade Association, Monaco is a member of the International Atomic Energy Agency, UNESCO, and the World Health Organization, and both Liechtenstein and Monaco belong to the International Telecommunication Union and the Universal Postal Union.

[31] Liechtenstein was denied membership in the League of Nations in 1920. Report of the Committee on Admission, First Assembly, 6 December 1920; see Green H. Hackworth, *Digest of International Law* (Washington, D. C.: Government Printing Office, 1940), vol. 1, pp. 48–49. Also see Michael M. Gunter, "Liechtenstein and the League of Nations: A Precedent for the United Nations' Ministate Problem?" *American Journal of International Law*, vol. 68 (July 1974), pp. 496–501. United Nations admission policy is summarized in Marjorie M. Whiteman, *Digest of International Law* (Washington, D. C.: Government Printing Office, 1963), vol. 2, pp. 46–47.

[32] For commentary on United States diplomatic relations with the Vatican, see Graham H. Stuart, *American Diplomatic and Consular Practice*, 2nd ed. (New York: Appleton-Century-Crofts, 1952), pp. 133–134; Elmer Plischke, *Conduct of American Diplomacy*, 3rd ed. (Princeton: Van Nostrand, 1967), pp. 94, 95; Martin F. Hasting, "United States-Vatican Relations," *Records of the American Catholic Historical Society of Philadelphia*, vol. 69 (March–June 1958), pp. 20–55; Howard R. Marraro, "The Closing of the American Diplomatic Mission to the Vatican and Efforts to Revive It," *Catholic Historical Review*, vol. 33 (1948), pp. 423–447. For a general but comprehensive account, see Robert A. Graham, *Vatican Diplomacy* (Princeton: Princeton University Press, 1959), esp. pp. 82–84 and 326–348, with extensive bibliography on pp. 397–419.

population, and the microentities. The first category consists of the following twenty territories and islands:

Western Hemisphere: British Honduras, French Guiana, Puerto Rico, and Surinam (Dutch Guiana).

Africa: Angola, Mozambique, Namibia (Southwest Africa), and perhaps the Cape Verde Islands, the French Territory of Afarsan and Issas, and the Spanish Sahara.

Asia: Brunei (Borneo), Hong Kong, and Sikkim (India).

Pacific Islands: British Solomons, French Polynesia, Guam, Micronesia (Marshalls, Mariannas, and Carolines), New Caledonia, New Hebrides, and Papua/New Guinea.

Some of these—such as Micronesia and New Guinea—are trusteeships, and Southwest Africa, a former League of Nations mandate, is administered by South Africa. In view of recent developments in nation building, state creation, and the proliferation of United Nations membership, some of these nineteen territories are likely to be added to the American diplomatic community. In 1974 Portugal granted or paved the way for the independence of Portuguese Guinea (Guinea-Bissau), Angola, and Mozambique. Other territories and archipelagoes, though less apt to achieve this status, cannot be discounted entirely, including, for example, the Virgin Islands in the Caribbean, Comoro and Reunion in the Indian Ocean, and American Samoa, Cook, Gilbert and Ellis, Niue, Wallis Futuna, and other islands in the Pacific.[33]

As a consequence, it is not beyond the realm of possibility that in the next decades United States diplomatic representation to foreign governments could be augmented by ten to twenty-five additional missions. This means that by the early years of the twenty-first century, the Department of State may be maintaining approximately 150 resident diplomatic missions to foreign governments. If diplomatic relations were established with all of the countries and islands mentioned, however, this number could be increased to some 170. Table A-3 lists potential additions to the American diplomatic community.

[33] For commentary on emergent independent countries since 1940 and ministates, see U.S. Department of State, *Profiles of Newly Independent States*, Geographic Bulletin no. 1, revised (Washington, D. C.: Government Printing Office, 1964), Patricia Wohlgemuth Blair, *The Ministate Dilemma*, Occasional Paper No. 6 (New York: Carnegie Endowment for International Peace, 1968), and Jacques Rapaport et al., *Small States and Territories: Status and Problems* (New York: Arno Press, 1971). Current commentary on trusteeships and dependent territory is to be found in the annual reports of the U.S. Department of State, *U.S. Participation in the UN*.

Additional Modes of Diplomatic Relations

The Department of State also accredits other types of diplomatic emissaries and missions. These include special presidential representatives, ambassadors at large, delegations to ad hoc and regularized international conclaves and conferences, and missions to international organizations. Dozens of special emissaries—originally called secret or special agents—may be dispatched abroad by each President, amounting to as many as twenty to twenty-five in a single year and numbering several thousand since 1789.[34] They are appointed without Senate confirmation and serve the President and secretary of state on special, nonresident assignments to foreign governments and in selected international negotiations. Serving a somewhat similar purpose but differing in essence, beginning with President Harry S. Truman's appointment of Philip C. Jessup in 1949, ten ambassadors at large also have been appointed. They are designated, with Senate confirmation, to continuing appointments, and function at a high level on whatever missions and in whatever capacity the President and secretary of state require.[35]

Finally, United States participation in international conferences imposes a substantial and growing demand on American diplomatic representation. Although represented at approximately 100 international conferences prior to 1900, averaging less than one per year, current United States conference attendance amounts to an annual average of 350 to 400. This includes occasional ad hoc gatherings, continuing conferences, and sessions of the agencies and principal subagencies of international organizations. By and large American

---

34 For additional information on the diplomatic special representative, see Maurice Waters, *The Ad Hoc Diplomat* (The Hague: Nijhoff, 1963); Henry M. Wriston, *Executive Agents in American Foreign Relations* (Baltimore: Johns Hopkins Press, 1929) and "The Special Envoy," *Foreign Affairs*, vol. 38 (January 1960), pp. 219–237; and Elmer Plischke, *Summit Diplomacy: Personal Diplomacy of the President of the United States* (College Park: Bureau of Governmental Research, University of Maryland, 1958), chapter 4 (republished by Greenwood Press of Westport, Conn., 1974). Statistics respecting presidential special representatives lie beyond the purview of this study.

35 In addition to Jessup, these include: Chester Bowles (1961–1963), Ellsworth Bunker (1966–1967), W. Averell Harriman (twice, 1961 and 1965–1969), U. Alexis Johnson (1973—), David M. Kennedy (1971–1973), Henry Cabot Lodge (1967–1968), George C. McGhee (1968–1969), and Llewellyn E. Thompson (1962–1966). Bunker was reappointed in 1973, and Robert J. McCloskey was appointed in 1974, increasing the number of appointees to twelve. For a list of appointments, see *United States Chiefs of Mission, 1778–1973*, p. 179; and for an intensive analysis of this diplomatic office, see Lee H. Burke, *Ambassador at Large: Diplomat Extraordinary* (The Hague: Nijhoff, 1972). McCloskey subsequently was also named assistant secretary for congressional relations, and thus held multiple high-level assignments simultaneously.

delegates to international conferences and meetings of international organizations serve in an ad hoc rather than a continuing residential capacity, and are therefore excluded from the statistics of this analysis.

However, with the creation of the United Nations, the Department of State began the practice of appointing resident missions to a selected group of international organizations. As in the case of United States embassies in foreign countries, such American diplomatic establishments are headed by "resident" or continuing chiefs of mission, such as the United States representative to the United Nations. Currently, such appointees are accredited to the following major international organizations: [36]

European Communities (Brussels, since 1959)

International Atomic Energy Agency (Vienna, since 1957)

International Civil Aviation Organization (Montreal, since 1947)

North Atlantic Treaty Organization (Brussels, formerly Paris, since 1952)

Organization for Economic Cooperation and Development (Paris, since 1961)

Organization of American States (Washington, D. C., since 1947)

United Nations (New York, since 1945)

United Nations Educational, Scientific and Cultural Organization (Paris, since 1961)

United Nations—European Office (Geneva, since 1958)

United Nations Industrial Development Organization (Vienna, since 1968)

At present the United States is a member of approximately seventy-five multipartite public international organizations, and in the next decades the Department of State may very well designate additional resident missions of this type. Column C of Table A-4

---

[36] Dates indicate appointment of U.S. representatives rather than presentation of credentials. Formal presentation applies only to general (as compared with specialized) international organizations, such as the Organization of American States and the United Nations. In any case, appointment and the presentation of credentials usually occur in the same year.

For a list of appointees and their appointments to these organizations, see *United States Chiefs of Mission, 1778–1973*, pp. 174–178. For analysis of the United States Mission to the United Nations see Arnold Beichman, *The "Other" State Department* (New York: Basic Books, 1967).

In addition to the missions listed, a regularized "office" is maintained in Rome to represent the United States to the Food and Agriculture Organization. Also see chapter 5, Table 3, for further comment.

provides summary aggregates, by decade, for the number of appointments as chiefs of mission to international organizations, while, for comparative purposes, other columns show appointees to senior offices in the Department of State, chiefs of mission to foreign countries, and ambassadors at large.

As of the early 1970s, the United States was dealing diplomatically with 132 foreign countries [37] and was appointing chiefs of mission to ten international organizations.[38] Assuming that in the next decades missions were established in all of the possible additional countries and islands mentioned earlier, as well as to a dozen more international organizations, the number of United States diplomatic establishments headed by resident chiefs of mission—together with several ambassadors at large—could number 200. This amounts to twenty-five times the number of diplomatic missions accredited by the United States in the 1770s.

As a consequence of this growth, the burden of maintaining full diplomatic representation is now far greater than would have been imagined even a few decades ago, and diplomatic relations are likely to continue to proliferate, but at a reduced rate. With the enlargement of the diplomatic community, competition for the attention and cooperation of dozens of foreign offices has intensified, and, as the membership of international organizations has expanded, the problems of American emissaries in coordinating among diplomatic missions and in influencing the collective policy formulation and voting of deliberative diplomatic agencies, have multiplied. The very expansion and development of the American diplomatic function, therefore, has transformed not only the extent, but also aspects of the nature of United States foreign relations.

37 As noted earlier, in the case of six countries, relations were temporarily suspended, but three of these were rescinded in 1974, and representation was withdrawn from Uganda. Subsequent to 31 March 1973, the United States also commenced diplomatic relations with the Bahamas, Grenada, Guinea-Bissau, East Germany, and the People's Republic of China, raising the total to 137.

38 The United States also is represented by "observer" missions to some international organizations, and, depending on the nature of the functioning of the organization, the Department of State could change some of these to resident missions. For an analysis of observership missions, see Jung Gun Kim, "Non-Member Participation in International Organizations," Ph.D. dissertation, University of Maryland, 1965.

2
UNITED STATES DIPLOMATIC APPOINTMENTS

By the time of its bicentennial, the United States will have made more than 3,000 diplomatic appointments—chiefs of resident diplomatic missions to foreign countries, top-level positions in the Department of State, chiefs of mission to international organizations, and ambassadors at large.[1] Of the 2,926 appointments from 1778 to 31 March 1973, some 364 (12 percent) were to senior offices in the Department of State, 55 (2 percent) to head missions to the United Nations and other international organizations, ten to ambassadorships at large, and the preponderant majority—2,497 (85 percent)—to the post of mission chief to foreign governments. Summary figures for these categories, with breakdowns by decades, are presented in Table A-4.

The largest numbers of diplomatic chiefs of mission have been appointed to the older European and Latin American countries. Perhaps somewhat surprisingly, more American emissaries have been accredited to Spain (sixty-five) and Russia/USSR (sixty-five)—the latter despite a lengthy break in diplomatic relations—than to any other countries. As might be expected, moreover, substantial numbers of appointments have also been made to Austria (fifty), France (fifty-eight), Great Britain (fifty-seven), the Netherlands (fifty), and Portugal (fifty-four), but equivalent numbers have similarly been dispatched to such Latin American countries as Argentina (fifty), Bolivia (fifty), Colombia (fifty-four), Guatemala/Central America

[1] The term appointment is used in several ways in this survey. In some cases it means nomination or designation by the President (even if not approved by the Senate), in others it refers to executive designation with Senate approval (although not fully consummated), and in still others it connotes presidential designation and formal commissioning and accreditation. These distinctions also apply to the term appointee. The sense in which the term is used will generally be apparent in the language and most frequently denotes nomination-appointment, but, where qualification or distinction is necessary, this will be indicated.

(fifty-three), and Mexico (forty-nine). Since 1778 the United States has named forty or more envoys to each of twenty-five countries—ten European and thirteen Latin American, together with China (forty) and Turkey (forty-one). It is interesting to note that sizeable numbers of appointments have also been made to Egypt (thirty-seven) and Iran (thirty-five) in the Middle East, Liberia (thirty-eight) in Africa, and Japan (thirty-two), and that some twenty-one appointments were made to independent territories that later were annexed to the United States—Hawaii (fifteen) and Texas (six).

Detailed statistics on the quantity of American appointments of chiefs of mission to foreign countries are presented in Table A-5, which indicates the number of appointments made to each foreign country, per decade, with totals for both the individual countries and each ten-year period. As the American diplomatic community developed and expanded, decade totals have shown an expectable rise in appointment totals. Sudden increases—as in the 1860s, 1880s, and since 1940—are due primarily to significant advances in the size of the American diplomatic community, but also reflect the usual flurry of new appointments attending changes in presidential administrations. In the 1860s and 1880s there were three presidential elections, and in each of these decades three Presidents made new appointments.

Equally interesting are significant declines from decade to decade, as in the 1870s, 1890s, and the period 1910–1920. Only one new President came to office in the 1870s and in the second decade of this century. During World War I, the decline is explainable in part by the severance of diplomatic relations with enemy countries and Russia, and in part by a desire to retain able diplomats in key posts for extended service and by not filling certain vacated positions immediately. The addition late in the decade (1919 and 1920) of states such as Czechoslovakia, Finland, and Poland also contributed to the increase in the following decade.

A comparison of the number of countries with whom the United States has maintained diplomatic relations (Table A-1) and the number of appointments of chiefs of mission made per decade (Tables A-4 and A-5) denotes substantial consistency for nearly two centuries in the number of such appointments per country per decade. These generally ranged between 2.5 and 3.5, and averaged approximately three appointments for each country each decade. A slight drop in the average occurred in the early twentieth century (during the Wilson, Harding, and Coolidge administrations), and a modest increase is noticeable since World War II, especially in the 1960s. During recent decades the overall annual rate of appointment of chiefs of mission to foreign governments by the President averages approximately thirty, or some two to three per month.

Although admittedly rare, illustrations of extremes include the appointment in a single decade of eight emissaries each to China (1850s), Ecuador (1860s), Luxembourg (1940s), Mexico (1860s), Russia (1880s), and Romania and Yugoslavia (1900s), and of twelve to Austria in the 1860s.[2] Except for Luxembourg, such exceptionally high numbers of appointments occurred prior to World War I. On the other extreme, examples of small numbers of appointments per decade have been more common, with many cases of only one or two diplomats accredited to a given country in a single decade, and with several cases in which an average of only two appointments per decade continue for extended periods of time.[3]

Senior Appointments in the Department of State

Statistics concerning appointments to the top-level positions in the Department of State are summarized in Table A-6 which presents figures per decade for fourteen categories of offices, with totals and career status of appointees. As of 1973 a combined total of 364 such appointments had been made. Presidents have made fifty-five appointments to the office of secretary of state,[4] a substantial number of whom have served for relatively short periods. Twenty-three (42 percent) held office for two years or less, and of these, twelve (22 percent) were in office for one year or less. Turnover has been substantial, and incumbencies have actually been as brief as two to three months—such as those of Jeremiah S. Black (17 December 1860–5 March 1961) and Robert Bacon (27 January–5 March 1909). The shortest of all was the eleven-day tenure of Elihu B. Washburne under President Grant (5–16 March 1869). In more recent times, relatively short periods have been served by Edward R. Stettinius (seven months), his successor James F. Byrnes (nineteen months), and Christian A. Herter (twenty-one months).

---

[2] Some of these represent unusual conditions. For example, eight of the twelve nominees to Austria were rejected by the Senate or declined appointment. These distinctions are considered more fully later (chapter 3).

[3] Of special note, in this respect, are China (only thirteen appointments between 1910 and 1970), Ethiopia (thirteen from 1909 to 1973), the Netherlands (twelve from 1782 to 1849), Portugal (ten from 1800 to 1849), and Sweden (eleven from 1900 to 1949). For discussion on the matter of average length of service, see later commentary in chapter 3.

[4] Prior to Henry A. Kissinger; his appointment was made after the period covered by this survey and is not included in these figures and analysis.

On the other hand, Cordell Hull, who occupied the office for the longest period of time, served one President for nearly twelve years. Five other secretaries held the position for eight-year periods.[5] Nine secretaries of state occupied the office under more than one President, and both Daniel Webster and James G. Blaine, who had split incumbencies, served three Presidents. In recent years only Stettinius and Dean Rusk served under two consecutive Presidents.

The office of under secretary of state—long the second ranking position in the department—was established shortly after World War I with President Wilson's appointment of Frank Lyon Polk in mid-1919. Since then, twenty-six appointments have been made to this office. In the 1940s additional under secretaries bearing functional titles—for example, for political or economic affairs—and deputy under secretaries began to be appointed, and in 1972 the super-level deputy secretary of state was created. To 1973, sixty-six appointments were made to these top-level offices—two deputy secretaries, twenty-six under secretaries, fifteen under secretaries with functional designations, and twenty-three deputy under secretaries. Tenure in these positions, as in the case of the secretary, also tends to be relatively short, generally averaging less than three years, with only 15 to 20 percent of the appointees serving for longer periods of time. It was exceptional, therefore, for Sumner Welles, formerly a career Foreign Service Officer, to remain under secretary for over six years during President Franklin D. Roosevelt's administration. George W. Ball, a noncareer officer, held the office for nearly five years in the 1960s, but he had also preceded it with a year as under secretary for economic affairs. The position of deputy under secretary has been held longest by Loy W. Henderson (six years) and Robert D. Murphy (four years), both career diplomats.

The primary level of departmental officers—the assistant secretaries—now head the basic structural units (called bureaus) of the department. Beginning in the 1850s, the second position after the secretary was a single assistant secretary; in 1866 he was supplemented with a single second assistant secretary, and eight years later by a third assistant secretary. This triumvirate constituted the only top-level officers to assist the secretary until the system was changed in 1924. During three-quarters of a century, thirty-three assistant secretaries, two second assistant secretaries, and twenty-one third assistant secretaries—totalling fifty-six—were appointed. Most of

[5] These include James Madison and John Quincy Adams, William H. Seward and Hamilton Fish during the era of the Civil War and Reconstruction, and Dean Rusk in the 1960s. John Hay occupied the post for more than six years at the turn of the century.

these also averaged less than three years' tenure, but it is worthy of note that, while only one in ten assistant secretaries remained more than three years, the length of service record was better for the lesser assistant secretaries. Thus, one-third of the third assistant secretaries remained more than three years, but the most remarkable record was set by the two second assistant secretaries who served for a combined period of fifty-eight years.[6]

During the two decades from 1924, when the system was changed, to 1944, some twenty-seven assistant secretaries were appointed, several serving simultaneously at equal rank—averaging more than one new appointment per year. Beginning in 1944, these assistant secretaries came to be denominated with specific functional designations as heads of the geographic and other bureaus of the department. Since then they have been appointed at the average rate of forty to fifty per decade, an incoming President normally commissioning ten or more during his first year in office. Currently, with approximately a dozen assistant secretaries serving simultaneously, this rate of appointment is likely to increase.[7]

The remaining senior Department of State positions are of relatively recent vintage, and generally the average number who remain in office for more than three years as counselor, legal adviser, chief of protocol, and similarly ranked officers, is greater than for assistant and under secretaries. The longest records are held by John F. Simmons, who was chief of protocol for more than six years in the 1950s, and Green H. Hackworth, the first legal adviser, who served for fifteen years.[8]

Multiple Appointments of Senior Department of State Officers

While Table A-6 lists fifty-five appointments to the office of secretary of state since 1789, the number of individuals holding this office was fifty-three by 1973,[9] inasmuch as Daniel Webster and James G. Blaine

---

[6] William Hunter for twenty years (1866–1886), and Alvey A. Adee for nearly thirty-eight years (1886–1924) which was preceded by four years as third assistant secretary, for a remarkable tenure of forty-two years for a single individual at these high ranks.

[7] As of 1974 there were eleven assistant secretaries for: Administration, Congressional Relations, Economic Affairs, Educational and Cultural Affairs, International Organization Affairs, Public Affairs, and such geographic areas as African Affairs, East Asian and Pacific Affairs, European Affairs, Inter-American Affairs, and Near Eastern and South Asian Affairs.

[8] Hackworth held the office from 1 July 1931, to 1 March 1946, when he was elected as a judge of the International Court of Justice.

[9] Prior to Henry Kissinger.

were appointed twice.[10] Twenty-six of these had prior diplomatic experience, either in the Department of State or as chiefs of mission in the field. Ten secretaries held prior Department of State appointments, the earliest serving ad interim.[11] Beginning with William R. Day shortly before the turn of the twentieth century, however, they functioned either as assistant or under secretaries, except for Robert Lansing, who previously held the office of counselor. In terms of previous departmental experience at a high level, Dean Acheson was especially well trained for the secretaryship, having served for more than six years as assistant and under secretary.

Nineteen secretaries of state (37 percent) also have held appointments as diplomats in the field. President Truman named General George C. Marshall as his special representative to China for thirteen months in the mid-1940s, and appointed Edward R. Stettinius, Jr., as his first ambassador to the United Nations in December 1945. The other seventeen functioned as resident chiefs of mission to foreign governments. Twelve gained their field experience prior to being named secretary,[12] whereas six of the nineteen served abroad after heading the department,[13] and James Buchanan held American diplomatic appointments abroad both before and after being named secretary. Most of these nineteen secretaries of state were designated to single field assignments, but John W. Foster was accredited to three foreign countries[14] and John Quincy Adams achieved the record of being appointed to five countries and serving abroad for fifteen years preceding appointment as secretary.[15] Such appointees were accredited primarily to Great Britain and France, but also to other European countries, China, Mexico, and, in the case of

[10] James Monroe had consecutive appointments (1811 and 1815) and served ad interim between these appointments; Hamilton Fish also held consecutive appointments. They are counted only once in the total. On the other hand, Daniel Webster (1841 and 1850) and James G. Blaine (1881 and 1889) are counted twice in the overall number of appointments.

[11] Five of the fifty-three also served as secretary ad interim, three prior to being appointed secretary (Timothy Pickering, Abel P. Upshur, and Robert Lansing), one was ad interim between two appointments as secretary (James Monroe), and one was so appointed following his tenure as secretary (John Marshall). None has served in this capacity since World War I.

[12] Aside from George C. Marshall, these included John Quincy Adams, Lewis Cass, Edward Everett, John Forsyth, John W. Foster, Frederick T. Frelinghuysen, John Hay, Thomas Jefferson, Frank B. Kellogg, James Monroe, and Louis McLane.

[13] Robert Bacon, Thomas F. Bayard, Edward Livingston, Edward R. Stettinius, Martin Van Buren, and Elihu B. Washburne.

[14] Mexico (1873–1880), Russia (1880–1881), and Spain (1883–1885).

[15] He was accredited to the Netherlands (1794–1797), Prussia (1797–1801), Russia (1809–1814), and Great Britain (1815–1817). He also was appointed minister plenipotentiary to Portugal in 1796, but did not serve in this capacity.

Stettinius, the United Nations. Except for Frank B. Kellogg,[16] no such appointment as chief of mission has been made since World War I. Assuming that this trend continues, it is possible to conclude that future secretaries of state are more likely to possess prior high level departmental responsibility than field experience as resident chiefs of mission to foreign governments.

Finally, it is relevant to note that, in the earlier history of the American republic, six secretaries used the office as a stepping stone to the presidency, namely, Thomas Jefferson, James Madison, James Monroe, John Quincy Adams, Martin Van Buren, and James Buchanan. Nine others—Secretaries John Jay, Henry Clay, Daniel Webster, John C. Calhoun, Edward Everett, Lewis Cass, James G. Blaine, William Jennings Bryan, and Charles Evans Hughes—also ran as presidential or vice-presidential candidates, but were unsuccessful.[17] Since the Civil War, on the other hand, no former secretary of state has been elected President, and the general belief that the office constitutes a back door to the White House has evanesced. Nevertheless, two secretaries have risen to the post of chief justice of the United States—John Marshall and Charles Evans Hughes—while both the latter and James F. Byrnes served on the Supreme Court prior to appointment to the secretaryship.

Other ranking Department of State officials, aside from the secretary, have also held multiple top-level diplomatic assignments. As noted, over the years sixty-six appointments were made to these senior departmental positions—deputy secretary, under secretary, and deputy under secretary. Of these, eleven served in more than one such rank, leaving a net of fifty-five individuals of whom only seventeen were single-assignment appointees,[18] whereas thirty-eight (70 percent) were named to diplomatic appointments as chiefs of mission in the field as well as to these senior departmental offices. Of these, four served twice as under secretary,[19] and one was named deputy under secretary twice.[20] Dean G. Acheson, Christian A. Herter,

---

[16] Aside from the specialized appointments of George C. Marshall and Edward R. Stettinius.

[17] This list is restricted to those presidential and vice-presidential candidates who were before the Electoral College, and does not include other aspirants. The matter of presidential aspirations of diplomats is dealt with more comprehensively in chapter 6.

[18] These seventeen represent only 25.76 percent of the total number of appointments to these positions.

[19] George W. Ball, C. Douglas Dillon, Joseph C. Grew, and William Phillips. The first two served as under secretary with functional titles as well as under secretary without such designations.

[20] U. Alexis Johnson.

Dean Rusk, and Edward R. Stettinius, Jr., also rose to become secretary of state, and four others functioned temporarily as secretary ad interim.[21]

Once appointed to this high level, the likelihood of additional appointment is substantial. Thus, of these thirty-eight multiple appointees, eleven held prior senior departmental office, six had previously served as chiefs of mission in the field, and seventeen had earlier gained both types of experience in preparation for achieving their highest State Department assignments, whereas only four had no such prior assignments, although two of these subsequently became secretary of state and two were later assigned as chiefs of mission in the field.[22] Since World War I, each of the thirty-eight multiple appointees held from two to eight high-level assignments in the department and the field, for a combined total of 167 appointments, averaging four to five for each such appointee.[23] This can only suggest that the upper levels of American diplomacy, so far as ranking departmental officers are concerned, devolve upon a refined if not an inner cadre of appointees, and it consists only partly of career officers who rise to this level as a consummation of their diplomatic careers.[24]

Multiple Appointments of Chiefs of Mission

Often United States diplomats accredited as chiefs of mission to foreign countries also serve in multiple assignments. These are of two basic types—sequential and simultaneous; statistics on such appointments are presented in Table A-7. Part 1 gives figures for several categories and for varying numbers of both types of such

[21] Charles F. Bohlen, Joseph C. Grew, H. Freeman Matthews, and Frank Lyon Polk.

[22] Of these thirty-eight multiple appointees to the higher departmental positions, sixteen held prior appointments either in the department as assistant secretaries or at higher ranks or as chiefs of mission in the field, four received subsequent but not prior appointments, and eighteen held such additional appointments both prior to and after serving in this high-level group—further substantiating the likelihood of reappointment at high levels once this elite group has been penetrated.

[23] Thus, ten appointees held two appointments, five held three, seven held four, three held five, five held six, five held seven, and three held as many as eight appointments. These last three include Joseph C. Grew, Loy W. Henderson, and William Phillips—all career officers.

[24] Sixteen of these thirty-eight multiple appointees (approximately 40 percent) were career officers, but some of the others, with extended, responsible assignments, can only be regarded as diplomatic professionals. This distinction is discussed in chapter 5.

multiple appointments. Part 2 is restricted to simultaneous diplomatic appointments, and part 3 presents overall totals for the various categories of multiple accreditation, the career status and sex of multiple appointees, and comparative percentages.

Of the total number of individuals designated as American chiefs of mission to foreign governments and international organizations, to top-level positions in the Department of State, and as ambassadors at large—amounting to 1,869 from 1778 to 1973—some 1,255 (67 percent) were named to single appointments and were later dropped from the senior posts of American diplomacy. On the other hand, 614 (33 percent) have been given multiple appointments. Of these, more than half (334) held two appointments, one of every five (124) had three appointments, and one-fourth (156) had four or more appointments, with seven recording as many as ten to fifteen per individual. A complete tabulation is given in line A, part 1, of Table A-7. Line B presents similar figures for multiple appointments solely as chiefs of mission in the field, eliminating departmental assignments. Inasmuch as 524 such appointments have been made, it is possible to conclude that since 1778 nearly three of every ten ranking American diplomatic appointees have served on such multiple assignments as chiefs of mission in the field. The figures in line C of Table A-7 exclude the cases of reappointment of individuals to the same foreign countries, therefore giving the net number of appointments as chiefs of mission to differing governments.

While a number of former secretaries of state were later elected to the presidency, as noted earlier, John Adams was the sole multiple diplomatic appointee (without previous experience as secretary of state) to be elected President, and George M. Dallas was the only candidate with multiple diplomatic experience abroad (in Russia and Great Britain) to be elected vice president. However, several other multiple appointment diplomats—including Andrew J. Donelson, Henry Cabot Lodge, Jr., Whitelaw Reid, and Richard Rush[25]—were unsuccessful presidential and vice-presidential candidates.[26]

Ninety-eight United States emissaries have held as many as five or more senior diplomatic appointments. Only eighteen of these served during the period prior to the outbreak of World War I, indicating that the level of reappointment is on the increase. Of the remaining eighty, most (sixty-five or 81 percent) were career diplo-

---

[25] Richard Rush, however, did serve as secretary of state ad interim for half a year in 1817.

[26] The overall relationship of diplomatic chiefs of mission to presidential and vice-presidential candidacy is discussed in chapter 6.

mats,[27] evidencing a marked trend toward employing career officers for such extended series of high-level missions. Of the fifteen remaining multiple-assignment noncareerist envoys since 1915, all but one held such appointments for eight years or more—with three serving approximately fifteen years each (David K. E. Bruce, Ellsworth Bunker,[28] and Boaz W. Long), one for more than twenty years (Lincoln MacVeagh), and another over a span of nearly twenty-five years (Laurits S. Swenson).[29] Altogether, these fifteen held ranking diplomatic and Department of State appointments for the remarkable combined total of approximately 190 years. While officially they are regarded as noncareerists at the time of appointment, in view of their extended service in high capacity, they can only be regarded as possessing the experience, if not the qualities of professionals.

Of the dozen and a half holding five or more appointments prior to 1915, only three, John Quincy Adams and James Monroe (both of whom became secretary of state and were later elected to the presidency) and Christopher Hughes, Jr. (who held diplomatic appointments to Sweden, Norway, and the Netherlands from 1819 to 1845), were appointed in the early history of the republic. The rest held their appointments between 1870 and World War I. The first of these, John L. Stevens, appointed in 1870, served for thirteen years during a period of a quarter of a century. Two others were commissioned in 1873, four in the 1880s, six in the 1890s, and only two after the turn of the century. The last of these were relieved of their positions in 1913. In all probability this development, which gained substantial momentum late in the nineteenth century, was brought to an end by a number of factors—the inauguration of Woodrow Wilson

---

[27] As defined by the Department of State; see chapter 5. These include, by way of example: George V. Allen, Willard L. Beaulac, Charles E. Bohlen, Philip Bonsal, Ellis O. Briggs, John M. Cabot, Selden Chapin, James R. Childs, James C. Dunn, Hugh Gibson, Loy Henderson, Alexander Kirk, Douglas MacArthur II, Thomas C. Mann, H. Freeman Matthews, Livingston T. Merchant, George C. Messersmith, Robert D. Murphy, John E. Peurifoy, William Porter, William Rountree, and Charles W. Yost.

Career officers with eight or more appointments include: Norman Armour, Jefferson Caffery, Joseph C. Grew, Raymond A. Hare, Donald R. Heath, U. Alexis Johnson, Arthur Bliss Lane, William Phillips, Rudolf Schoenfeld, and George Wadsworth. Ellis O. Briggs also was appointed eight times, but his last nomination (to Spain) was not consummated.

[28] Bunker also was reappointed ambassador at large after he left Vietnam in 1973, which is not included in the statistics of this survey.

[29] The remainder include Anthony J. Drexel Biddle (eleven years), Chester Bowles (ten years), Spruille Braden (nine), Angier Biddle Duke (nine), Averell Harriman (ten), Robert Hill (eight), Henry Cabot Lodge (eleven), William B. Macomber, Jr. (eleven), and George C. McGhee (twelve). Only Henry F. Grady, of this group, served for a shorter period (six years).

in 1913, the changes in American diplomacy resulting from World War I, and especially the commencement of the designation of the diplomatic career status by 1915.

While these eighteen pre-World War I multiple appointees represented a variety of backgrounds, several were careerists, such as Eugene Schuyler, who had previous consular experience for a dozen years, and William W. Rockhill who, after holding two ranking departmental posts, was accredited to six countries between 1897 and 1913 in addition to a special mission as President William McKinley's commissioner to China to participate in the settlement of Boxer Rebellion indemnities. David J. Hill, previously president of Bucknell and Rochester universities, was named assistant secretary in 1898 (then the second highest officer in the department) and as chief of mission to four countries over a period of thirteen years, and John G. A. Leishman was accredited to three European countries and Turkey, serving continuously as chief of mission for sixteen years. Others generally were chiefs of mission for shorter periods, and the criticism has been made that the appointment of some of these, as well as certain single-mission appointees, resulted from the American spoils system.

The presumption that multiple-assignment emissaries are normally appointed to countries of the same geographic area, culture, language group, or political character, is far from valid. Since the early decades, when appointments were confined largely to Europe and Latin America, it has been unusual for American diplomats to be assigned to multiple missions solely to related countries, and in those exceptional cases where this has occurred, diplomats have continued to be assigned primarily to Europe (where French was the common language of diplomacy until World War I), and to Latin America (where Spanish was nearly universal), although occasionally an emissary also was restricted to the Middle East.[30] However, with the increase of opportunities in Africa and Asia, this may become a more prevalent American diplomatic practice.[31] Nevertheless, in the past it

[30] By way of illustration—each of the following having at least five appointments to at least four different countries—H. Freeman Matthews served entirely in West-Central Europe; Norman Armour, William Dawson, Henry C. Hall, Cornelius A. Logan, Boaz W. Long, Romualdo Pacheco, and Walter C. Thurston served entirely in Latin American capitals; whereas Raymond A. Hare and James S. Moose had a similar tenure limited to the Mideast, and the same appears to be possible for Hermann Eilts.

[31] For example, a trend may be portended by Alan W. Lukens, who headed multiple missions only to Africa in the 1960s and by Walter P. McConaughy, Jr., appointed to the governments of Central and East Asian countries in the 1950s and 1960s.

was more common for appointees to a high number of multiple missions to be accredited to a variety of assignments.[32] Among the reasons for such disparity are the nature and level of vacancies when appointees—especially careerists—become available for transfer or reappointment, the interests of the specific diplomats and their competition for particular posts, and their acceptability to receiving governments. These, naturally, do not always coincide.

Simultaneous Multiple Diplomatic Appointments

By way of comparison with the substantial number of sequential appointments to both the Department of State and the field, part 2 of Table A-7 indicates that a relatively small number of American diplomats are appointed to multiple missions simultaneously. To a limited extent, this practice was employed during the revolutionary period, with the simultaneous commissioning, for example, of John Adams to participate in negotiating the peace treaty with Great Britain as well as arranging a loan from, and a treaty of commerce with, the Netherlands, and of Benjamin Franklin, who served simultaneously as minister plenipotentiary to France, commissioner to negotiate the peace treaty with Britain, and minister plenipotentiary to Sweden. It might be presumed, therefore, that many early American diplomats held such simultaneous missions, but this was not the case. A review of all appointments to the eight European countries [33] to which the United States commissioned emissaries from the 1780s to 1825 indicates that, although thirty-seven diplomats were appointed, only seven of them held multiple appointments,[34] and these were all sequential except for three years of overlap in the appointments of

[32] Illustrative of apparently unrelated assignments are the records of such non-careerist emissaries as: Anthony J. Drexel Biddle, Jr. (Norway, Poland, France, Belgium, the Netherlands, Norway, Yugoslavia, Czechoslovakia, Greece, the Netherlands and Norway, Yugoslavia, Czechoslovakia, and Spain—in order of appointment) and Ellsworth Bunker (Argentina, Italy, India and Nepal, the Organization of American States in Washington, ambassador at large, Vietnam, and, subsequent to 31 March 1973, again as ambassador at large to deal, in part, with the Panamanian treaty and arms limitation negotiations).

The same may also pertain to career diplomats, however, illustrated by: Ellis O. Briggs (Czechoslovakia, Korea, Greece, and four Latin American countries) and Donald R. Heath (Bulgaria, Vietnam, Cambodia, Laos, Lebanon, Saudi Arabia, and Yemen). Even an expert on the Soviet Union, such as careerist Charles E. Bohlen, may not be able to avoid appointment to such an unrelated post as the Philippines.

[33] France, Great Britain, the Netherlands, Portugal, Prussia, Russia, Spain, and Sweden.

[34] John Adams (two appointments), John Quincy Adams (four), David Humphreys (two), James Monroe (two), William Pinckney (two), Jonathan Russell (three), and William Short (three).

John Adams to the Netherlands and Great Britain in the mid-1780s. From the very outset, therefore, the United States established the practice of normally designating separate chiefs of mission to individual countries.

In nearly two centuries, aside from Adams, only eighty-four appointees (4 percent of the total) were named to simultaneous missions conjointly—with sixty-nine of these diplomats accredited simultaneously to two governments, twenty-four to three governments, three to four governments, and five to five governments—totalling 101 such appointments.[35] Half of these appointees served in this capacity prior to 1915 and, while approximately one-third of the total are designated as career officers by the Department of State, they account for two-thirds of such appointments since 1915, which means that currently noncareerists are only infrequently named to such simultaneous missions. Some of these eighty-four multiple-appointees were commissioned to two and even three such simultaneous missions.

The reasons for simultaneous appointments vary, but generally appear to fall into six categories: (1) because the countries concerned are neighbors with interlinked or similar interests and needs; (2) because representation to one or more of the countries is less demanding than to require a full-time ranking emissary, and therefore can be handled simultaneously; (3) because one or more of the countries involved is newly emergent in the family of nations, so that an emissary serving primarily in an established country may also care for United States interests in other nearby countries on an interim basis; (4) because of a shortage of qualified diplomatic personnel; (5) because, in exceptional cases, it is expedient to deal simultaneously at one place with a number of governments in exile, which occurred during World War II; (6) because the Department of State is obliged to economize.

One of the most protracted experiences of United States simultaneous diplomacy involved the appointment of a series of multiple representatives to the Central American Republics for more than three-quarters of a century.[36] Other nineteenth century examples of

---

[35] From the 1780s to 1905, emissaries were credited to the single court of Sweden and Norway, and they are not regarded as multiple representatives. Norway separated in 1905 and envoys have since been accredited individually to both Sweden and Norway.

[36] During most of the period from 1825 to 1890 (except for a time in the 1860s), a single envoy represented the United States to all five Central American Republics, either collectively or individually. From 1891 to 1907, one American emissary was accredited to Costa Rica, El Salvador, and Nicaragua (resident at Managua), and another to Guatemala and Honduras (resident at Guatemala City). Since 1908 a separate emissary has been sent to each of the five countries.

simultaneous representation in Latin America include United States relations with Haiti and Santo Domingo,[37] and with Uruguay together with either Argentina or Paraguay.[38] The President made similar multiple appointments to a dozen European governments. These involved various combinations of southeastern European countries (Bulgaria, Greece, Montenegro, Romania, Serbia, and Yugoslavia) prior to World War I,[39] the Baltic states of Estonia, Latvia, and Lithuania between the two world wars,[40] and Luxembourg together first with the Netherlands and later with Belgium.[41]

During World War II the United States became involved in a most unusual diplomatic experience with simultaneous multiple diplomacy, when it handled its representation conjointly to the governments in exile of nine countries (Belgium, Czechoslovakia, Denmark, Greece, Luxembourg, the Netherlands, Norway, Poland, and Yugoslavia) through representatives stationed in London, Cairo, and Ottawa. When Poland was attacked by Germany in 1939, its government fled first to France and then to Great Britain, and Ambassador Anthony J. Drexel Biddle, previously American ambassador to Warsaw, accompanied it, and in Britain he eventually was accredited simultaneously to seven of these governments in exile. He remained

[37] An emissary was stationed in Haiti from 1862 to 1883 when, diplomatic relations having been established with Santo Domingo, the same man was accredited to both countries. This continued until 1904, when separate envoys were sent.

[38] United States representatives to Argentina (resident at Buenos Aires) also were accredited to Uruguay from 1867 to 1870, and emissaries to Paraguay (resident at Montevideo) similarly were accredited to Uruguay from 1870 to 1914, when the United States commenced sending chiefs of mission to both countries.

[39] American representatives served these six states as follows: a single emissary to Greece, Romania, and Serbia from 1883 to 1902, and to these countries plus Bulgaria from 1903 to 1905; one emissary to Greece, Montenegro, and Bulgaria, and another to Romania and Serbia from 1905 to 1907; separate emissaries to Greece and Montenegro from 1907 to 1914 and to Bulgaria, Romania, and Serbia from 1907 to 1920. Representation to Montenegro ceased at the end of World War I, and thereafter separate emissaries were accredited individually to Bulgaria, Greece, Romania, and Yugoslavia.

[40] From 1922 to 1937 one emissary (resident at Riga) was accredited to the three countries; then separate envoys were assigned to Lithuania and to Estonia and Latvia until 1940 (when they were taken over by the Soviet Union).

[41] From 1903 to 1922 the American emissary represented the United States simultaneously to the Netherlands and Luxembourg (resident at The Hague), and from 1923 to 1940 he was accredited simultaneously to Belgium and Luxembourg (resident at Brussels). During World War II the three countries were occupied by German forces and their governments fled into exile. For a few years after the war (1946–1949), Ambassador Alan G. Kirk revived dual representation to Belgium and Luxembourg, but in 1949 President Truman appointed Perle Mesta as the first American emissary accredited solely to Luxembourg.

until 1943, when Rudolf E. Schoenfeld replaced him as chargé d'affaires.

In 1940 Denmark was occupied by the Nazis, and the American envoy, Ray Atherton, left Copenhagen. In 1943 when he was appointed United States emissary to Ottawa, he was recommissioned to represent the United States to the Danish government through its preinvasion envoy to Canada. He was also accredited to the government of Luxembourg for several months in 1943, until it transferred to London where Ambassador Biddle took over. In the meantime, the Greek government left Athens in 1941, transferring first to London and then to Cairo in 1943, where Alexander C. Kirk, United States envoy to Egypt, simultaneously represented American interests to the Greek government in exile. The Yugoslav government also fled to London, where for a time Ambassador Biddle handled American interests, but in 1943 it also moved to Cairo and then returned to London the following year where it dealt with Chargé Schoenfeld. Ambassador Lincoln MacVeagh succeeded Ambassador Kirk as representative to both Greece and Yugoslavia in 1943, and he resided in Cairo until October 1944 when he moved to Athens.

Late in 1944 the Department of State accredited separate emissaries to the exile governments of the Netherlands (Stanley K. Hornbeck), Norway (Lithgow Osborne), and Yugoslavia (Richard C. Patterson, Jr.) at London, and they accompanied these governments back to their capitals at the conclusion of hostilities. In this extraordinary manner the United States handled its wartime diplomacy with these nine exile governments in three locations, primarily by means of the multiple appointments of Ambassadors Biddle, Atherton, Kirk, and MacVeagh, and Chargé d'Affaires Schoenfeld pending the revival of more normal relations.

In addition, beginning at the time of World War II, as many new nations were being established, the United States expanded its earlier practice of utilizing a single diplomatic appointee to represent it simultaneously to two or more governments, either on a temporary or a continuing basis. Since 1939, for example, the Department of State has established a network of such simultaneous multiple representations to Egypt, Saudi Arabia, and half a dozen other countries on the Arabian Peninsula.[42] Similarly, for a time (1942–1947) the

[42] The American representative to Egypt was simultaneously accredited to Saudi Arabia from 1939 to 1943, when a separate emissary was accredited to the latter, but he was also commissioned to Yemen from 1946 to 1959, when the ambassador to Egypt was assigned to replace him with respect to Yemen for two years (1959–1961), at which time the United States envoy to Saudi Arabia was made

American envoy to Lebanon (resident at Beirut) also represented the United States to Syria. After World War II, the same practice was employed in Asia for multiple representation to India and Nepal,[43] to Ceylon (now Sri Lanka) and the Maldives,[44] and for a few years to Vietnam, the Khmer Republic (Cambodia), and Laos.[45] Recently, as new states emerged in Africa, this practice of simultaneous representation was again employed, but often only temporarily. Since 1960 such multiple missions were accredited in the cases of Senegal, Mauritania, and the Gambia; [46] Ivory Coast, Dahomey, Niger, and Upper Volta; [47] the Congo (Brazzaville), the Central African Republic, Chad, and Gabon; [48] and Bostwana, Lesotho, and Swaziland.[49] The practice of temporary multiple representation to new countries, pending the appointment of separate emissaries to them, may be essential to the early consummation of diplomatic relations and, therefore, is likely to continue. In the case of some smaller countries, however, such multiple representation may be extended for some years, as was the case with Nauru after it become independent in 1968.

---

responsible also for Yemen and Kuwait (1961–1963). In 1963 Kuwait was sent its own emissary, and when relations, following a break of five years, were revived with Yemen in 1972, it received its own American ambassador. However, as relations were initiated with Bahrain, Oman, Qatar, and the United Arab Emirates in 1971–1972, the American representative to Kuwait was also accredited to them, until 1974.

[43] Six emissaries (resident at New Delhi) also represented the United States to Nepal from 1947 to 1959, when a separate envoy was commissioned to Kathmandu.

[44] Since 1964 four emissaries (resident at Colombo) have also represented the United States to the Maldives.

[45] Relations with these three Southeast Asian governments commenced in 1950, and Donald R. Heath (resident at Saigon) represented the United States to all three until 1954, when separate envoys were commissioned to each of these countries.

[46] Representation to Senegal (resident at Dakar) commenced in 1960. The American ambassador was also accredited to Mauritania in 1961 and a separate emissary was sent to it in 1965, but that year the emissary to Senegal also commenced to represent the United States to the Gambia.

[47] United States representation to Ivory Coast began in 1960, with temporary simultaneous accreditation to Dahomey, Niger, and Upper Volta, but separate envoys were sent to these three countries the following year.

[48] American diplomatic relations were begun with the Congo (Brazzaville) late in 1960, and within a few days the United States ambassador was accredited additionally to the Central African Republic, Chad, and Gabon, but the following year (1961) separate appointees were named to these three countries.

[49] In 1971 the United States appointed a single emissary to these three African countries (resident at Gaborone).

Reappointments to the Same Countries

A final point relating to multiple diplomatic appointments is that some American emissaries are accredited to a given country more than once. Of 135 such appointees, a substantial majority, ninety-three (69 percent), were reappointed simply with a change of diplomatic rank—usually an increase of personal title or a higher status necessitated by the elevation of the American mission from a legation to an embassy.[50] Rarely has reappointment of a given emissary been accompanied by a reduction of diplomatic rank.[51] In a few cases reappointment involved a change of title to accommodate the adding or deleting of consular to diplomatic responsibilities.[52] Only occasionally—sixteen of the 135 appointees (12 percent)—are American emissaries formally reappointed or recommissioned to continuing assignments with unchanged ranks. When this occurs, it simply reflects such technical changes as modification of the title, government, or regime of the country to which the envoy is accredited, or it indicates reappointment to a different combination of Central American or Balkan countries, or it denotes recommissioning following Senate confirmation or upon expiration of a recess appointment.

The remaining twenty-six (19 percent) such reappointments to the same countries entailed interruptions during which either the American emissary had himself held intervening appointments to other assignments (and other American envoys were accredited to those countries in the interim), or occasionally the emissary was recalled to service at a later date.[53] Some of the two dozen countries to which these American emissaries have been reappointed may be

---

[50] The matter of diplomatic titles and ranking of missions is discussed more fully in chapter 5.

[51] This was the case, however, in 1876 with a series of American emissaries—to Denmark, Greece, Paraguay, Portugal, Switzerland, and Uruguay—whose status was changed from minister resident to chargé d'affaires. In several other cases, the rank was reduced from envoy extraordinary to minister resident, as in Nicaragua (1858), Romania and Serbia (1892), and Iran (1893).

[52] The title of Thomas O. Osborn in Argentina in 1884 was changed from minister resident by adding that of consul general, whereas the consular designation was dropped from the reappointment rank of envoy extraordinary of William W. Rockhill to Greece, Romania, and Serbia in 1898.

[53] Such as the appointments of Chester Bowles to India (1951 and 1963), Myron T. Herrick to France (1912 and 1921), Rufus King to Great Britain (1796 and 1825), Henry Cabot Lodge to Vietnam (1963 and 1965), Oscar S. Straus to Turkey (1887 and 1898), and William W. Thomas, Jr., who held three noncontinuous appointments to Sweden and Norway (1883, 1889, and 1897).

regarded as among the preferred assignments—such as Argentina, Brazil, Canada, France, Germany, Sweden, and the United Kingdom—but, on the whole, they represent a fairly broad spectrum of possible assignments, particularly in northern Europe and South America.[54]

[54] In addition to those named, multiple appointments of a single emissary have been made to such countries as Afghanistan, Chile, Colombia, Greece, Uruguay, and Yemen, and Llewellyn E. Thompson was twice commissioned to Moscow. Reasons other than the desirability of location—such as the special qualifications of the appointee, his acceptability and credibility to the receiving government, and national need—therefore, may also contribute to the making of such unusual appointments.

3

DIPLOMATIC APPOINTEES: COMMENCEMENT, DURATION, AND TERMINATION OF MISSIONS

Having reviewed the evolution of American diplomatic representation and the nature and distribution of diplomatic appointments, it is possible to concentrate more directly on the corps of United States diplomats themselves. This and the following chapters are concerned with the 1,869 persons who, since 1778, have been named to 2,926 appointments—both in the aggregate and as individuals—examining the commencement, duration, and termination of their missions, their geographic origins (that is, the states from which they were appointed),[1] their sex, their age upon appointment, their diplomatic ranks and career status,[2] their presidential and vice-presidential aspirations, their prior congressional experience, and their literary endeavors.

The Appointment Process

When a diplomatic envoy of the United States is decided upon by the President, under the Constitution the appointment must be confirmed by the Senate, and in accordance with international practice, the nominee must be acceptable to the government to which he is accredited. The power of appointing and receiving diplomats is an important political prerogative and is customarily accorded to the executive branch of government. The Constitution provides that the President "shall nominate and, by and with the advice and consent of

---

[1] In this context the term "states" refers to the fifty states and the District of Columbia.

[2] As explained in chapter 5, U.S. diplomats fall into three categories: pre-1915 undesignated appointees, careerists, and post-1915 noncareerists.

the Senate, shall appoint ambassadors, other public ministers, and consuls." [3]

As a political and pragmatic function, nomination for office needs to be distinguished from actual appointment. The nomination is exclusively the prerogative of the chief executive. Early in the history of the republic it was suggested that the Senate propose nominations, but this was opposed as being contrary to the clear wording of the Constitution and violative of the separation of powers doctrine. The consummation of diplomatic appointment, however, necessitates Senate approval, although the Constitution authorizes the President to make "interim appointments" of a temporary nature in order to fill vacancies which occur while Congress is not in session. Accordingly, the President is empowered "to fill up all vacancies that may happen during the recess of the Senate, by granting commissions which shall expire at the end of their next session." [4] As a consequence, when a vacancy exists in some ambassadorial post during such recess, the President may fill it immediately, and the appointment is valid pending the reconvening of the Senate. If the interim appointee is not confirmed by the Senate during its next session his temporary appointment expires.

The following appointment procedure has been followed. Candidates for the posts of heads of missions to foreign governments and international organizations and as ambassadors at large are formally nominated by the President and appointed by him with the approval of the Senate. Generally, but not invariably, the Senate grants its endorsement as a routine matter, even though some diplomats are purely political appointees, and it usually does so with considerable dispatch.[5] Appointments to the career Foreign Service—to be distinguished from designation as a chief of diplomatic mission or to a ranking position in the Department of State—likewise are made by the President with Senate approval. For the career service, nominations are determined on the basis of special examinations, and normally neither the President nor the Senate exercises any serious

---

[3] U.S. Constitution, Article II, Section 2, Clause 2. The same clause also stipulates that Congress may by law vest the appointment of "inferior officers" in the President. For discussion of the process of appointing "inferior officers" as this pertains to diplomacy, see Plischke, *Conduct of American Diplomacy*, pp. 89–91.

[4] U.S. Constitution, Article II, Section 2, Clause 3.

[5] Nominations are passed upon by the Senate Foreign Relations Committee. It is congressional custom that usually no opposition is raised to the appointment of a former senator, either in the committee or in the Senate itself, and, in order to accord proper courtesy to an incumbent senator, when his name is placed in nomination by the President for a diplomatic post, confirmation is considered by his colleagues without even sending it to committee.

discretion in the matter. Both Congress and the President have approved this method in a series of statutes which established this selection system.[6] When an FSO is designated as a chief of mission, however, such appointment is subject to the same nomination and confirmation procedure that applies to noncareer diplomats.

As part of the appointment process, the President is constitutionally empowered to "commission all the officers of the United States," including its diplomats.[7] Official appointments to major positions in the government, therefore, are acknowledged by the issuance of commissions, which are legal authorizations empowering appointees to perform their official duties. They are signed by the President or some other official designated by him, and those issued to diplomatic representatives as a rule bear the presidential signature. Technically, the appointment is not effective until the commission has been properly issued, but this is essentially a formality attesting, so far as the United States is concerned, that the appointment is legally verified and complete.

Although international law and practice do not specify hard and fast rules concerning the personal qualifications and character of those appointed as diplomats—inasmuch as these are determined on the basis of domestic constitutional and political considerations—no sending state has the right to demand that a receiving state accept a particular individual. If a government elects, for good and sufficient reasons, to refuse to receive a certain envoy, this is entirely within its prerogatives. In other words, a diplomatic representative must be acceptable, or *persona grata*, to the receiving government. States usually do not oppose suggested appointees, but they do refuse to receive their own citizens or subjects as the envoys of foreign countries,[8] or individuals whose powers or activities are deemed to be incompatible with the institutions or way of life of the receiving state. For example, in the past, Protestant countries—including the United States—have usually refused to receive regular resident Papal envoys.

To obviate the problems and delay that might flow from the refusal to receive a particular emissary, the custom has developed

---

[6] Current legislation respecting the Department of State and Foreign Service is contained in *Legislation on Foreign Relations: With Explanatory Notes*, produced in an annually updated version by the Senate Foreign Relations Committee and House Foreign Affairs Committee (Washington, D. C.: Government Printing Office, annually), section on the Department of State.

[7] U.S. Constitution, Article II, Section 3.

[8] This has been traditional United States practice. More precisely, the Department of State recognizes as valid the appointment of an American as a member of a foreign mission in Washington providing that he is not the chief of mission.

whereby the sending state consults in advance with the receiving government concerning the matter. In technical language, the process for determining such acceptability prior to appointment is called *agréation,* and the approval is known as *agrément.*

During most of the nineteenth century the United States did not adhere to this practice, because none of its diplomatic envoys had a rank higher than that of minister and, perhaps, because American conduct was influenced by the turnover of ranking diplomats occasioned by frequent elections and changes of administration. Since adopting the policy of appointing diplomats with ambassadorial rank, however, the Department of State has followed the custom of ascertaining acceptability through *agréation,*[9] and in 1961 this process was made a treaty requirement by the Vienna Convention on Diplomatic Relations.[10] The traditional procedure is for the secretary of state to contact the head of the foreign government to which an appointment is pending to determine whether a particular nominee will be acceptable, and if he is, the President submits the name to the Senate for confirmation.[11] It is contrary to accepted protocol for a receiving government to assume the initiative and intimate to the sending state its preference for or willingness to accept a specific individual.[12]

When the receiving government has given *agrément,* the diplomat is furnished with a number of credentials and official documents in addition to his commission. One of the most important is his "letter of credence," evidencing the envoy's representative character, signed by the chief executive, which is addressed to and formally presented to the head of the receiving state. In the case of chargés d'affaires, it is addressed by the secretary of state to the foreign minister of the country to which the chargé is accredited. The letter of credence identifies the envoy, indicates the general object of his mission, acknowledges confidence in his management of the affairs with which he is charged, and requests the receiving state, in return, to accord full faith and credit to the matters he handles for the United States.

---

9 For further discussion, see Graham H. Stuart, *American Diplomatic and Consular Practice,* pp. 139–141.

10 Article 4 specifies: "The sending State must make certain that the *agrément* of the receiving State has been given for the person it proposes to accredit as head of the mission to that State. The receiving State is not obligated to give reasons to the sending State for a refusal of *agrément.*"

11 For illustrative and explanatory documents, see Plischke, *Conduct of American Diplomacy,* p. 603, and Elmer Plischke, *International Relations: Basic Documents,* 2nd ed. (Princeton: Van Nostrand, 1962), p. 14.

12 However, sometimes foreign governments indicate their impatience if a government delays unduly in naming a successor diplomat.

The letter of credence of a resident diplomat often contains "full powers," or this may be confined to a separate document. The full powers define the limits within which the envoy may negotiate and to what extent his acts may be considered binding, with a reservation at least implied concerning subsequent ratification by the government of the United States. In addition, the diplomat may be furnished with written and oral "instructions," or directions for the guidance of his mission. These usually are supplied at the outset of his appointment and may be supplemented, suspended, or replaced at any time. He also is provided with a "diplomatic passport" by the Department of State—to identify his special status while en route to the receiving country; in some cases in the past diplomats were furnished a "safe conduct"—an authorization granting permission to pass unmolested through the territory of a belligerent state in time of war.[13]

Nonconsummation of Appointment

As a consequence of these United States and international procedures and documentation, entailing a number of specific stages in the process of consummating diplomatic representation to foreign governments, diplomatic appointees need to be distinguished from nominees, and those who are appointed must be differentiated from those who are formally accredited, are officially received, and actually assume their responsibilities as American chiefs of mission. Of the total number of 2,497 nominations-appointments of chiefs of mission since 1778, approximately 2,270 (91 percent) served in their appointments, whereas 227 (9 percent) failed to do so. In other words, somewhat less than one of every ten, although nominated for appointment, went unapproved, was otherwise not commissioned or accredited, or was not officially received. This failure to consummate diplomatic appointment is attributed to several reasons, political and personal, which are listed in Table A-8.

Inasmuch as purpose and action are required on the part of not only the President, but also the Senate, the receiving government, and the nominated candidate, these reasons for failure to effectuate nearly one in ten diplomatic nominations and appointments fall into

---

[13] For a more detailed discussion of these matters respecting appointment and credentials (and for copies of appointment and accreditation documents, together with U.S. procedures), see Plischke, *Conduct of American Diplomacy*, pp. 295–297, and Appendices IX–XI, XIII, and XVI–XVII, and Plischke, *International Relations: Basic Documents*, chapter 2. These have also been reproduced in Robert B. Harmon, *The Art and Practice of Diplomacy: A Selected and Annotated Guide* (Metuchen, New Jersey: Scarecrow Press, 1971), pp. 228–233, 240–241.

four general categories. The first of these flows from the basic American separation of powers system, requiring legislative-executive cooperation in the making of presidential appointments. In approximately one-third of the 227 cases the difficulty lay with Senate consideration. While only twenty nominations have been overtly rejected by the Senate in nearly two centuries,[14] twenty-four others were tabled or simply remained unconfirmed—both of which are tantamount to rejection, albeit by lack of action—and twenty-nine were withdrawn by the President, often but not always because Senate approval seemed unlikely. However, even if all of these are attributable to Senate action or inaction, in combination they amount to less than 3 percent of all nominations and appointments as chiefs of mission since 1778, and, keeping in mind that the Senate confirmed most of the other nominations, this represents a high degree of legislative-executive cooperation.

Once successfully nominated and confirmed, the diplomat is almost invariably appointed and commissioned. There appear to be only three cases in which appointment was aborted because commissioning was withheld by the chief executive,[15] and only one emissary's letter of credence, having been signed by the President, was cancelled.[16]

Also noteworthy is the fact that only on three occasions have receiving governments turned down American diplomatic appointees. One of the most striking examples of the refusal to accept a particular envoy involved Anthony M. Keiley, whose accreditation was refused by both the Italian and Austrian governments. Upon designation as minister to Italy in 1885, he was not accepted because some years earlier he had publicly protested Italy's annexation of the Papal States. Subsequently, when commissioned to Austria-Hungary, that country objected on the ground that, since he was wedded to a Jewess

---

[14] Exceptional was the case of John A. McClernand, former congressman, named minister to Mexico in the 1860s, who was not commissioned because his nomination was twice rejected by the Senate.

[15] William Van Murray, whose nomination as minister to France late in the eighteenth century was superseded (because of certain pressures in the Senate) by a new nomination of Murray and two others (including Chief Justice Oliver Ellsworth) to serve on a joint three-member commission to settle outstanding difficulties with the French government prior to appointing a new regular resident emissary. George N. Erving, who had previously served in Denmark and Spain, was nominated as the first American emissary to Turkey in 1830, and, although he was approved by the Senate, he was not commissioned. Aaron A. Sargent, who had previously served in Germany, was not commissioned as envoy to Russia in the 1880s, even though his nomination was confirmed by the Senate.

[16] In the late 1860s David Armstrong was named chargé d'affaires to Vatican City, but pending commissioning, his letter of credence, dated 30 April 1869, was cancelled.

by civil marriage, he would unfortunately prove socially unacceptable in Vienna. Although the State Department refused to accept this as proper justification for rejection, Mr. Keiley resigned and another appointment was made, whereupon Keiley was named a judge on the International Tribunal of Egypt. Another case involved former Senator Henry W. Blair who was named minister to China in 1891 but, because of his earlier opposition to Chinese immigration and his participation in the enactment of oriental exclusion legislation, the Chinese government found him to be *persona non grata,* and his appointment foundered.

Since the introduction of the process of *agréation,* this problem has been eliminated. By and large, very few potential appointees are rejected by foreign governments. In 1913, however, when President Woodrow Wilson sought to send James W. Gerard as ambassador to Mexico, the receiving government refused to accept him because of alleged mistreatment of labor on his Mexican mining property. Gerard was then appointed ambassador to Germany, and the United States failed to name a new envoy to Mexico for three years.[17] All told, these categories account for merely eighty cases (35 percent) in which nominations for diplomatic appointment failed to be consummated.[18]

The primary reasons for the failure of designated chiefs of mission to serve under their commissions come from the appointees themselves. Some fifty declined their appointments, forty-seven were accredited but did not proceed to their posts, and thirty-six either failed to present their credentials to the receiving governments or did not otherwise serve under their commissions—for a total of 133 (or 59 percent). A number of those who fall into the last three categories were named as recess appointees—politically a somewhat equivocal status—which left Senate action in abeyance.[19] About two dozen of those who did not present their credentials or assume responsibilities in particular posts were multiple assignment appointees, serving in one or more countries but not in all of those to which they were appointed.[20]

---

[17] For additional information concerning these and other illustrations, see Stuart, *American Diplomatic and Consular Practice,* pp. 141–144.

[18] Items 1–6 and 10 of Table A-8.

[19] Nevertheless, a good many others did serve under such recess appointments and were recommissioned after Senate confirmation.

[20] This was particularly true of emissaries accredited simultaneously to two or more of the Central American Republics, but also pertained to those accredited to some combination of the Balkan countries prior to the end of World War I (i.e., Bulgaria, Greece, Montenegro, Romania, Serbia, and Yugoslavia), to Luxembourg as well as to either Belgium or the Netherlands, and to Saudi Arabia and Yemen.

Finally, twelve appointees (5 percent) died prior to commencing their diplomatic assignments—six in the United States before proceeding to their posts, three en route, and the remaining three after arriving in the countries to which they were designated but prior to taking charge of their missions.[21] More than half of these involved appointees to Latin American countries, of which three were named as emissaries to Guatemala and two to Ecuador.[22]

Two early American diplomats—John Jay, appointed to Spain in 1779, and Francis Dana, accredited to Russia the following year—were technically unable to consummate their missions, at least in a formal sense, in that they were not officially received. Nevertheless, they remained in these countries for several years before their missions expired. They constitute a unique category in that, although they were not formally acknowledged by the receiving governments, they carried on their functions and, as in the case of special envoys and presidential agents, their missions ended without formal action respecting termination or supersession.

As a consequence of the United States appointing and accrediting process, resulting in the failure to effectuate a substantial number of diplomatic appointments, it may be presumed that the government was left unrepresented by chiefs of mission in a good many countries for extended periods of time. This suspension of top-level American representation has involved sixty-seven countries—amounting to somewhat less than half (48 percent) of the states with which diplomatic exchanges have been established since 1778. Because only one or two nominees have been involved in the case of approximately half of these countries (thirty-one of sixty-seven), such nonappointment of diplomats has not been a serious problem in United States relations with them. However, five or more nominees failed to serve in each of seventeen states—mostly European and Latin American countries with which the United States has had the lengthiest records of diplomatic relations, but also including China and Liberia. The states most seriously affected in this respect include (with the number of cases in parentheses):

Europe: Austria (10), Russia (10), and Spain (8)

---

21 One of these died prior to presenting his credentials, and another before being officially received.

22 The United States had difficulty initially in staffing its mission to Guatemala in that, during the four decades from 1825 to 1865, of eighteen nominees-appointees, only six actually served, and one of these died at his post. Difficulty also was encountered in Ecuador between 1867, when the American minister died, and 1875; during this period of less than a decade, seven nominees failed to be appointed and received in Quito and the one appointee who assumed his duties died in service.

Latin America: Guatemala (13), Ecuador (9), Honduras (9), Argentina (7), and Mexico (7)

Others: China (8) and Liberia (6)

These ten states account for nearly 40 percent of the 227 cases of nonconsummation of diplomatic appointments. On the other hand, this problem has been virtually nonexistent in the relations of the United States with most countries, including a good many of those with which extended diplomatic exchanges have been maintained.

The primary diplomatic difficulty resulting from nonconsummation is the break in top-level diplomatic representation. This occurred at the commencement of diplomatic relations with fourteen countries and delayed the establishment of adequate representation at chief of mission level.[23] Early representation to a number of additional states also were interrupted by nonconsummation of appointment. In the case of Guatemala, for example, although the first envoy was nominated on 7 March 1825 and the President submitted seven nominations in approximately eight years, only one of them was formally appointed prior to 1833 so that during this period the United States was represented by a chief of mission for only seven months. On the other hand, although the first American diplomat to Liberia was named in March 1863 and only two of the initial six nominees were appointed, they served as American emissaries for seven years during the nine-year period to the spring of 1871.

The actual time gap in diplomatic representation, therefore, is of greater import than the number and sequence of nonconsummations of appointment. Often, as a matter of fact, the nomination of one diplomat is so timed in relation to the termination of his predecessor's tenure that in reality little or no hiatus occurs in top-level American representation. During the period, for example, in which three candidates were nominated for appointment to Liberia in the late 1860s, the incumbent minister resident continued at his post, keeping the break in representation to less than nine months. Similarly, in Yugoslavia, although three of six nominees either declined appointment or did not otherwise enter upon their duties during the period

[23] The first two nominees to Costa Rica, El Salvador, Honduras, and Mexico either declined appointment or were not fully accredited or received. The single initial nominees to China, Greece, Guatemala, Iran, Liberia, Mali, New Zealand, Nicaragua, Peru, and Turkey also failed to be appointed or to assume their responsibilities. In five cases the nominations were withdrawn from the Senate, one nominee was not commissioned, two declined appointment, one died en route, and one suffered the consequences of a change of statehood in the country to which he was being accredited.

from 1902 to 1909, the interruption of United States representation continued for only eight months. Moreover, whereas eight consecutive nominees failed to be appointed to Austria in the 1860s—primarily because the Senate failed to approve them—the lack of representation lasted only fifteen months.[24]

On the other hand, protracted if not deleterious gaps do occur. For example, for twelve years of the nineteenth century the United States had no chief of mission to represent it in Argentina,[25] and for more than eighteen years of a four-decade period of the same century there was no American chief of mission in Guatemala.[26] Unless such breaks in diplomatic representation result from war and the severance of diplomatic relations, or, for policy reasons, they are created by design, they may result in serious adverse effects upon the diplomacy of the United States with such countries.

Of greater political significance internally is the timing of these 227 cases of appointment nonconsummation. Table A-9 presents statistics by decade, from which four important interrelated conclusions may be drawn. Most noteworthy is the high number of cases materializing in the mid-nineteenth century, with one-fourth of all nonconsummations clustered in the single decade of the 1860s. Furthermore, nearly 60 percent of all nonconsummations occurred during the first century of American diplomacy, when the total number of countries with which the United States maintained diplomatic relations amounted to less than one-third of the states presently involved, so that the ratio of cases was much greater than is apparent in the figures presented. Conversely, not only has the number of cases per decade been modest since 1910, but the ratio of nonconsummations to the number of countries concerned and to the overall quantity of appointments made has also declined substantially in the twentieth century. As a consequence, it appears that greater care is being exercised in the manner of selecting and nominating candidates, that the President and the Senate are cooperating more effectively in the appointment process, and that the problem of nonconsummation is of declining political importance. It is likely to decline even more as the percentage of career appointees increases.

---

[24] 14 June 1867 to 25 September 1868.

[25] 26 September 1832 to 15 November 1844, during which period two nominees remained unappointed.

[26] 1 December 1826 to 17 December 1833; 23 June 1849 to 14 February 1855; 8 May 1856 to 13 July 1858; 17 March 1860 to 28 May 1861; and 22 June 1864 to 26 June 1866. Eleven nominees failed to be fully appointed during this period.

Duration of Diplomatic Missions [27]

In view of the problems and delay involved in the nominating and appointing procedures and the time necessary for a diplomatic emissary to learn to know the country to which he is assigned, to gain the confidence of its leaders, to establish his professional and personal credibility, and to achieve useful diplomatic results, it would seem that a chief of mission would optimally remain in his post for several years—normally not less than three and preferably at least four or five. This is not borne out by the record, however. Reviewing the average length of service of United States envoys—determined by computing the ratio between the total number of American diplomats who served in each foreign country and the length of time the United States has maintained diplomatic relations with it—as indicated in column H of Table A-2, it is possible to conclude that the overall duration of American diplomatic missions averages between two and one-half and three years. More precisely, over a span of nearly two centuries, the arithmetical mean—counting all countries, including those with which diplomatic relations had just commenced,[28] is 3.1 years. If one excludes the eleven countries with which diplomatic relations had just commenced for which initial emissaries were accredited for one year or less, the overall average is 3.12 years. Were the time gap between departing and replacement emissaries to be included in the equation, the tenure average would be somewhat lower. In any case, this means that, on the whole, since 1778 American chiefs of mission have been replaced in three years or less.

These averages differ from country to country, and from region to region. Specific figures are given in Table A-2, and they indicate that, of the 141 countries with which the United States had established diplomatic representation over the years, in one-third of them (fifty—or 35 percent) the average length of American missions was two and one-half years or less, whereas it exceeded three and one-half years in fewer than one-fifth of them (twenty-eight or less than 20 percent). For the remaining sixty-three (45 percent) the average tenure ranged from two and one-half to three and one-half years. Individual country mission duration varies from such rapid turnover averages as 1.33 years (in Equatorial Guinea and Texas),

---

[27] This section is concerned with the length of tenure of diplomatic appointees to individual countries. The matter of tenure longevity of individuals in the diplomatic service of the United States is dealt with in chapters 2 and 4.

[28] This excludes Bangladesh, however, with which diplomatic relations were being launched but to which no American emissary had been accredited by 31 March 1973.

1.5 years (the Maldives), and 1.75 years (Gambia and Malta) to a high of four years or longer. The lengthiest averages have applied to China, Cyprus, and Ecuador (4.0 years), the Netherlands (4.13), Norway (4.19), Sweden (4.39), and Israel (4.8). The ratios may change considerably for those countries on both extremes of the scale with which diplomatic relations have been of relatively short duration. However, the high averages for such countries as China, Ecuador, the Netherlands, and the Scandinavian countries extend over protracted periods.

Turning from individual countries to broader geographic considerations, Table 2 summarizes the diplomatic mission duration averages given in column H of Table A-2. The fact that Europe has the highest regional record, and that the Western Hemisphere is second, may mean that diplomatic posts in these areas are regarded as among the more desirable and emissaries are therefore inclined to remain longer. Nevertheless, these also are the regions with which the United States has maintained the lengthiest diplomatic exchanges. Where relations have been established only recently with many of the countries within the other three regions, especially in sub-Saharan Africa, the duration figure is lowest. It may be concluded, therefore, that tenures tend to be shorter at the commencement of diplomatic relations or, more likely, that length of service is generally decreasing.

Table 2

AVERAGE DURATION OF DIPLOMATIC MISSIONS BY GEOGRAPHIC AREA

Region	**Countries** [a]	**Diplomats Who Served** [b]		**Mission Duration** (Years) [c]
Western Hemisphere	26	751		3.33
Europe	34	858		3.36
Middle East and North Africa	16	210		3.14
Sub-Saharan Africa	33	192		2.66
Asia and Pacific	21	256		3.01
Total	130	2,267	Overall Average	3.10

[a] This excludes the eleven new countries with which diplomatic relations were maintained for one year or less as of 31 March 1973.

[b] Based on totals contained in column G of Table A-2.

[c] Based on totals contained in column H of Table A-2.

Source: Summary totals derived from Table A-2.

Because this analysis concerns only comprehensive averages, it does not take account of a number of important factors, such as periods of time between the departure of an emissary and the commencement of the mission of his successor. More concrete assessment can be derived from an examination of the specific duration of the individual missions themselves. Table A-10 provides statistics for the length of time American chiefs of mission to foreign governments have actually held their posts, giving, in part 1, the number of diplomats who remained from one to fifteen years or more, and indicating separately, in part 2, the missions which have been shorter than one year. Summary totals are given in part 3.

Of the 2,154 appointees who actually served in their posts and whose tenure can be calculated,[29] 222 (10 percent) remained for less than one year. Among the remainder, the preponderant majority (1,365 or 71 percent) served from one to four years. Of these, 457 (21 percent) held their posts for only twelve to twenty-four months, and 908 (42 percent) remained for periods ranging from two to less than four years. Only 381 (18 percent) were accredited for four or five years, and the balance of 186 (9 percent) lasted for six years or more, with twenty-four achieving the record of persevering in a single mission for ten years or longer.

It is clear from Table A-10 that American diplomatic tenures tend to be relatively short. Somewhat exceptional are the cases of Ecuador, where during a period of thirty-four years (1913–1947) six appointees averaged five to six years each, and Turkey, where during a thirty-nine-year period (1831–1870) six emissaries held their posts for periods ranging from more than three to nearly twelve years. On the other hand, also atypical, of the first seven envoys to Panama (1903–1913) only one held his mission for more than two years, and of the twenty-seven appointees to that country to 1973, only six continued for three years or more, whereas five survived for less than a year. Similarly, of the fifty-five chiefs of mission accredited to Russia/Soviet Union, only fifteen (27 percent) served for more than three years, whereas twenty-two (40 percent) remained less than two years.

The longest tenures of American chiefs of mission were held by career officer Edwin V. Morgan, who served as ambassador to Brazil for more than twenty-one years (1912–1933) and by George P. Marsh, envoy extraordinary and minister plenipotentiary to Italy,

[29] The figure is the total of parts 1 and 2 of Table A-10; it differs from the total of 2,155 in Table A-11 in that the latter includes a nomination for appointment to Bangladesh which was pending as of March 1973.

who might have exceeded the twenty-one years and four months (1861–1882) of his tenure had he not died in office. Maxwell Blake, also a career officer, held two nonconsecutive appointments as diplomatic agent and consul general to Morocco for a combined total of twenty years.[30] Others with extended mission tenure, ranging between twelve and fourteen years, include: John A. Bingham (Japan, twelve years), Claude G. Bowers (Chile, fourteen years), John R. Clay (Peru, thirteen years), Charles Denby (China, thirteen years), William L. Merry (Costa Rica, fourteen years),[31] and David Porter (Turkey, nearly twelve years).

Of the two dozen envoys serving for ten years or more, fourteen were appointed before 1915, and of the remainder seven were careerists, each of whom, aside from Blake and Morgan, served in his post from ten to twelve years. The countries to which these twenty-four chiefs of mission were assigned lay primarily in Europe (nine appointments) and Latin America (eight appointments), but also included China (two appointments) and Japan, and Israel, Liberia, Morocco, and Turkey. Nevertheless, there appears to be little discernible pattern respecting geographic distribution, and much the same can be said concerning the historical periods in which these long-tenured diplomats were serving. Nearly three-fourths were appointed prior to World War I, and none were designated in the 1940s and 1950s, but Walworth Barbour, a career diplomat, was accredited to Israel in 1961 and remained for nearly twelve years (to January 1973).

Far more numerous are those American diplomats who serve for short periods. Part 2 of Table A-10 lists, by number of months, the 222 who remained less than a year in their assignments. Nine of these had their missions aborted by death or assassination, one was declared *persona non grata,* and in ten cases missions were terminated early by Axis invasion, the wartime transfer of the locale of an exile government, or a change in the legal status of the receiving country (as explained in the following section). Aside from these few whose appointments expired for reasons beyond their control, more than 200 American emissaries served for such brief periods for other reasons, including, in a few cases, the establishment of new diplomatic missions in emergent countries by envoys who may have been commissioned on an interim basis pending the appointment of more permanent chiefs of mission.

---

[30] These ran from 1917 to 1922 and from 1925 to 1940.

[31] Merry was also commissioned simultaneously to Nicaragua for eleven and to El Salvador for ten of these fourteen years, which renders this an exceptional multiple appointment, amounting to a combined total of thirty-five years of service.

Perhaps even more significant is the fact that approximately seventy-five American diplomats have remained at their posts for merely half a year or less, in some dozen instances for only one or two months. Among the shortest appointments were the ten-day tenure of Marcus Otterbourg in Mexico (1867) and the four-day mission of Kenneth Franzheim in Tonga (1972).[32] In addition, Tilghman A. Howard, chargé accredited to Texas in 1844, had his mission terminated by death after serving for only two weeks. The majority of these very short appointments have occurred since 1930, and most of the emissaries concerned have been careerists.

The professionalization of the senior ranks of American diplomacy does not reduce the problems of short tenure and rapid turnover. As a matter of fact, of the seventy-four who have held their posts for six months or less, thirty-eight (or more than half) have been careerists, twenty-seven were pre-1915 appointees, and only nine were post-1915 noncareerists. Consequently, it appears that both the total number of such short tenures and the percentage of careerists involved are on the increase. Even though each of the 222 cases of less than a year's tenure—amounting to more than one in every ten diplomats designated since 1778—may be deemed to be individually justifiable, and some certainly are, as a widespread practice with a substantial aggregate, this must be not only costly, but also detrimental to the diplomacy of the United States and should, therefore, be resolutely reduced. To the extent to which this condition represents poor selection of noncareerists from outside the Foreign Service or personal jockeying by careerists for preferred posts, which may in either case produce a protracted chain reaction of reassignments, it might profitably be eliminated entirely.

Termination of Diplomatic Missions

Once a diplomatic mission has been established and has run its course, normally it is concluded by the sending government on its determination or at the behest of the diplomat. The decision to terminate is entirely an executive action and requires no legislative approval. Sometimes the mission may be brought to an end by the receiving government. In general, the process of termination is somewhat less

[32] These are computed from the time of presentation of credentials to termination of mission. Ambassador Franzheim had also been serving in New Zealand since 1969, as well as in Fiji and Western Samoa, and his appointment to Tonga was made at about the same time that he was leaving his primary post in New Zealand, so that he never did present his credentials at Nukualofa. The reason for Minister Otterbourg's early departure is not clear.

formal and complicated than that of appointment and accreditation, but certain standard procedures have been widely used.

Diplomatic missions may be ended for a variety of reasons, some pertaining to the mission per se and others relating to the tenure of the incumbent. Sometimes missions expire in accordance with the terms of letters of credence which fix a time limit for their duration, but this would be more applicable to special assignments than to regular resident emissaries to foreign governments. Missions may terminate, of course, when diplomatic relations are suspended temporarily pending the recognition of a new government in the host country, when diplomatic relations are formally severed, when war breaks out between the two countries, when the mission of a diplomat is ended by flight of the receiving government in the face of foreign invasion and occupation, when there is a change in the fundamental legal status of the country to which the envoy is accredited, or when the diplomat becomes *persona non grata* or dies.

The normal and most frequent modes of termination, however, involve the determination of the sending government to dismiss or transfer the diplomat, or the latter resigns. Technically, such action is accomplished by the process known as recall, usually certified to by a formal "letter of recall." Before quitting a foreign capital, envoys often have a final audience with the head of state and present their letters of recall. In return, they may receive letters of recommendation, and, in some capitals, gifts or decorations.[33] American practice has differed somewhat from this general procedure. Although the President often has received departing foreign diplomats in an informal ceremony, letters of recall have only exceptionally been conveyed personally by the retiring envoy. They usually are trans-

[33] The giving of presents has been disappearing from diplomatic practice, but the bestowal of decorations and honors is sometimes still practiced. The Constitution of the United States (Article 1, Section 9), and legislation to implement it, prohibit an officer or employee of the United States, including diplomats, to ask for, or without the consent of Congress, receive any presents (including decorations), emoluments, pecuniary favors, offices, or titles from any foreign government. While Congress initially was loathe to grant its approval, in the course of time its attitude has become more liberal. However, gifts, decorations, and other displays of honor are taken into custody by the Department of State, and, because there is no similar constitutional prohibition respecting private individuals, diplomats may receive such gifts and decorations upon retirement from public service. For the text of the law and additional comment, see *United States Code*, Title 22, Par. 804; Green H. Hackworth, *Digest of International Law* (Washington, D. C.: Government Printing Office, 1942), vol. 4, pp. 475–478.

In 1957, as a consequence of the acceptance by the wife of an American diplomatic official of an expensive automobile from the King of Saudi Arabia, the Department of State issued a new directive barring diplomats from accepting gifts from foreign dignitaries and instructing emissaries to discourage such gift giving.

mitted by the successor at the time the latter presents his letter of credence.

The Department of State ascribes a variety of reasons for the termination of diplomatic appointments and missions. Some of these evince rather concrete and obvious reasons for expiration, whereas others—such as a diplomat leaving his post, the leaving of the country to which the emissary is accredited, the relinquishment of charge, and supersession—are more ambiguous and may be formal explications rather than basic justifications. Twenty-one categories of diplomatic mission termination are provided in Table A-11. Only one of these—resignation—clearly suggests the wishes of the diplomat, and while the requesting of passports appears to imply volition on the part of the envoy it may really be instituted on Department of State instructions. Two of these categories—requesting that the envoy be recalled, and dismissal because the emissary is regarded as *persona non grata*—are initiated by the host governments.

Table A-11 indicates only one case in which an American chief of mission is specified by the Department of State as having resigned (but note that because George Williamson held simultaneous appointments to the five Central American Republics, all of his five missions were terminated by his resignation on 31 January 1879). Although resignation may have been the main reason for a good many other terminations, they were formally handled in other ways, and therefore are covered by other departmental termination designations. Appearing to reflect process rather than motivation for termination, in 1842 Richard Pollard "requested his passports" from the Chilean government after serving as chargé d'affaires in Valparaiso for nearly eight years.[34]

In a period of nearly two centuries, only fourteen (less than 1 percent) American diplomats had their appointments terminated on the initiation of the host governments, generally because they ceased to be acceptable to the receiving authorities. Diplomats may become *persona non grata* for alleged criticism of government officials, meddling in domestic (especially political) affairs, violating local laws, disparaging the government or people, or committing acts inimical to their interests or security. Usually the offended host government transmits a request to the sending government to recall its emissary,

---

[34] In early modern times the receiving government often issued the foreign emissary a passport to enter and leave its territory. Consequently, when the diplomat became *persona non grata*, he was "handed his passports," or if the envoy wished to terminate his mission, he "requested his passports" to depart the country. This is no longer the case, and when these expressions are still used, this is done figuratively.

which if made in good faith and for cause, is normally honored. If it is declined, however, the receiving government may simply inform the envoy that it will no longer deal officially with him, or it may summarily dismiss him. In any event, an American envoy whose recall has been requested can be of little further effective service in the capital to which he has been sent, so that there is minimal advantage in refusing to comply with the recall request.[35]

On eight occasions foreign governments have "requested the recall" of American diplomats. These included Gouverneur Morris, an early emissary to France whose withdrawal the French government solicited in the 1790s because of his antipathy to the excesses of the French Revolution, and Joel R. Poinsett, first United States minister to serve in Mexico, who was requested to leave in 1829, after serving for more than four years; in 1835 the Mexican government also requested the recall of his successor, Chargé Anthony Butler. These Mexican actions probably were due to major policy differences with the United States concerning the boundary and Texas questions. There appears to be no particular pattern to the issuance of requests for recall, each case having its own reasons. Three involved Latin American governments, and four have occurred in this century, two as late as the 1960s.[36] In addition, while differing little in effect, but varying in formality if not in purpose, in 1971 the Madagascar (Malagasy) government "requested the departure" of Ambassador Anthony D. Marshall. All but two of the nine emissaries involved in these actions were noncareerists, including six whose recall antedated 1915.[37]

Only five American diplomats have been overtly dismissed by foreign governments, ostensibly for being *persona non grata.* The first was Thomas Russell, who was informed by the Venezuelan government in 1877 that it refused to have any further dealings with

---

[35] The 1961 Vienna Convention on Diplomatic Relations, specifies in Article 9: "The receiving State may at any time and without having to explain its decision, notify the sending State that the head of the mission or any member of the diplomatic staff of the mission is *persona non grata* or that any other member of the staff of the mission is not acceptable. In any such case, the sending State shall, as appropriate, either recall the person concerned or terminate his functions with the mission. A person may be declared *non grata* or not acceptable before arriving in the territory of the receiving State.

If the sending State refuses or fails within a reasonable period to carry out its obligations under . . . this Article, the receiving State may refuse to recognize the person concerned as a member of the mission."

[36] Aside from those mentioned, given chronologically, these include: Albert G. Jewett, Peru (1846); Francis B. Loomis, Venezuela (1901); Charles E. Mitchell, Liberia (1933); Donald A. Dumont, first Ambassador to Burundi (1965); and Weymberley DeR. Coerr, Ecuador (1967).

[37] The careerists were Dumont and Coerr.

him. The remaining four dismissals occurred after World War I. T. Sambola Jones, a noncareerist, was dismissed by Honduras in 1920, and the remaining three—each a career officer of some distinction—were emissaries to Eastern European Communist countries during the cold war, when a veritable battle of attrition was being waged on diplomatic staffs. In this battle the United States was at some disadvantage. A Communist country could force the recall of a valuable emissary, leaving the Department of State in a difficult position, because at the time it had few diplomats who were adequately familiar with that part of the world and conversant in the languages. Also, newly designated emissaries and their staffs were severely circumscribed by onerous local security regulations behind the Iron Curtain.[38]

Early in 1949 the Hungarian government demanded that the United States recall Selden Chapin, its minister to Budapest, on the grounds that he had cooperated with Cardinal Mindszenty, who was tried and sentenced by a Hungarian court to life imprisonment for alleged treason. The charges against the American minister were denied officially by the United States government, but it recalled him, and he left his post. The following year, the Bulgarian government's request for the recall of Minister Donald R. Heath led to the severance of diplomatic relations with that country, and they remained in abeyance for a decade.

Doubtless the most celebrated case in recent American experience was that involving Ambassador George F. Kennan. On 3 October 1952 the Soviet government informed the United States that two weeks earlier, at Tempelhof airport in West Berlin, after only a few months at his post, Ambassador Kennan made certain critical remarks to the press comparing the status of members of the American diplomatic mission in Moscow with that he allegedly experienced when interned by the Nazis in Germany in 1941 and 1942. The Soviet Union regarded these statements as "slanderous attacks" and a "rude violation of generally recognized norms of international law," and it declared the ambassador to be *persona non grata.*

The formal record of the unacceptability of only seventeen American emissaries—both prior to appointment and recalled on request or dismissed—is rather impressive, amounting to less than 1 percent

---

[38] For additional commentary, see Jean E. Spencer, "Soviet and European Satellite Treatment of Resident United States Diplomatic Personnel Since the Second World War," M.A. thesis, University of Maryland, 1961, and Cecil B. Jones, Jr., "Mistreatment of Foreign Diplomats in the United States Since World War II," M.A. thesis, University of Maryland, 1963. Also see Clifton E. Wilson, *Cold War Diplomacy* (Tucson: University of Arizona Press, 1966).

of all Americans nominated and appointed as chiefs of mission. Nevertheless, in some instances an emissary who might have become *persona non grata* was recalled or replaced on American initiative, and still others left their posts, resigned, or requested reassignment without awaiting formal dismissal or enforced recall action.[39]

The termination of appointment of the preponderant majority of American diplomats is on the action of the United States government. The principal reasons ascribed by the Department of State (see Table A-11) are that the emissary either left his post or the country to which he was accredited, that he presented his letter of recall or had a final audience with the head of state, that he relinquished charge of his mission, that he was superseded, or simply that his appointment or his mission was terminated. Each of these designations appears to have an obvious meaning, and yet there are a number of subtle differences and apparent traditional usage patterns.

The normal procedure for the presentation of letters of recall, or having a farewell audience or interview with the head of state, thereby terminating the diplomat's mission, was a well-established practice when the United States entered the diplomatic arena. A letter of recall is a formal document, signed by the President, and addressed to the head of state of the receiving country, informing him of the termination of the diplomat's mission.[40] This procedure was first used by American emissaries in France, the Netherlands, Portugal, Spain, and Great Britain in the late eighteenth century, and in Germany in 1801. It was freely employed as the normal procedure for mission termination until late in the nineteenth century. The quarter century from 1890 to World War I constituted a transition period, during which some terminations continued to be made by this recall submittal procedure, and in a number of isolated cases it was

---

[39] Often governments cooperate respecting the manner in which the termination of the appointment of a particular diplomat is handled. For example, in a celebrated case during the presidential campaign of 1888, the British minister Lord Sackville-West found himself the victim of an electioneering hoax. In reply to a private letter received from one purporting to be a naturalized Anglo-American, requesting his advice as to the candidate most likely to benefit British interests in the United States, he advised voting for Grover Cleveland, and the response was published and used against Cleveland in the campaign. The minister's recall was requested by the Department of State, but when the British government intimated that it preferred having him dismissed, because that would be less injurious to the emissary's diplomatic career, the United States obliged by "sending him his passports."

[40] For American procedure and examples of the letter of recall, see Plischke, *Conduct of American Diplomacy*, p. 607; Plischke, *International Relations: Basic Documents*, pp. 18–19; and Harmon, *The Art and Practice of Diplomacy*, pp. 235–239.

continued into the 1940s.[41] This mode of bringing diplomatic missions to an end, therefore, was common for more than a century, and accounts for some 446 (21 percent) mission terminations. It was used most frequently in United States relations with Europe and Mexico.[42]

The current designation commonly applied by the Department of State is simply to specify that the chief of mission "left his post." As of 31 March 1973 the missions of nearly 1,200 American emissaries (55 percent) have expired in this fashion. Although this designation was used as early as the eighteenth century,[43] was relied upon for the initial American appointees to at least a dozen countries in the nineteenth century, and was employed on an occasional basis throughout the nineteenth century (when the recall presentation procedure was well established in United States practice), it did not become the standard denomination for mission termination until the transitional period beginning in the 1890s.

In a few countries, such as Brazil, the United States replaced the recall presentation procedure much earlier,[44] in China the Department of State used it only once,[45] and although American diplomatic relations with Cairo date back to 1848, Washington never used it in Egypt.[46] In such cases, the transition to the designation "left post" occurred much earlier. Because of the wholesale conversion to this expression prior to the turn of the twentieth century, most emissaries to those countries with whom relations were established since World War I have had their missions terminated for this reason.

---

41 Among the latest cases in which this recall submittal procedure was used occurred in France (1933), Spain (1939), the Dominican Republic (1940), Cuba (1942), and Greece (1943). There are no such listings for mission termination since World War II.

42 The European countries included Belgium, Denmark, France, Germany, Greece, the Netherlands, Portugal, Russia, Spain, Sweden, Switzerland, and the United Kingdom. It was also used fairly freely in Turkey.

43 For example, it has been applied to the missions of Thomas Jefferson (France, 1789), and William Short (the Netherlands, 1792, and Spain, 1795).

44 In the case of Brazil this occurred in the 1860s. It was also used more freely at an early date in such Latin American countries as Argentina, Bolivia, Colombia, and Peru.

45 This applied to Minister Plenipotentiary Charles Denby in 1898. Perhaps the reason that the designation "left post" was used regularly as early as the 1850s for China is explained by the fact that until 1857 American emissaries generally held the rank of commissioner rather than that of minister, and American emissaries did not present their credentials to the chief of state of China until the 1890s, by which time the transition from recall presentation was under way.

46 American emissaries to Egypt held the rank of diplomatic agent/consul general from 1848 to 1922, by which time the recall presentation procedure had been superseded.

A variant, simply indicating that the emissary left the capital or country to which he was accredited, has been employed by the Department of State in nearly 200 cases. In combination, these designations, accounting for 1,389 (64 percent), appear to serve as generalized rubrics and fail to reveal the real reasons for termination; however, in this respect they do not differ materially from the earlier process of recall presentation. Nor can it be assumed that no recall letters were transmitted on their behalf to the host governments in such cases, because currently these documents are usually presented by successor appointees. This change in procedure may eliminate the formal departure audience. Whereas such receptions may not have been regarded as too demanding when there were only a few foreign emissaries in each national capital and often they served for lengthy periods, at present, in a major capital, such as Washington, this formality could involve an average of at least one departure ceremony per week.

Two other modes of mission termination—which the Department of State designates as "relinquished charge" and "superseded," and which account for 137 (6 percent) cases, may be somewhat more expressive of actual purpose. The designation "superseded" was used as early as 1785 for the conclusion of Benjamin Franklin's pioneering mission to Paris, and for several appointments to France and the Netherlands in the 1830s, and the expression "relinquished charge" was first employed for envoys to Portugal and Texas in the 1840s. The latter designation was utilized most frequently in the 1880s and 1890s at the commencement of the transition period, presumably as a generalized alternative to the recall presentation procedure. At times there were specific reasons for using it as a norm, as for terminating the mission of a chargé d'affaires accredited to a country where American diplomats customarily held a higher rank,[47] of a chargé d'affaires who served without a commission or who failed to present his credentials to the receiving government,[48] and of an envoy who functioned without Senate approval.[49] Such usage, though understandable, was exceptional. These designations have been employed more widely in cases of multiple appointments, in which an emissary, assigned simultaneously to two or more countries, relinquishes charge

[47] Such as the mission of Levett Harris in France in 1833.

[48] Such as the missions of Aaron Vail, chargé ad interim in the United Kingdom in 1836, for whom there is no record of his presentation of credentials as chargé *en titre,* and of Albert Rhodes, chargé in the Netherlands in 1866, who served briefly although he was not fully commissioned. For the distinction between chargés *en titre* and ad interim, see chapter 5.

[49] Such as the mission of Thomas N. Stilwell in Venezuela in 1868, whose nomination was tabled by the Senate.

or is superseded by appointees to one or more of them while he remains accredited to others.[50] The reasons for the use of these denominations, however, is less clear for the majority of cases, which may signify that toward the end of the nineteenth century they were regarded as being experimental and were subsequently replaced by the broader appellation—"left post."

Other designations—including the termination either of appointment or of the diplomatic mission [51]—applied by the Department of State to twenty-one cases, have been used occasionally since 1859, but were relied upon most frequently during the Franklin D. Roosevelt administration and the 1950s. To these may be added isolated examples of the use of such equally unrevealing expressions as having a successor appointed, being relieved of one's diplomatic functions, being recommissioned, and going on leave—as well as having a recess appointment expire (although this is somewhat more specific).

A few designations for diplomatic mission termination are more concrete and explicit. In thirteen cases American missions were brought to an end by the severance of diplomatic relations,[52] usually caused by the outbreak of war.[53] An additional sixteen American emissaries had their missions aborted by the "interruption" of diplomatic relations.[54] In 1858 the United States legation "suspended

---

[50] This practice of mission termination was used in 1911 and 1913 for emissaries commissioned to Luxembourg as well as the Netherlands, for various Balkan countries in the decades preceding World War I, and especially for various newly emergent countries since World War II. For example, Louis G. Dreyfuss, accredited to Iran and Afghanistan was superseded by Cornelius Van H. Engert in the latter in 1942 but remained in Iran for another year, and W. Wendell Blancké, ambassador to the Central African Republic, Chad, and Gabon, as well as to the Congo, was superseded in all but the Congo in 1961, where he remained for another two years.

[51] This designation represents the end of an individual's diplomatic mission, not the suspension or severance by the United States of its diplomatic relations with the foreign government.

[52] This figure represents the number of times the severance of diplomatic relations brought representative missions to an end, not the total number of cases in which such relations were severed.

[53] These involved Great Britain (1812), Mexico (1845), Spain (1898), Germany and Turkey (1917—an American chargé d'affaires was serving in Austria at the time), several European countries and Japan (during World War II), and five countries in 1967 (at the time of the Arab-Israeli War). The case of Franklin Mott Gunther, minister plenipotentiary to Romania, is unique in that this Balkan country declared war on the United States on 12 December 1941 and the American emissary died at Bucharest ten days later.

[54] This figure represents the number of times relations were interrupted bringing representative missions to an end, not the total number of cases in which such relations were interrupted. Additional cases of protracted interruption of relations are not included in this figure, such as Cuba in 1961, because a chargé d'affaires was on duty at the time and no chief of mission was involved.

political relations" with the Mexican government, two years later similar action was taken in Peru, and on fourteen occasions United States missions ended when relations were temporarily interrupted pending American recognition of a new government in the receiving country.[55] Usually such interruptions have been short-lived, but in the case of the Soviet Union, it continued for sixteen years (1917–1933).[56]

Nine American diplomats saw their missions terminated when the countries in which they served were occupied by foreign military forces. These included the Italian occupation of Ethiopia in May 1936,[57] and eight countries invaded by Axis powers during World War II.[58] Certain diplomatic aspects of United States representation to the governments of these occupied countries in London, Ottawa, and Cairo have been mentioned earlier, but six American diplomatic missions also terminated when such governments in exile moved from one location to another.[59]

In addition, United States missions succumbed permanently in the three Baltic states of Estonia, Latvia, and Lithuania when they were annexed by the Soviet Union in 1940. In six other cases, diplomatic missions expired when the countries to which American diplomats were accredited experienced a significant change of legal status. Four of these countries were annexed by others and their independent diplomatic relations ceased. Chronologically, these include the Two Sicilies which was absorbed by Italy in 1860, Hawaii which was annexed by the United States in 1898, Korea which was taken over by Japan in 1905, and Montenegro which was incorporated into Yugoslavia in 1918.[60] Moreover, early in the twentieth century, when Norway separated from Sweden, the United States minister to Stockholm ceased to function as emissary to Norway, to which an independent envoy was accredited in 1906. In 1958 Syria joined the United

---

[55] Aside from Portugal (1910), China (1912), Russia (1917), and Greece (1920), all of these cases of the interruption of diplomatic relations involved Latin American countries, and occurred most frequently in Mexico (1858 and 1913), and Peru (1860, 1865, and 1962).

[56] Suspension also was more than momentary in Costa Rica (1917–1922) and Greece (1920–1924).

[57] United States diplomatic representation to Addis Ababa remained in abeyance until 1943.

[58] Albania was occupied by Italian forces in 1939; Belgium, Czechoslovakia, Denmark, Luxembourg, the Netherlands, and Norway were occupied by Germany in 1939 and 1940; and Thailand was occupied by Japan in 1941.

[59] These included Greece (twice), Luxembourg, and Yugoslavia (three times).

[60] The dates indicate the years when United States diplomatic missions terminated.

Arab Republic and United States diplomatic representation was handled in Cairo, with the American embassy in Damascus temporarily converted into a consulate general.[61]

Finally, seventy-six missions were brought to an end by the death of American emissaries. Because the diplomats were serving dual missions in three cases, the number of persons involved amounted to seventy-three. These, together with the twelve nominees referred to earlier who died before entering upon their duties, constitute nearly 5 percent of all nominees-appointees. The ratio of those who died in service, compared to the number of appointments made, was highest in the 1840s (when it reached nearly 9 percent) and the 1860s and 1870s (when it averaged approximately 6.5 percent).

The first American diplomat to die in service was Joel Barlow, minister to France, who passed away at Zarnowiec the day after Christmas in 1812, while en route to Paris from consultations with French officials in Russia. The next two were the first United States emissaries to Argentina (Caesar A. Rodney, 1824) and Colombia (Richard C. Anderson, 1826). It may be of interest to note that, between 1824 and 1858, six of the diplomats who died in service were the first appointees and three were the second American emissaries appointed to the countries concerned. Three or more American diplomats died in service accredited to each of seven countries—Bolivia, France, Germany, Guatemala, Japan, Liberia, and Peru, and in 1844 two of the six emissaries of the United States accredited to Texas (during the short period from 1837 to 1845) also died in service. An extraordinarily high death rate has applied to envoys accredited to Liberia, where since 1866 eight of thirty-two appointees—or one in every four—died in service, including four who died there during the short period between 1881 and 1893.

Since 1915, of the twenty-six chiefs of mission who died in service, eleven were career diplomats and fifteen were noncareerists. Among the latter were such emissaries as Bert Fish, who served as minister to Egypt, Saudi Arabia, and Portugal (1933–1943); Myron T. Herrick, who was the American ambassador to France (1912–1914 and 1921–1929); and Albert H. Washburn, minister to Austria for eight years (1922–1930). Among the careerists were Monnett B. Davis (Denmark, Panama, and Israel, 1945–1953); John G. Erhardt (Austria and South Africa, 1946–1951); Albert F. Nufer (El Salvador, Argentina, and the Philippines, 1947–1956); John E. Peurifoy (assistant secretary of state and ambassador to Greece, Guatemala, and Thailand, 1947–1955); and J. Butler Wright (assistant secretary of

[61] Separate representation to Syria was revived in 1962.

state and minister to Hungary, Uruguay, Czechoslovakia, and Cuba, 1923–1939).[62]

Tragically, two American diplomats had their missions extinguished by assassination: John Gordon Mein and Cleo A. Noel, Jr., both of whom were career officers serving on their first assignments as chiefs of mission. On 28 August 1968 Ambassador Mein, who had just left his residence in the suburbs of Guatemala City, was forced out of his car at gunpoint. As he turned to flee he was shot in the back, and he died within moments—one of many victims of Guatemalan political extremists.

Five years later, on 2 March 1973, as guests were leaving the villa of the Saudi Arabian ambassador in Khartoum, seven Palestinian Black September guerrillas attacked the group. They wounded newly arrived U.S. Ambassador Noel and Belgian Chargé d'Affaires Guy Eid. They seized as hostages Ambassador Noel and FSO George Moore, together with the emissaries of Belgium, Saudi Arabia, and Jordan. They then levied a series of unconscionable demands on several governments, which were not met, and within hours they assassinated the American and the Belgian diplomats.[63]

In addition, careerist Rodger P. Davies, newly appointed ambassador to Nicosia, was shot and killed by rioting Greek Cypriots who attacked the United States embassy in August 1974. Press reports indicate that an anti-American mob of hundreds marched on the embassy, set fires near the building, blew up a number of American vehicles, and pumped high-powered rifle fire into the ambassador's office. While seeking shelter from the attack in the corridor near his office, the ambassador was struck in the chest and a Cypriot secretary who tried to help him also was killed. Whether the ambassador's death was a random murder resulting from a freak shot or was a calculated attempt to assassinate him may not be clear, but the killing was senseless and wanton. Although extreme, these incidents characterize the degree of retrogression that has set in respecting the personal safety and political immunity of diplomats in recent times.

To summarize, since 1778 the United States has made 2,497 nominations-appointments to foreign governments, of which 227 nominees failed to have their nominations approved or did not other-

---

[62] Other careerists who died in service include Franklin M. Gunther (Romania, 1941), Paul Knabenshue (Iraq, 1942), Jay Pierrepont Moffat (Canada, 1943), William C. Burdett (New Zealand, 1944), William A. Hoyt (Uruguay, 1967), and Samuel Z. Westerfield (Liberia, 1972).

[63] Eventually the assassins surrendered to Sudanese forces, and the remaining diplomatic hostages were freed.

wise assume their duties, two others (early diplomats) served without being officially received, and 2,155 appointments were either fully consummated or in the process of accreditation as of March 1973. Of these, 2,012 were eventually terminated for reasons and by processes which are normal to the practice of diplomacy. Only in the case of request for recall, dismissal, the temporary interruption or formal severance of diplomatic relations, the arbitrary suspension or termination of relations required by military occupation or change in the legal status of countries, and the death of the diplomat—numbering 143—has termination been other than routine. As of 31 March 1973, the remaining 113 appointees continued in their appointments.[64]

[64] This involved appointments to 110 countries; in three cases—Australia, Honduras, and Turkey—there were dual appointees not having been fully accredited and received as of this date and with the predecessor appointees not yet having been superseded.

4
GEOGRAPHIC ORIGIN, SEX, AND AGE OF DIPLOMATS

Geographic Origin of Diplomats

It is generally presumed that American diplomats hail largely from the northeastern states and, while a substantial number do, this impression is an exaggerated one. Factors which have influenced the place of birth or legal residence of diplomatic appointees include the length of time individual states have been in the union, the population size and economic status of the states, and political influences brought to bear by the President, the secretary of state, the Senate, and political party leadership. In more recent times, the increasing appointment of career Foreign Service Officers, and their concentration of legal residence in the national capital and the surrounding area has been of importance. Table A-12 presents statistics, by decade, identifying the states from which American diplomatic representatives have been appointed, with totals per state, per decade, and for career officers, and indicating the year in which each state joined the Union.

The earliest American diplomats were, naturally, appointed from the original thirteen states and from other states as they were admitted into statehood. Appointment since then has been uneven, however. Up to 1820, forty-seven of the fifty-one initial envoys came from only eleven of twenty-three states,[1] with the largest numbers being provided by Massachusetts (twelve), Virginia (seven), Maryland (five), New York (five), and South Carolina (five). Since 1778, of the total number of appointments made, some 1,144 (46 percent) of all appointees have been drawn from the original thirteen eastern sea-

[1] The following states had been added to the Union by 1820: Alabama, Illinois, Indiana, Kentucky, Louisiana, Maine, Mississippi, Ohio, Tennessee, and Vermont. One appointee came from the District of Columbia, and the state of origin was unspecified for three diplomats.

board states,[2] while only ninety-two (4 percent) have been named from the twelve states which entered the Union since 1888 [3] and only thirty-three have been made from the five states which joined after 1900.[4] Fifty percent (1,256) have come from the eastern seaboard,[5] whereas the smallest numbers have been recruited from fourteen of the West-South-Central, Mountain, and Pacific states.[6]

By far the largest number of diplomats have been appointed from New York (353, or nearly 15 percent). Other states with high appointment records include Pennsylvania (164), Illinois (129), California (123), Massachusetts (106), and Maryland (100). These six states, together with the District of Columbia (157), have been listed as the official residences of 1,132 (45 percent) appointees, and, together with Ohio, have produced nearly half of all appointees since 1778. Five of these states and the District of Columbia,[7] together with Connecticut,[8] have the highest level of appointments since 1940 (511, or 51 percent), indicating considerable consistency, with New Jersey and Virginia also gaining status in the list of recent high contributors.

On the other hand, as of 1973, no diplomats had been appointed from Alaska, Hawaii, or Idaho, only one heralded from North Dakota over a period of nearly eighty-five years, ten or less came from each of half a dozen other states,[9] and eleven to twenty were appointed

---

[2] Connecticut (fifty-four), Delaware (twenty-two), Georgia (thirty-six), Maryland (100), Massachusetts (106), New Hampshire (forty-two), New Jersey (eighty-six), New York (353), North Carolina (thirty-eight), Pennsylvania (164), Rhode Island (thirty-four), South Carolina (thirty), and Virginia (seventy-nine).

[3] The states which entered the Union during its second century include: Alaska (none), Arizona (thirteen), Hawaii (none), Idaho (none), Montana (eight), New Mexico (ten), North Dakota (one), Oklahoma (ten), South Dakota (ten), Utah (fourteen), Washington (nineteen), and Wyoming (seven)—totaling ninety-two, of which half (forty-six) were named from the three states of Arizona, Utah, and Washington.

[4] Alaska, Arizona, Hawaii, New Mexico, and Oklahoma.

[5] This embraces the New England states (Connecticut, Maine, Massachusetts, New Hampshire, Rhode Island, and Vermont); the Middle Atlantic states (New Jersey, New York, and Pennsylvania); three of the South Atlantic states (Delaware, Maryland, and Virginia); and the District of Columbia.

[6] West-South-Central states: Arkansas (seventeen) and Oklahoma (ten); Mountain states: Montana (eight), Idaho (none), Wyoming (seven), Colorado (seventeen), New Mexico (ten), Arizona (thirteen), Utah (fourteen), and Nevada (nine); Pacific states: Washington (nineteen), Oregon (twenty), Alaska (none), and Hawaii (none). Exceptions include Louisiana (forty-four), Texas (fifty-four), and California (123).

[7] California, Illinois, Maryland, New York, Pennsylvania, and the District of Columbia.

[8] Superseding Massachusetts and Ohio.

[9] Montana (eight), Nevada (nine), New Mexico (ten), Oklahoma (ten), South Dakota (ten), and Wyoming (seven)—totalling fifty-four.

from each of eleven additional states.[10] Thus only 227 (9 percent) have been selected from twenty-one of the states during nearly two centuries. This situation also has remained relatively constant since 1940, with twenty-five states providing only 109 (11 percent) of the appointees.[11] In other words, recent practice indicates that about 90 percent of American diplomats have been legal residents of only half of the states and the District of Columbia.

The population of states, although theoretically a relevant influence, is not as important as might be thought. Several of the most populous states—such as California, Illinois, New Jersey, New York, Pennsylvania, and Virginia—are indeed among the leading states so far as high diplomatic appointment is concerned, both overall and in the recent period since 1940. But although Massachusetts is fifth and Ohio is eighth in the total number of appointees, they drop out of the top ten for the period since 1940. Moreover, several heavily populated states, including Texas and Michigan, are not in the top ten. At the same time, seven of the ten least-populated states are in the group which provided the fewest diplomatic envoys.

Appointments have averaged nearly two per year from New York since 1788, and one per year from California. All other states fall below this level, with eight to nine appointments per decade from Illinois and Pennsylvania, approximately six per decade from Maryland and Massachusetts, and other states ranging downward to an average of one or less per decade for such states as Mississippi (twelve in 156 years), Montana (eight in 84 years), Nevada (nine in 109 years), North Dakota (one in 84 years), Vermont (twelve in 182 years), and Wyoming (seven in 83 years).

Within such broad generalizations, a number of more special statistical factors are apparent in Table A-12. One of these is the declining contributory role of several states in the twentieth century. For example, while Arkansas provided twelve appointees in the last half of the nineteenth century, only five have been named from that state since 1900, and Mississippi has had a similar experience. Also noticeable is the increase since 1940 of appointees from certain states, such as California, Connecticut, Maryland, and the District of Columbia, and a similar increase appears in the records of Florida,

[10] Alabama (eighteen), Arizona (thirteen), Arkansas (seventeen), Colorado (seventeen), Mississippi (twelve), Nebraska (twelve), Oregon (twenty), Utah (fourteen), Vermont (twelve), Washington (nineteen), and West Virginia (eighteen)—totalling 172.

[11] Arizona and Colorado have dropped from the original list of twenty-one, and Delaware, Mississippi, Nebraska, South Carolina, Tennessee, and Wisconsin have been added—each of which had less than ten appointees during this period.

New York, and Texas since 1930. In some cases there is steadiness in the figures, while on the other hand, prolonged gaps appear in the records of certain states, including Alabama, Arizona, Mississippi, and Vermont.[12]

Diplomatic appointments from secessionist states declined for some time as a consequence of the Civil War. The number of appointees from the eleven members of the Confederacy dropped from forty-eight appointments in the 1850s to less than half that number in the 1860s and even less in the 1870s.[13] Substantial declines were experienced by Alabama, Arkansas, Georgia, Mississippi, South Carolina, and Virginia, but the contributions of some, such as Tennessee and Texas, remained fairly constant, and those of Louisiana continued relatively high. At the same time, the number of nominees from several non-Confederacy states commenced a sharp increase during this period, especially California and Illinois, and, because of the relatively large number of appointments made during the 1860s, certain other states achieved a noticeable peak during this decade, including Kentucky, Missouri, New York, Ohio, Pennsylvania, and Wisconsin.

Also noteworthy is the fact that diplomatic emissaries were appointed from the District of Columbia as early as 1811,[14] and District residents have been appointed regularly each decade since the 1840s, except for the 1860s. Quite surprising is the steadily increasing number of envoys named from the District of Columbia since the 1920s, so that in the 1940s it was exceeded by only four states, and since the 1950s it has become the second largest contributor, exceeded only by New York.[15] If the recent trend continues, the District of Columbia may very well become the legal residence of the largest number of diplomatic appointees.

On a number of occasions, several nominees to a specific foreign government have been appointed in succession, or in close sequence, from a given state. For example, five of a sequence of six nominees from New York were named to Austria in the 1860s,[16] three nominees from Ohio and three from Tennessee were designated to Ecuador in

---

12 Alabama, 1900s to 1930s; Arizona, only one appointee from 1900 to the 1940s; Mississippi, only one appointee since 1920; and Vermont, only one appointee in half a century, 1900 to 1950.

13 There were twenty-one from these eleven states in the 1860s, and only eighteen in the 1870s.

14 Joel Barlow was named minister plenipotentiary to France, 27 February 1811.

15 In the 1960s the District of Columbia virtually equalled New York.

16 The first four of whom either were rejected or tabled by the Senate, or declined the appointment.

the 1860s and 1870s,[17] and a series of four appointees accredited to Russia in the 1830s were from Pennsylvania.[18] Although this may have been fortuitous, it appears to suggest either some attempt to appoint diplomats from specific states at particular times in order to manage the selection of emissaries in terms of geographic representation or, more likely, that political influences were brought to bear in favor of certain states.

Few envoys from the eastern states were appointed to serve in Hawaii,[19] and most of those accredited to Texas were from the Midwest.[20] In all likelihood, because of the Scandinavian population of Minnesota a number of envoys to the Scandinavian countries have been appointed from that state.[21] However, there is little reliable evidence to verify any substantial or direct relationship between the states from which diplomats are recruited and the countries to which they are sent.

As noted earlier, the identification of the state of residence was not available for some appointees. Nearly forty diplomats fall into this category, three-fourths of whom were appointed prior to 1900. This is understandable for early times, in view of the less certain record keeping system and the nature, in certain instances, of the appointment process. Although this is no longer a serious problem, there have been nine such cases since 1940; these have primarily involved military officers, including Admiral Alan G. Kirk and Generals Mark Clark and Walter Bedell Smith. A few appointees have had their legal residences in such American territories as Puerto Rico or the Virgin Islands, and they are included in the forty for whom no state of residence is identified.

Column G of Table A-12 indicates the number of career diplomats appointed from each state. One in eight of these appointees has maintained his residence in the District of Columbia, and half of the career diplomats list six states, together with the District, as their

---

17 One from Ohio and the three from Tennessee either were not approved by the Senate, or did not proceed to Quito, and therefore did not serve.

18 Similar sequential appointments involved four Californians among ten appointees named to represent the United States in Afghanistan between 1941 and 1967, three in sequence from Kansas were appointed to Chile in the 1870s, three of four from Pennsylvania were designated to Spain between 1921 and 1933, followed by three of four from Connecticut in the 1950s, and the first three emissaries commissioned to Thailand were from Missouri.

19 Most came from Arkansas, Colorado, Georgia, Illinois, Indiana, Kentucky, Ohio, Nevada, and Oregon, with only three from Massachusetts and Maine.

20 Appointments were made from Indiana, Kentucky, Ohio, and Tennessee, but also one from Louisiana.

21 Four to Denmark, three to Norway, and two to Sweden—approximating 20 percent of all appointments from Minnesota.

places of residence.[22] On the other hand, no careerists have been named from five states,[23] and less than ten have been selected from each of some twenty-one states, which means that more than half of the states have supplied only 105 career diplomats (13 percent of the total). These figures are similar to the overall appointment figures mentioned earlier. Differences are probably due, in part, to the multiple appointment of career officers and the transfer in some cases of the legal residences to the Washington area because of the tax advantages provided by the District of Columbia.

Finally, it may be interesting to speculate on the relationship of the territorial origin of diplomats and the geographic background of appointing Presidents. There appears to be little statistical verification, however, of such relationships. The first six Presidents were from Virginia and Massachusetts, and collectively they appointed larger delegations of diplomats from these two states than from any others,[24] with President Washington evidencing some partiality toward Virginians and John Quincy Adams toward appointees from Massachusetts. However, Adams also named as many from New York as from his native state, and Presidents Madison and Monroe recruited three times as many from Massachusetts as from Virginia. As a matter of fact, beginning with Madison, these early Presidents appear to have deliberately avoided excessive appointments from their own states.

Appointments from New Jersey, and New York as well, dropped in the Wilson years.[25] They increased somewhat from New York during Franklin D. Roosevelt's administration, as did selections from Massachusetts and Texas in the 1960s. Appointments from Pennsylvania dropped considerably during the Eisenhower decade, but the number of candidates from Kansas rose noticeably. Nevertheless, it must be concluded that factors other than geographic origin influence presidential appointment of diplomatic chiefs of mission, and the state of legal residence from which an emissary is named seems to be a matter of no consequence in the increasing appointment of career diplomats to serve the United States abroad as ranking emissaries.

[22] Aside from the District of Columbia, these include New York (eighty-eight), California (sixty-eight), Maryland (forty-four), Pennsylvania (thirty-nine), Illinois (thirty-six), and New Jersey (twenty-nine). Four other states—Maine, Massachusetts, Ohio, and Virginia—accounted for an average of some twenty-five to twenty-seven career appointees, and all other states fell below twenty.

[23] Alaska, Hawaii, Idaho, North Dakota, and Vermont.

[24] This amounted to approximately one-fourth—twenty-five of ninety-one.

[25] This may have reflected a general numerical decline in the period 1910–1920, but increases may be noted for other states, such as Missouri and South Carolina.

Women Diplomats

According to Graham H. Stuart, in the United States, although women had for many years been eligible for a variety of political positions, there seemed to be little desire on their part to enter the diplomatic service until after World War I. One noteworthy exception was Marilla Ricker, a New Hampshire lawyer, who publicly announced her desire to be appointed envoy to Colombia during the second Grover Cleveland administration. Reportedly she told a newsman that, "If Luther McKinney [United States minister to Colombia at the time] can fill the place, I can overflow it." However, she was not nominated for the position.[26]

It was not until 1933 that President Franklin D. Roosevelt named the first American woman chief of mission, when he accredited Ruth Bryan Owen to Copenhagen.[27] In the subsequent forty years only fifteen women were named to nineteen ranking diplomatic posts.[28] President Roosevelt also accredited Florence Jaffray Harriman as minister to Oslo in 1937, and in 1949 President Truman designated Eugenie Anderson to Denmark as the first full-fledged woman ambassador of the United States and, as noted earlier, that same year he sent Perle Mesta as the first American minister accredited solely and directly to Luxembourg.[29] President Eisenhower named the first careerist woman, Frances E. Willis, as minister to Switzerland (1953) and later to Norway (1957), and he also accredited noncareerist Clare Boothe Luce to Italy in 1953 with the rank of ambassador—the first women to be commissioned to a major foreign power. Later in his administration, he nominated Mrs. Luce to be ambassador to Brazil but, even though the Senate gave its approval, in view of the bitter

---

[26] Stuart, *American Diplomatic and Consular Practice,* p. 145.

[27] The Soviet Union set a precedent ten years earlier when it sent Alexandra Kollontay, daughter of a Czarist general, to Oslo, and later to Mexico City, and Stockholm. See E. Wilder Spaulding, *Ambassadors Ordinary and Extraordinary* (Washington, D. C.: Public Affairs Press, 1961), p. 179. For commentary on other early foreign women diplomats, see Stuart, *American Diplomatic and Consular Practice,* pp. 144–145.

[28] For commentary on women in the Foreign Service who serve at various ranks and positions abroad—as distinguished from chiefs of mission—see Plischke, *Conduct of American Diplomacy,* pp. 252–254, with some statistics given in footnote 43.

[29] Previously American emissaries represented the United States conjointly also to either Belgium or the Netherlands. Perle Mesta's mission was popularized by the musical *Call Me Madam,* and she was memorialized by Irving Berlin in the hit song "The Hostess with the Mostes' on the Ball."

public debate the nomination engendered, she declined the appointment.

In the 1960s new avenues were opened with the commissioning of women as chiefs of mission to such non-European countries as Barbados, Nepal, and Ceylon (Sri Lanka), and in 1973 and 1974 also to Ghana, Togo, and Zambia. Presidents Johnson and Nixon designated women diplomats as representatives to a major international organization and to high office in the Department of State.[30] Thus, since the 1930s the horizons have slowly but perceptibly been broadened for women diplomats. Nevertheless, the number appointed—both absolutely and relatively—remains miniscule, amounting to less than 1 percent overall, and merely 1.3 percent since 1930.

Two women diplomats—Ruth Bryan Owen and Clare Boothe Luce—had prior congressional experience, both in the House of Representatives.[31] While all early women diplomatic appointees were noncareerists, as of 1973 five of the fifteen have been careerists. One of these, Frances E. Willis, held three consecutive appointments—to Switzerland, Norway, and Ceylon—and Carol C. Laise, former ambassador to Nepal, was named the first careerist assistant secretary of state (for public affairs) in 1973, and in 1975 she was named director general of the Foreign Service.[32] For general statistics on American women diplomats, see column G of Table A-4, for designation of the countries to which women have been accredited as chiefs of mission, see column E of Table A-5, for figures on multiple appointments, see part 3 of Table A-7, for the states from which women diplomats have been selected, see column F of Table A-12, and for women diplomats as authors, see column C of Table A-16.

In *Ambassadors Ordinary and Extraordinary,* E. Wilder Spaulding concluded that diplomacy was a man's profession. However, this appears to be changing. Whereas in the past women diplomats were conspicuous by their absence, more are likely to be appointed in the future, especially as more are recruited by, and rise within, the

---

30 In 1968 President Johnson appointed Barbara M. Watson, noncareerist as administrator of the Bureau of Security and Consular Affairs, an appointment which continued until 1974, and in 1971 President Nixon named Betty Crites Dillon as chief of the United States mission to the International Civil Aviation Organization.

31 See chapter 6 for discussion of congressmen-diplomats.

32 These departmental appointments, however, were made after the cutoff date of 31 March 1973 employed for the statistics of this analysis and therefore have not been counted in the preceding figures. In addition, in 1974 Shirley Temple Black was named ambassador to Ghana and careerist Nancy V. Rawls became ambassador to Togo.

Foreign Service, and as additional countries evidence their willingness to receive and deal effectively with them.[33]

Age of Diplomats

As might be anticipated, the age factor of United States diplomats conforms with the normal bell curve. Table A-13 presents statistics for the 1,869 individuals who have served in the positions under discussion. The youngest appointees were only twenty-four years of age at the time of their original accreditation, and the oldest was seventy-eight. Within this span of more than fifty years, a substantial majority of appointees were in their forties or fifties as they launched their diplomatic careers. Those in their twenties and seventies together amounted to only 3 percent of the total, those in their thirties and sixties jointly totaled 26 percent, while those in their forties amounted to 35 percent, and the largest group were in their fifties, accounting for 36 percent. Thus, more than 70 percent of United States diplomats were middle-aged, and the largest number fall within the range of forty-seven to fifty-three at the time of their appointment.[34]

Twenty-three American diplomats (1 percent) were under thirty when commissioned. The youngest—at the age of twenty-four—were Washington Barrow, who served as chargé d'affaires to Portugal (1841–1844), Charles Denby, who became envoy extraordinary to China in 1885 and remained for thirteen years, and E. Rumsey Wing, who was named minister resident to Ecuador in 1869 and died at his post five years later. John Quincy Adams, at the age of twenty-seven, was named minister resident to the Netherlands in 1794, and after serving in Prussia, Russia, and the United Kingdom, he was made secretary of state in 1817, in which office he remained for eight years.

These younger diplomats fall into three main groups. The first—and by far the largest—consists of those who were appointed as regular chiefs of mission to foreign governments. A few—such as William W. Crump, who was twenty-five when appointed chargé d'affaires to Chile in 1844, and Rowland B. Mahany, who was three

---

[33] For additional commentary on women diplomats, see Spaulding, *Ambassadors Ordinary and Extraordinary*, chapter 7, and Stuart, *American Diplomatic and Consular Practice*, pp. 144–147. Also see Herbert Wright, "Can a Woman Be a Diplomat?" *American Foreign Service Journal*, vol. 17 (August 1940), pp. 454–457, 469.

[34] Unless otherwise specified, age is calibrated as of the time of nomination-appointment or the commencement of the diplomatic mission, and in cases of multiple assignments, as of the beginning of the first mission.

years older when accredited as envoy extraordinary to Ecuador in 1892—were named to single appointments and, after a short time, disappeared from the diplomatic arena.

The majority of the younger appointees, however, were given multiple appointments. Some of them, once commissioned, held a series of sequential assignments. Lloyd C. Griscom, for example, was twenty-nine when accredited to Persia in 1901 and, during the next eight years also served as chief of mission to Japan, Brazil, and Italy. Others, such as John Randolph Clay, enjoyed a long tenure in a single post. He was twenty-eight when first appointed, and after a year as chargé d'affaires to Russia (1836–1837), was named chief of mission to Peru, where he remained for thirteen years, and subsequently, in the 1860s, an additional nomination for appointment to Liberia went unconfirmed by the Senate. Others, originally appointed in their 30s, also were reappointed to multiple missions. These include noncareerists Angier Biddle Duke, Hugh S. Gibson, and Laurits S. Swensen, and careerists Joseph C. Grew, Arthur Bliss Lane, and Charles W. Yost.[35] All but four of these appointees retired from such diplomatic posts before they reached the age of sixty.[36]

The second category of younger American diplomats consists of those who were appointed to ranking Department of State positions at an early age. For example, both Walker Blaine and John Bassett Moore became third assistant secretaries of state at the age of twenty-six in the 1880s, and later Moore was also named assistant secretary in 1898 and counselor some fifteen years later. A dozen appointees, most of whom were reappointed to multiple diplomatic assignments, were commissioned to departmental posts while in their thirties. These included such noncareerists as Richard Rush in the early nineteenth century and William B. Macomber and George C. McGhee after World War II.[37] Occasionally young careerists also have commenced

[35] Duke, five missions (1952–1969); Gibson, seven missions (1919–1938); Swensen, five missions (1897–1934); Grew, eight missions (1917–1945); Lane, eight missions (three of which were simultaneous, 1933–1943); and Yost, six missions (1945–1971).

[36] The single-mission envoys—Crump and Mahany—were still in their twenties when their diplomatic careers expired. Griscom was still in his thirties, while Clay, Duke, and Lane were in their fifties, and the rest were in their sixties when they retired from such assignments. Only one of these emissaries—Swensen—was approaching seventy years of age.

[37] Rush—secretary of state ad interim (1817) and then chief of mission to the United Kingdom and France; Macomber—assistant secretary (1957–1961) and then chief of mission to Jordan and Turkey, as well as other departmental offices; and McGhee—assistant secretary (1949–1951) and then chief of mission to Turkey and Germany, as well as other positions in the Department of State and ambassador at large.

their careers in senior Department of State offices, such as Leland Harrison, William Phillips, and William M. Rountree.[38] All of these were under forty years of age when appointed to their first ranking posts and then established extended high level diplomatic careers. However, there are others, such as Nelson A. Rockefeller, named assistant secretary for American republic affairs in 1944, at the age of thirty-six, whose subsequent service was limited to that of personal representative of the President, although he also was considered for other regular appointments, including the secretaryship of state, and in 1974 was appointed to the vice-presidency.

The third category of young appointees involves those who had the right credentials and were in the strategic places at the right time, so that they could take over on a contingent basis as chargé d'affaires ad interim. They have been careerists, and for some of them—such as Stuart E. Grummon (Haiti, 1928–1930), Wells Stabler (Jordan, 1949), and Charles W. Thayer (Afghanistan, 1942)—these were their sole and usually brief diplomatic appointments at the chief of mission level. The preponderant majority of such careerists, however, have been given subsequent ranking assignments, often with some interval between their initial and later appointments, the duration of the gap depending largely on their age when they were first named chargés d'affaires. For example, Walter C. Thurston, only twenty-seven when he became chargé d'affaires ad interim to Costa Rica in 1921, was approaching fifty when he began a series of tours as chief of mission to four Latin American countries, and Bernard A. Gufler was thirty-seven when named chargé d'affaires ad interim to Lithuania in 1940, and it was not until 1959 when he was in his mid-fifties that he was appointed ambassador to Ceylon (Sri Lanka). As a consequence, it appears that early accreditation of careerists to ad interim appointments rarely assures them early designation to regular posts as chiefs of mission, and in some cases they never achieve this status throughout their entire careers in the Foreign Service.

All but five of the diplomats (nearly 80 percent) who were in their twenties when designated, were appointed in the nineteenth century, and no such appointments have been made since the 1920s when three of the four were careerists named as chargés ad interim. William J. O'Toole, envoy extraordinary to Paraguay (1922–1924),

---

[38] Harrison—assistant secretary (1922–1927) and then chief of mission to Sweden, Uruguay, Romania, and Switzerland; Phillips—third assistant secretary (1909, 1914–1917) and then chief of mission to the Netherlands, Luxembourg, Belgium, Canada, and Italy, as well as other posts in the Department; and Rountree—assistant secretary (1956–1959), and then chief of mission to Pakistan, Sudan, South Africa, and Brazil.

was the last of the young emissaries accredited as regular chiefs of mission. The trend, therefore, appears to be against selecting young envoys, except on a provisional and short-term basis, and as the size of American diplomatic missions increases, usually older and more experienced careerists are available for chargé ad interim assignments. Moreover, since World War II, very few American diplomats, other than those named to interim posts, have been as young as in their thirties. The principal exceptions have been a few noncareerists appointed to positions in the Department of State, such as assistant secretaries Macomber and McGhee, as noted, and Tyler Abell, Lloyd Nelson Hand, and James W. Symington, who were named chief of protocol.[39]

Turning to the other end of the age scale, the number of United States diplomats who have been over sixty years of age when originally appointed attests to a growing reliance on maturity and experience. This older group numbers 205 (11 percent) of which thirty-one were seventy or older when commissioned. Only one of these was accredited prior to 1800 and, while the number increased as the size of the American corps of diplomats grew, it is interesting to note some decline in the 1870s, a significant upsurge in the 1880s and 1890s (when the number achieved a level not equalled until the 1940s), and the achievement of the largest number reached in the 1950s.[40] This may suggest that certain Presidents tend to be more liberal than others in selecting older emissaries.

Many of those assigned to their first posts as chief of mission while in their sixties and seventies are noncareerists. By the time an FSO reaches the age of sixty, he normally will have risen in the ranks, received high-level appointment, and be approaching the end of his career. Retirement age is fixed by law for career diplomats.[41] Only seven careerists have been given their first ambassadorial appointments after reaching the age of sixty, all but one of whom

39 Chiefs of protocol have usually been relatively young appointees, and to date none has held this post at an advanced age.

40 These are absolute figures and do not reflect relative percentages.

41 The Foreign Service Act of 1946, as amended, specifies a maximum retirement age of sixty for FSOs who are below the career ambassador and career minister levels, and a retirement age of sixty-five for career ambassadors and career ministers—except for those serving as chiefs of missions or on other presidential appointments with Senate confirmation. If it be "in the public interest" the secretary of state may extend an emissary's service for an additional period not to exceed five years. See Foreign Service Act, secs. 631 and 632. In 1974 Congress considered amendments to reduce the maximum retirement age of career ministers from sixty-five to sixty, leaving only career ambassadors at sixty-five.

were commissioned in the 1940s and 1950s.[42] Therefore, unless the law is changed, it will be exceptional for careerists who have reached the age of sixty to be newly designated as chiefs of mission or senior Department of State officers, and those who have attained the age of sixty-five are unlikely to be appointed to sequential missions at this level.

Most of those first designated to such senior positions after reaching seventy years of age have served in single appointments as chiefs of mission. More than half of their missions have been to European countries,[43] and the remainder were accredited to Western Hemisphere governments and to China and Thailand. These appointments are illustrated by the unusual missions of Thomas Sumter, who, at seventy-five when commissioned as minister plenipotentiary to Portugal in 1809, served in this capacity for approximately a decade, and Josephus Daniels, who at the age of seventy-one was accredited to Mexico in 1933, where he remained for more than eight years. In addition to Sumter, the oldest single-mission appointees include John Rowan (seventy-five when he became chargé d'affaires to the Two Sicilies in 1848), Andrew W. Mellon (seventy-seven when accredited as ambassador to the United Kingdom in 1932), and Douglas Maxwell Moffat (seventy-five when named ambassador to Australia in 1956, who died in office that same year).

A few American diplomats who were seventy years of age or older when initially appointed have also served on multiple diplomatic missions. For example, Benjamin Franklin, at seventy-two, was accredited as minister plenipotentiary to France in 1778 and, four years later was commissioned to Sweden while remaining accredited to France. He served in this capacity until he was approximately eighty years of age. Frederick Douglass, already high in his seventies, was named simultaneously minister resident to Haiti and chargé d'affaires to Santo Domingo in 1889, and he served in this joint assignment for two years. Two others held sequential diplomatic missions—Herman B. Baruch, appointed at seventy-three to represent the United States in Portugal and the Netherlands for more than four years, and Alphonso Taft, commissioned at seventy-two and served in Austria and Prussia for three years. The only other older multiple-mission

[42] These include John K. Caldwell, Jefferson Patterson, Kenneth S. Patton, George W. Renchard, Henry E. Stebbins, Thomas M. Wilson, and North Winship. All of these were in their early sixties except Patterson who was sixty-five, and his appointment to Burundi was made in 1968. Stebbins was also named to a second mission when he was sixty-one, and he served for another three years.

[43] The following have been favored: Portugal (four such appointments), and Ireland, the Netherlands, the Soviet Union, and the United Kingdom (two each).

diplomat was R. Walton Moore, designated assistant secretary of state when he was seventy-four and then as counselor at the age of seventy-eight. He was over eighty when he left the Department of State. Two other appointees in this age category were selected to head United States missions to international organizations, namely, Warren R. Austin, as ambassador to the United Nations, and Paul F. Foster, as ambassador to the International Atomic Energy Agency.

By and large, the age factor of American women diplomats has conformed with the general norm. Six of the fifteen were in their forties when appointed, and seven were in their fifties. The remaining two—Ruth Lewis Farkas and Florence Jaffray Harriman—were beyond sixty-five years of age when recruited. The careerists ranged between forty-five and fifty-four. Most of these women diplomats served on a single mission. To 1973, only one careerist, Frances E. Willis, has remained in such ranking appointments until she reached the retirement age of sixty-five.[44]

The age curve for secretaries of state varies somewhat from that of chiefs of mission to foreign capitals. Although Robert R. Livingston was only thirty-five, and John Jay only thirty-nine, when appointed secretary of foreign affairs, this proved to be most unusual. The overall average age of secretaries of state, on appointment, is somewhat higher than that of diplomats in the field. Only nine secretaries (17 percent) were in their forties when appointed, including six of the first twelve—namely, Thomas Jefferson, Edmund J. Randolph, John Marshall, Henry Clay, Martin Van Buren, and Louis McLane. Robert Bacon and Edward R. Stettinius have been the only secretaries below the age of fifty to be appointed since the turn of the twentieth century. Approximately half of the secretaries (twenty-seven, or 50 percent) have been in their fifties on appointment. By way of illustration, these included John Quincy Adams (who was only twenty-seven when he began his diplomatic career), James Monroe, John Forsyth, and John W. Foster (who had been appointed chiefs of mission to foreign governments while they were still in their thirties), and Dean G. Acheson, Dean Rusk, and William P. Rogers. Henry A. Kissinger also was fifty years of age when appointed secretary of state in September 1973.

A dozen and a half secretaries of state (34 percent) were sixty or over when appointed. The earliest of these was Edward Livingston, who was sixty-seven, and subsequently he also was named envoy

[44] This, naturally, will change as more women careerist diplomats, who hold ranking appointments, reach retirement age. For example, subsequent to March 1973, Carol C. Laise, appointed to Nepal at the age of 49 was later named assistant secretary in 1973 and two years later was nominated to head the Foreign Service.

extraordinary to France (1833). Prior to the twentieth century only nine other secretaries belonged to this category,[45] whereas, since the designation of Frank B. Kellogg in 1925, all but four secretaries have been in their sixties at their commissioning.[46] As a consequence, it appears that the general trend has been to recruit older secretaries of state—rarely in their forties, sometimes in their fifties, but most often in their sixties.[47]

Of the secretaries of state appointed since the 1890s, eight had previous departmental experience at high levels—two as under secretary (Edward R. Stettinius and Christian A. Herter), one as counselor (Robert Lansing), and the remainder as assistant secretaries (William R. Day, John Hay, Robert Bacon, Dean G. Acheson, and Dean Rusk). All of these except Lansing and Herter were in their forties when they commenced their departmental assignments, and the same applies to Henry A. Kissinger when he became assistant to the President for national security affairs in 1969.

The secretaries who were most advanced in years on appointment include John Sherman (over seventy) and Frank B. Kellogg, Edward Livingston, and William L. Marcy (in their upper sixties). Sherman served for only a year, while Kellogg remained four years. Although Cordell Hull was over sixty on appointment, he served for more than eleven years, and John Foster Dulles, in his mid-sixties when appointed, served for six years. All except Livingston were in their seventies when they left the secretaryship. (Livingston subsequently contributed an additional two years as envoy extraordinary to France.)

The final point is the age of American emissaries at the conclusion of their diplomatic service. As might be expected, careerists normally end their tenure as chiefs of mission and ranking departmental officers when they reach the statutory retirement limits of the mid-sixties.[48] A few may remain a number of additional years, such

---

[45] This group included John C. Calhoun, William L. Marcy, William H. Seward, Hamilton Fish, Frederick T. Frelinghuysen, Walter Q. Gresham, Richard Olney, John Sherman, and John Hay. They were all appointed between 1844 and the end of the nineteenth century.

[46] Those under sixty years were Stettinius, Acheson, Rusk, and Rogers. Henry A. Kissinger, appointed secretary at the age of fifty after March 1973, must be added to this small group.

[47] Nevertheless, beginning with Dean Rusk, a reversal of this trend may be under way.

[48] This has been the case even with such multiple-mission careerists as Willard L. Beaulac, Charles E. Bohlen, Ellis O. Briggs, John M. Cabot, Selden Chapin, James C. Dunn, Joseph C. Grew, Foy D. Kohler, H. Freeman Matthews, George S. Messersmith, Robert D. Murphy, William Phillips, and Llewellyn E. Thompson. Some, such as George F. Kennan, are retired earlier.

as Norman Armour, Jefferson Caffery, and Loy W. Henderson, who retired in their late sixties. The legislative restriction on maximum retirement age has not applied to noncareerists, however. Consequently, some of these diplomats, in their seventies when commissioned—such as Warren R. Austin, Josephus Daniels, Andrew W. Mellon, Douglas Maxwell Moffat, and John Rowan—were seventy-five years or older when they left the diplomatic service, and Thomas Sumter reached the advanced age of the mid-eighties when he presented his letter of recall to the Portuguese government.

The multiple-mission emissaries often were younger when first appointed, but several reached their late sixties by the time they retired from their diplomatic careers—such as Anthony J. Drexel Biddle, Chester B. Bowles, Henry F. Grady, and Henry Cabot Lodge—and a few of these were seventy-five or older, including Herman B. Baruch, David K. E. Bruce, and Alphonso Taft. Quite unique in this respect, in addition to Sumter's, were the diplomatic careers of Benjamin Franklin, Robert W. Moore, and W. Averell Harriman, who were approaching or over eighty years of age when they concluded their diplomatic ventures. Also remarkable in recent times, Ellsworth Bunker, beyond the mid-fifties when first appointed as ambassador to Argentina in 1951, and after serving as chief of mission to five countries, as ambassador at large, and as representative to the Organization of American States, was reappointed ambassador at large in 1973, and he continued to serve in this capacity although he was then in his eighties.

It is apparent, therefore, that most American diplomatic appointees are in their middle years and, while appointment and reappointment to ranking posts of individuals who are over sixty-five years of age is somewhat exceptional, it is not without precedent. However, such appointments as emissaries to foreign governments and international organizations, as ambassadors at large, and as secretary of state have been restricted largely to noncareerists. Without gainsaying the value and accomplishments of such diplomats as Warren Austin, Ellsworth Bunker, David K. E. Bruce, Josephus Daniels, and Averell Harriman, one must wonder whether there may not be an occasional careerist of comparable quality and experience who might profitably be retained in active service for additional high-level diplomatic assignments. If not, then perhaps the program of mid- and upper-career level guidance and training of FSOs requires serious attention. In any case, by itself, age is only an arbitrary and rudimentary qualifying standard, whereas proven competence should be given the greatest weight despite the career status of the candidates concerned.

5
DIPLOMATIC RANKS, TITLES, AND CAREER STATUS

The sensitive questions of ranks and career status of American emissaries, especially those in the professional service, have been widely discussed and debated. The ranks and titles accorded to chiefs of mission often resulted in imbuing them with second-rate status and placing them in inferior positions within the diplomatic community. The facts that American diplomats often are political appointees and that the career service was late in being established contributed to the problem of the professional qualification and performance of diplomatic envoys. The following paragraphs are not intended either to explain or to suggest a formula for resolving these issues, but rather to present factual developments respecting the ranks, titles, and career status of American diplomats.

Diplomatic Ranks and Titles

There have been two basic types of resident diplomatic establishments —called embassies and legations—headed by chiefs of mission bearing, respectively, the generic titles of ambassador and minister. This reflects a protocolary and functional distinction between two fundamental levels of diplomatic representation, and an individual emissary bears a rank and designation commensurate with the status of the resident mission.

Historically, however, additional refinements have been recognized. Thus, a traditional resident ambassador has been called "ordinary," whereas emissaries sent on particularized, often temporary, missions of significance were deemed to be "extraordinary." This differentiation has virtually disappeared, so that at present, resident chiefs of mission accredited to foreign governments universally bear the title ambassador extraordinary and plenipotentiary, the qualification plenipotentiary having been added to connote broad authority to conduct the normal panoply of diplomatic relations. The rank of minister has been refined to distinguish two basic categories—the envoy extraordinary and minister plenipotentiary and the minister resident—and at times additional variants of this rank have been employed.

When the United States was emerging into the foreign relations arena, matters of diplomatic rank were fluid and governmental attitudes toward matters of protocol and precedence were very touchy. Diplomatic status and titles were neither ordained by international convention nor by customary transnational law, so that during the revolutionary period, American envoys bore a number of pragmatically determined designations, including minister plenipotentiary (then the highest rank), commissioner (usually to negotiate a treaty or for coequal members of a diplomatic team), diplomatic agent, and chargé d'affaires. Following the establishment of regularized resident diplomatic relations, and until 1815, the United States generally appointed emissaries at the ministerial level to the eight European countries with which it exchanged envoys. Of forty-one appointments during this period, thirty carried the rank of minister plenipotentiary, five were ministers resident, four were chargés d'affaires, and only two were envoys extraordinary and ministers plenipotentiary. The designation envoy extraordinary was first applied to American representatives to the Netherlands (1814) and Russia (1815).

At the Congresses of Vienna and Aix-la-Chapelle (1815 and 1818), the major European powers agreed to establish the ranks of diplomats in four standard categories, in descending order of precedence, as follows:

1. Ambassadors extraordinary and plenipotentiary, and Papal legates or nuncios.
2. Envoys extraordinary, ministers plenipotentiary, and Papal internuncios.
3. Ministers resident.
4. Chargés d'affaires and chargés d'affaires ad interim.

The third level of emissary—the minister resident—added at Aix-la-Chapelle, served theoretically in an observer capacity rather than as an active representative and negotiator. Although this rank was used widely by the United States in the nineteenth century, it has fallen into disuse. Consequently, the ranks generally employed at present are ambassador extraordinary and plenipotentiary, envoy extraordinary and minister plenipotentiary, and chargé d'affaires.[1] In diplomatic practice a distinction also is made between the chargé d'affaires ad hoc or *en titre,* appointed on a continuing or permanent basis, and the chargé d'affaires ad interim, who functions temporarily, usually during the absence of the chief of mission, or pending the accreditation of a permanent emissary.[2]

These determinations of the early nineteenth century respecting diplomatic ranks produced several changes in American practice. Because the United States elected not to employ the ambassadorial title until late in the century, the rank of envoy extraordinary and minister plenipotentiary was usually but not universally ascribed to its diplomats accredited to the eight European countries.[3] Early American appointments to Latin America were less consistent. Emissaries accredited to Mexico were given the rank of envoy extraordinary and minister plenipotentiary from the outset (1825) and continued to bear this title throughout most of the century. On the other hand, as relations were commenced with Argentina, Chile, and Colombia in 1823, the first envoy to each of them was given the rank of minister plenipotentiary, but their successors, as well as early appointees to Bolivia, Brazil, Guatemala, Peru, and Venezuela were designated at the lower rank of chargé d'affaires. In general, this situation continued until the 1840s when mission chiefs to Brazil and Chile were changed to envoys extraordinary and ministers plenipotentiary, whereas diplomats accredited to the other countries were titled ministers resident.[4] It appears, therefore, that international political

[1] The titles of diplomatic ranks used in this analysis and in Table A-14 are those employed by the Department of State; see U.S. Department of State, *United States Chiefs of Mission, 1778–1973* including the glossary of abbreviations in Appendix F, p. 229.

[2] Statistics and analysis in this survey do not encompass the host of American diplomats appointed to serve as chargés d'affaires ad interim.

[3] While this rank of envoy extraordinary and minister plenipotentiary appears to have been generally preferred and came into American usage in Europe at the time of the Congress of Vienna (1815), appointees to Spain and Portugal continued at the minister plenipotentiary level for approximately another decade (when those to Spain were raised to envoy extraordinary and minister plenipotentiary and those to Portugal were reduced to chargé d'affaires. Envoys to the Netherlands and Sweden also were designated chargés d'affaires until the 1850s when they were changed to ministers resident. However, as relations were revived with Prussia, in 1837 American emissaries to this country were also given the rank of envoy extraordinary and minister plenipotentiary.

[4] The conversion from chargé d'affaires occurred first in Brazil (1841) and Chile (1849), and the others followed between 1850 and 1854.

considerations were influential from the outset in fixing diplomatic ranks, and that the United States was content to have its emissaries at the lowest rank commensurate with the requirements of their responsibilities. Table A-14, column C, provides statistics concerning the rank and titles of American diplomats, by country to which they were accredited.

A major upgrading of diplomatic appointees seems to have occurred in the early 1850s, when a series of envoys to Europe and Latin America were raised in rank from chargé d'affaires to minister resident.[5] In the same decade emissaries to several countries were elevated to that of envoy extraordinary and minister plenipotentiary.[6] During the next quarter century, the United States raised the status of its diplomats to the rank of envoy extraordinary and minister plenipotentiary only on a rare and occasional basis, as in the case of Japan in 1870. Another wave of diplomatic upgrading was instituted in the 1880s and early 1890s, when emissaries to approximately two dozen countries were raised to the rank of envoy extraordinary and minister plenipotentiary,[7] so that by the mid-1890s some thirty-seven—or approximately 85 percent—of United States emissaries held this rank.

A notable advance came in the 1890s when the Department of State commenced appointing its initial ambassadors extraordinary and plenipotentiary, and joined the major powers in employing this highest of diplomatic ranks. This change was authorized by legislation in 1893, which provided that the President, when advised by a foreign government that it wished to be represented in Washington by an emissary with the title of ambassador, he might, at his discretion, decide that the representative of the United States to that government bear the same designation. The upgrading began that very year with four European countries—France, Germany, Italy, and the United Kingdom—and was followed in 1898 with Mexico and Russia. In the early twentieth century, prior to 1913, Austria, Brazil, Japan, and Turkey were added, and President Woodrow Wilson elevated the diplomatic level of five more.[8]

The most sweeping and decisive change was instituted by President Franklin D. Roosevelt who raised the rank of American

[5] Belgium, Bolivia, Denmark, Ecuador, Guatemala, Nicaragua, Portugal, Sweden, and Venezuela, where the change was made in 1853 and 1854.

[6] Austria, China, and Peru; the change in Italy occurred in 1861.

[7] Nine in Europe, twelve in the Western Hemisphere, Hawaii, and Turkey.

[8] Argentina, Belgium, Chile, Peru, and Spain.

emissaries to the ambassadorial level in all of Latin America,[9] in most of the European countries aligned with the wartime United Nations as well as the countries occupied by the Axis powers during World War II,[10] and in several other states, including Canada and China. He did not include new states with which the United States was commencing regular diplomatic relations during his administration—such as Afghanistan (1935), Australia (1940), Saudi Arabia (1940), Iceland (1941), Lebanon (1942), New Zealand (1942), and Syria (1942).[11] All told, he elevated the rank of twenty-three American diplomatic missions, increasing to forty (70 percent) the total number of countries with which the United States had diplomatic exchanges at this most prestigious level.[12]

Since World War II the United States has continued the trend of raising the status of its resident envoys and diplomatic missions to the highest level. The number of remaining legations, headed by envoys extraordinary and ministers plenipotentiary, gradually diminished and were converted to embassies headed by ambassadors; usually as new missions were created they also were accorded embassy status. Among the last to be elevated were the American missions to Romania (1964), Bulgaria (1967), Hungary (1967), and Yemen (1972). By 1970 all American resident diplomatic envoys to foreign governments were at the ambassadorial rank (see Table 3).[13] The

[9] He began by elevating American missions to the ambassadorial rank in Colombia, Panama, and Venezuela in 1939, added Uruguay in 1941 and Bolivia, Ecuador, and Paraguay in 1942, and, in a single year during World War II (1943), he raised the status of diplomatic establishments to the remaining Central American and Caribbean countries—Costa Rica, Dominican Republic, El Salvador, Guatemala, Haiti, Honduras, and Nicaragua.

[10] In 1942 and 1943 Roosevelt elevated to embassy rank United States missions to five European countries warring against or occupied by Germany, including Czechoslovakia, Greece, the Netherlands, Norway, and Yugoslavia. Late in the war he added Portugal, although it was technically neutral. But other neutrals—including Sweden and Switzerland—were not so favored. Similarly, a number of Axis powers, with which diplomatic relations had been severed, were not involved—namely, Finland, Hungary, Romania, and Bulgaria.

[11] Dates indicate the years in which the first United States emissaries were officially received.

[12] Actually, due to temporarily severed relations with Austria, Germany, Japan, and Poland, as of 1945 the United States was dealing at the ambassador extraordinary and plenipotentiary level with thirty-six of its fifty-four diplomatic missions, as noted in Table 3.

[13] The apparent inconsistency respecting Yemen is due to the fact that Yemen severed relations with the United States in 1967, and when they were revived in 1972, the rank of the mission was raised to an embassy. By March 1973 there were 126 diplomats at this rank, and emissaries to the six countries with whom relations then were severed (Algeria, Congo/Brazzaville, Cuba, Egypt, Iraq, and Syria) also had previously been at this level.

Table 3

DEVELOPMENT OF STATUS OF U.S. DIPLOMATIC MISSIONS

Diplomatic Missions	1930	1935	1940	1945	1950	1955	1960	1965	1970	1975
Embassy	14	16	20	36	58	69	79	111	116	134[c]
Legation	41	45	38	17	15	7	4	2	0	0
Mission[a]	0	0	0	1	2	2	3	8	9	9
Office of Political Adviser[b]	0	0	0	0	1	1	0	0	0	0
Total	55	61	58	54	76	79	86	121	125	143[c]

[a] These represent the United States missions to international organizations as listed in chapter 1, minus the mission to UNESCO. The *Foreign Service List* identifies the representative agencies to UNESCO and the Food and Agriculture Organization as "offices" rather than "missions."

[b] These missions were established in occupied countries: three in 1947, four in 1948, and five in 1949, but reduced to one in 1950.

[c] These figures do not include the liaison office to the People's Republic of China.

Source: *Foreign Service List,* January issues through 1970, and February issue for 1975.

United States has reached the point of universal diplomatic representation at the highest level.

A number of special cases in American history do not accord with these general developments respecting the ranks of United States diplomatic emissaries and resident missions. For example, the initial American chiefs of mission to a few countries were accorded titles other than those of chargé d'affaires, minister plenipotentiary, minister resident, and ambassador extraordinary and plenipotentiary. Francis Dana, the first envoy to Russia, has the distinction of being the only chief of mission to a foreign court designated by the Department of State simply as "Minister." [14] In several cases the initial American emissaries to a country were accredited either as commissioner or as diplomatic agent. Although Caleb Cushing, first chief of mission to serve in China was originally named envoy extraordinary and minister plenipotentiary and commissioner in 1843, the following year his rank was reduced simply to commissioner, and five successors also bore this title until it was changed back to envoy extraordinary and minister plenipotentiary in 1857.

Similarly, the first appointee to Paraguay carried the rank of commissioner for nearly two years (1861–1863), and for a decade (1853–1863) the first three envoys to Hawaii also held this rank, but it was then changed to minister resident and eventually (1890) was elevated to envoy extraordinary and minister plenipotentiary. On the other hand, all United States emissaries to Texas carried the lesser title of chargé d'affaires. During the first decade of diplomatic exchanges with Bulgaria (1901–1910) the President named six emissaries with the rank of diplomatic agent. The first of these, Charles M. Dickinson, serving as consul general in Constantinople where he resided, was given the appointment to Bulgaria as an additional simultaneous assignment.

Although unusual, several American chiefs of mission simultaneously held both diplomatic and consular assignments to a single capital, and therefore they carried multiple ranks and titles. The most exceptional records were established in Egypt where, over a period of nearly three-fourths of a century (1848–1922), twenty-four representatives were appointed as joint "agent-consul general," and in Liberia where, for sixty-eight years (1863–1930), twenty-eight emis-

[14] See *United States Chiefs of Mission,* p. 136. However, the *Register of the Department of State, October 1, 1937,* p. 335, identifies him as "Minister Plenipotentiary."

saries were designated with dual titles.[15] Joint diplomatic-consular appointments were also made to certain other countries: for short periods at the commencement of American diplomatic relations in the case of Lebanon (1942–1944), Romania (1880–1891), and Syria (1942–1947), and for more extended periods in Haiti (1862–1897) and Morocco (1917–1956). All of these envoys were accredited with joint titles combining their diplomatic rank with the position of consul general.[16]

The reasons for these exceptional rank designations for resident chiefs of mission are obvious in those instances where diplomatic and consular responsibilities have been combined, and it is not difficult to comprehend the justification for employing the lesser titles of commissioner or diplomatic agent when first establishing diplomatic relations. However, the purposes served by thereafter varying from chargé d'affaires to commissioner and diplomatic agent are less apparent. It appears that the designation chargé implied substantial expectancy of permanence in diplomatic relations and that the rank of commissioner denoted negotiations looking toward such permanence, whereas the title diplomatic agent, where employed over an extended period, as in the case of Bulgaria at the turn of the twentieth century, signified diplomatic responsibility as a part of multiple accreditation with the primary assignment to a different country. A complementary reason for using the rank of commissioner to China in the early days may have been because, as noted, prior to 1898 American emissaries did not present their credentials directly to the head of state.

On rare occasions, where the quantity and complexity of diplomatic responsibility has warranted it, the United States has recently introduced the practice of supplementing the chief of mission with a deputy ambassador. For example, near the end of Ambassador William C. Bullitt's term of service in France, Anthony J. Drexel Biddle (former ambassador to Poland who accompanied its government when it fled to France in 1939 and continued as American representative to the Polish government in exile) acted as deputy ambassador to France for a short time.[17] More recently, during the Vietnam War, a series

[15] Such conjoint diplomatic-consular designations are not included in the statistics and analysis concerned with multiple diplomatic appointments discussed in chapter 2.

[16] Their titles generally were agent-consul general, diplomatic agent-consul general, or commissioner-consul general. In the case of Haiti and Liberia, however, the President appointed a succession of ministers resident-consuls general (ten to Haiti and twenty-six to Liberia).

[17] 13-25 June 1940.

of deputy ambassadors were appointed to Saigon to assist the American ambassador.[18]

Since 1778, in summary, the United States has assigned the following ranks to its resident chiefs of mission to foreign countries (see Table 4):

Table 4

RANKS OF U.S. DIPLOMATS, 1778–1973

Rank	Number	Percentage
Ambassador extraordinary and plenipotentiary	1,011	40.49
Envoy extraordinary/minister plenipotentiary	901	36.08
Minister resident	300	12.02
Chargé d'affaires	189	07.57
Minister plenipotentiary	36	01.44
Commissioner	17	00.68
Agent, diplomatic agent, and others	43	01.72
Total	2,497	100.00

Note: Detailed statistics respecting the ranks of American chiefs of mission are presented in column C of Table A-14, which lists all such appointments by ranks for each country with which the United States has maintained diplomatic relations since 1778, together with overall totals and percentages.

The common titles at the ministerial level initially employed by the Department of State were minister resident and minister plenipotentiary, but in the aggregate they have accounted for only approximately one-fourth of all ministerial-level appointments. Once the changes wrought by the Congresses of Vienna and Aix-la-Chapelle began to be implemented by the United States, the President commenced appointing envoys extraordinary and ministers plenipotentiary to head American legations. While some ministerial-level appointees continued to be named simply as ministers plenipotentiary or ministers resident, a preponderant majority—some 901—were given the superior rank.

More significant, however, is the fact that when the United States decided to elevate its diplomatic missions to the status of

[18] These deputy ambassadors included U. Alexis Johnson (June 1964–September 1965), William J. Porter (September 1965–May 1967), Eugene M. Locke (May 1967–January 1968), Samuel D. Berger (March 1968–March 1972), and Charles S. Whitehouse (March 1972–1973). All except Locke were career officers, whereas the ambassadors during this period—Maxwell D. Taylor, Henry Cabot Lodge, and Ellsworth Bunker—were noncareerists. Graham A. Martin, careerist, was appointed ambassador in 1973.

embassies and began appointing ambassadors extraordinary and plenipotentiary late in the nineteenth century, and as existing positions were advanced to this rank and as it was also applied when diplomatic relations were commenced with newly emergent countries, this became the universal rank of American emissaries. As a consequence, since the 1890s more than a thousand diplomats have been accorded this title and, in a dozen years or so, with the accreditation of as many as thirty to forty each year, it will exceed all the other ranks combined.

Because the practice of appointing chiefs of mission to international organizations began only after World War II, when the trend to elevate American representatives to the ambassadorial level was well advanced, it is not surprising to note that a good many United States resident emissaries to these organizations carry the rank of either ambassador or ambassador extraordinary and plenipotentiary. This pertains not only to representatives to the United Nations, but also to the Organization of American States, the North Atlantic Treaty Organization, and several other international institutions.[19] However, American representatives to the specialized agencies of the United Nations generally have held the rank of minister.[20]

The United States has not contributed a great deal of innovation in the designation of its traditional resident emissaries. One exception has been its widespread use of nonresident presidential special representatives, but they too have usually held the rank of ambassador extraordinary or minister plenipotentiary, although in the early years they sometimes were simply designated as special agents or commissioners. In recent years the White House also has appointed special assistants to the President with the personal rank of ambassador. The titles of such special emissaries are determined by the chief executive in keeping with the nature of their diplomatic assignments.[21]

Aside from such exceptional appointments (not included in this analysis, as noted earlier) the major contemporary deviation from customary practice respecting diplomatic ranks is the commissioning of a number of ambassadors at large. This title, however, is more indicative of an internal constitutional/political designation or assignment than it is of a new internationally agreed upon supergrade

[19] Such as the European Communities, the International Atomic Energy Agency, the Organization for Economic Cooperation and Development, and the Geneva office of the United Nations.

[20] These include the International Civil Aviation Organization, UNESCO, and the United Nations Industrial Development Organization.

[21] For additional discussion on the ranks and titles of presidential special emissaries, see Elmer Plischke, *Summit Diplomacy: Personal Diplomacy of the President of the United States*, pp. 48–50.

diplomatic rank, even though in some cases it may in fact serve this purpose. If used widely in the future, it may eventually come to constitute such superior rank.[22]

Career Status of Diplomats

The literature on American diplomacy has debated and often criticized presidential appointment of noncareer outsiders, the professional competence of United States diplomats, and their career status. It has been disputed whether diplomacy is an art or a science—whether the artful negotiator is more essential than the systematic policy maker and implementer. The presumption is that if diplomacy is primarily an art, it can best be practiced by carefully selected and trained members of an efficient career service. Although American diplomacy may be regarded as having been emancipated from earlier confinement as the preserve of the wealthy, some still deem it to be excessively the stepchild of the spoils system—or, at least, as being insufficiently professionalized.

E. Wilder Spaulding, writing after a lifetime of concern with American diplomatic practice, concludes that it may be easier to evolve a formula for the "ideal ambassador" than it is to recruit him.[23] It may appear to be relatively simple to assess the success of a particular appointee at the conclusion of his service, but it is far more difficult in most cases to foresee accomplishment or failure—or even ability or latent inadequacy—at the time of appointment. Little comfort may be found in the illusory proposition that the only solution is the invariable appointment of the right man to the right assignment at the right time. These—the man, the post, and the moment—together with other identifiable variables and imponderables in the appointing equation render the process both uncertain and difficult. Given the need to designate an average of some thirty to forty diplomats each year and to accredit them to disparate countries, and having in mind not only the problems of the availability of qualified candidates at the moment of need[24] and their acceptability to particular governments, but also existing political relations and un-

[22] For analysis of the origin and development of this type of American appointment, see Lee H. Burke, *Ambassador at Large: Diplomat Extraordinary.* David M. Kennedy, previously secretary of the treasury, even retained his cabinet position and rank on appointment as ambassador at large.

[23] Spaulding, *Ambassadors Ordinary and Extraordinary,* p. 286. But also see footnote 28.

[24] It must be remembered that the transfer of a career diplomat from one foreign capital to another is likely to produce a chain reaction of reassignments.

foreseeable probabilities, it would take consummate genius and inordinate luck to achieve such a goal.

In retrospect, the United States is fortunate to have been blessed with so many able diplomats, some of whom may have emerged despite, rather than because of, the prevailing system. At the same time, it cannot be gainsaid that more unfortunate appointments were made than should have been the case. Those charged with recruiting and developing able diplomatic careerists and with appointing equally competent noncareerists to high positions in the Department of State and as chiefs of diplomatic mission bear a heavy burden of responsibility.

This analysis is less concerned, however, with devising a formula for dealing with such issues, or with passing judgment on either the system or specific individuals, than it is with reviewing the career status of American diplomats. In doing so, several fundamental distinguishing designations need to be clarified. The first of these—the "career diplomat"—generally reflects the status of an individual as a member of a formal career service, which, at present, means a Foreign Service Officer. They enter the Foreign Service with the intention of making diplomacy their profession and, rising through the ranks, they may ultimately be appointed as chiefs of mission to foreign governments or to other top-level posts. In principle, this appears to be straightforward and uncomplicated. Prior to 1946, however, FSOs were required to resign from the career service when they accepted appointment as an ambassador or minister, and technically they ceased being career diplomats.[25] To allow for this and to provide a rule of thumb for designating career diplomats, the Department of State has determined that the appellation "career diplomat" be accorded to all those who were members of the Foreign Service when appointed chief of mission and to certain others who qualified for the designation at the time of the enactment of the law (15 February 1915) which restructured the Diplomatic and Consular Services.[26] In this survey, consequently, three categories of designation are used,

[25] Since the enactment of the Foreign Service Act of 1946 this requirement has been rescinded, so that FSOs appointed as chiefs of mission now retain their status in the career service.

[26] Such others include those who, serving in 1915, had at least ten years of continuous diplomatic service, or, if appointed later, had at least five years experience in the Foreign Service or the earlier Diplomatic and Consular Services prior to appointment. The career designation has also been assigned to those few individuals who had served as diplomatic secretaries, who had then been commissioned before 1915 as chiefs of mission or as presidential appointees in the Department of State, who were not serving as chiefs of mission in February 1915, but who were subsequently appointed or reappointed to head diplomatic missions. For these specifications, see *United States Chiefs of Mission*, pp. iii–iv.

namely, the pre-1915 appointees, the careerists, and the post-1915 noncareerists. Statistics for these categories of careerism are provided in Tables A-4 and A-6 (by decades and by type of appointment), Tables A-5 and A-14 (by country to which appointed), and Table A-7, column 3 (for multiple appointments).

A second distinction to bear in mind is that of the "professional diplomat." Defined in one sense, all diplomatic careerists are professionals, but if the latter concept is limited solely to careerists, then the United States had no professional diplomats prior to 1915, which cannot be maintained. Even if all careerists are deemed to be professionals, there are a good many others who, in terms of length of service or accomplishment, must equally be regarded as professional diplomats.

This applies to certain chiefs of mission in the pre-1915 period, some of whom served for extended periods in a variety of missions, as already noted. Some of these—such as Benjamin Franklin, John Quincy Adams, James Monroe, James Buchanan, and Richard Rush in our early history, Charles Francis Adams and John Bigelow in the 1860s, and Joseph H. Choate, Arthur S. Hardy, David Jayne Hill, and William W. Rockhill at the turn of the century—because of the nature of their service and achievement occupy a status in American history as professional diplomats well above that of a contemporary FSO who may cap his career with a few years as a chief of mission, even though he is designated a career diplomat. Equally significant is the post-1915 appointee who may enjoy an extensive record of service at the highest levels but, because he is not an FSO, is regarded as a noncareerist. Illustrations, again to mention but a few, include George W. Ball, Anthony J. Drexel Biddle, David K. E. Bruce, Ellsworth Bunker, W. Averell Harriman, Henry Cabot Lodge, George C. McGhee, and Laurence A. Steinhardt.[27]

While the career/noncareer distinction is necessary and important, its limitations as compared with the differentiation between the professional and the amateur—a category which some brand as dilettantism—are obvious. The point is, simply, that some careerists are professionals only in a limited and formal sense, and not all noncareerists are diletantes—again except in the sense that they may not be long-lived Foreign Service Officers; in reality, they may be first-rate professionals.

The concept of professional diplomat, as related to service as chiefs of mission and at high levels in the Department of State, might

[27] Among a great many others who might be included are Spruille Braden, Wilbur J. Carr, William R. Castle, Angier Biddle Duke, Henry F. Grady, Stanton Griffis, Lloyd C. Griscom, Robert C. Hill, Alan G. Kirk, and Lincoln MacVeagh.

usefully be defined arbitrarily as being based on a minimum number of years of service in such assignments, or on a minimum number of such assignments, or on a combination of these factors. However, to identify the genuine professionals among both the careerists and noncareerists, other criteria would be needed. These might include reputable experience, acknowledged negotiatory achievements, management ability, facility at functioning at the highest political or other professional levels and the like, but it is not the purpose of this analysis to define or attempt to apply such criteria.[28] Moreover, even if they were to be established and applied, the categorization of careerist professionals and nonprofessionals, and noncareerist professionals and nonprofessionals could create greater complexity and confusion. Suffice it to say that there have been and are diplomatic professionals—or professional diplomats—who are not careerists, and that the limitations of the concept of careerism must be acknowledged.

Table A-4 presents statistics concerning the career status of all appointees to senior positions in the Department of State, as chiefs of mission to foreign governments and international organizations, and as ambassadors at large, distinguishing between the pre-1915 (or undesignated) appointees and the post-1915 careerists and noncareerists. Figures are provided for each category of appointees by decades since 1778, with overall totals and percentages. Of the 2,926 appointments made, 1,202—or 41 percent—predated 1915, and since then 935 (32 percent) of the total number of appointments were of careerists, with the remaining 789 (27 percent) being accorded to noncareerists.

In keeping with this differentiation, an aggregate of some 1,991 of 2,926 (68 percent) are technically regarded as noncareerist American diplomats. More significantly, however, of the 1,724 appointments since 1915, more than half (54 percent) have been careerists. This means, on the one hand, that, even if post-1915 professional noncareerists are added to this number, the extent to which nonprofessional noncareerists are appointed is still high—to some analysts, even excessive. Nevertheless, evidencing an important trend, the ratio

[28] E. Wilder Spaulding addresses himself to the difficult question of defining the requisites and qualities of a good ambassador in the last chapter of his *Ambassadors Ordinary and Extraordinary*, and he quotes a good many others—including Francois de Callières, J. Rives Childs, Jules Jusserand, Sir Ernest Satow, Charles W. Thayer, Sir Henry Wotton, and the like. Also see John S. Creaghe, "Personal Qualities and Effective Diplomatic Negotiation," Ph.D. dissertation, University of Maryland, 1965. The problem of fixing scientifically the qualities essential to distinguish effective diplomats, and determining a pragmatic method of applying them in assessing performance systematically is difficult and may well be impossible.

of careerists appointed to high level diplomatic positions since 1940 has increased, overall, to nearly 60 percent.

In view of the number of appointments made to the secretaryship of state and the other senior department officers prior to 1915, and the very nature of these positions, it is not surprising that, in the aggregate, only 30 percent of these appointments have gone to careerists. Of greater consequence, however, are the facts that since 1920 the number of careerists has amounted to nearly 40 percent of these departmental appointees, and that during this half century the number of careerists approximated half the appointees during two decades, the 1920s and 1950s.

Since 1920 the record with respect to chiefs of mission to foreign governments is far more favorable to careerism in that 799 of 1,315 (61 percent) have been careerists. In the 1940s the ratio of careerists reached 64 percent and since 1950 it has approximated or exceeded 65 percent each decade, so that together with the professional noncareerists, they currently account for more than two-thirds of American resident chiefs of mission.[29]

Aside from such general statistics, a number of detailed developments are material to understanding the nature of, and trends regarding, the career status of American chiefs of mission. For example, one of the criticisms of ranking United States diplomats is that presidential appointments to the principal capitals of the world represent an undemocratic stronghold of exclusiveness and wealth in government service. The widespread belief that certain diplomatic posts are the guaranteed preserve of noncareerists is valid, but only to a very limited extent. True, no careerist has been appointed to the United Kingdom, and since 1915 only six of thirty-one appointees to France and Germany have been FSOs. Yet, noncareerist professionals like David K. E. Bruce, William C. Bullitt, George C. McGhee, and Henry Cabot Lodge have held such appointments. Other posts favored with an exceptionally high proportion of noncareerist appointees include Ireland (with only one of fourteen appointees chosen from the career ranks), Australia, Denmark, India, the Philippines, and Spain—to each of which two-thirds or more have been noncareerists.[30] Belgium, Luxembourg, the Netherlands, Norway, and Japan have also been favored somewhat for noncareerist appointments.

[29] To be precise, according to the *Foreign Service List*, published periodically by the Department of State, in January 1970 careerists held more than 70 percent of the ambassadorial posts, and in February 1974, with eighteen positions vacant, careerists held more than 65 percent of such posts.

[30] To these, tentatively, may be added Jamaica and Malta, with only one of four appointees in each case selected from among careerists, but this encompasses too short a period to warrant any useful predictions.

After diplomatic relations were revived with the Soviet Union in 1933, the United States appointed seven noncareerists over a period of nearly two decades, but has named only careerists since 1952. Moreover, three of the noncareerists were former military officers—Admirals William H. Standley and Alan G. Kirk and General Walter Bedell Smith—and three others—William C. Bullitt, Laurence A. Steinhardt, and W. Averell Harriman—may be ranked among the acknowledged professionals. Nearly two-thirds of American chiefs of mission to the Eastern European Communist countries have been careerists. While in the case of Poland the number of noncareerists approximated that of careerists after 1915, since World War II only five of thirty-four (15 percent)) appointees to these six countries have been noncareerists.[31] Thus, the President tends overwhelmingly to accredit careerists and other professionals to the Communist countries of Eastern Europe.

The United States has also appointed more careerists than noncareerists as its chiefs of mission to countries in the Western Hemisphere. Only in the case of four of the twenty Latin American countries has the number of noncareerists exceeded the careerists, and then only by one or two appointees per country;[32] moreover, half of the emissaries accredited to Canada since relations were established in 1927 have also been careerists. An unusually high proportion of careerists has been assigned to such countries as Haiti and Uruguay,[33] and the number also has been substantial (two-thirds or more) in the case of Brazil and the Dominican Republic. The largest numbers of noncareerist appointments in the Western Hemisphere have been to two new countries—Jamaica, and Trinidad and Tobago, and they are likely to change. The notion, therefore, that such posts as Buenos Aires, Mexico City, Rio de Janeiro, and Ottawa are the sanctuary of noncareerists cannot be sustained. Even including Canada—where the ratio of careerists remains approximately 50 percent—careerists have increased each decade since 1940, rising from some 55 percent to nearly 70 percent.

The degree to which American diplomatic appointments to the Middle East, to sub-Saharan Africa, and to the newer countries of

[31] Bulgaria, Czechoslovakia, Hungary, Poland, Romania, and Yugoslavia. The United States has sent no resident emissaries to Albania since World War II. Among the five noncareerists were Eugenie Anderson, appointed to Bulgaria in 1962, Stanton Griffis, who served as ambassador to four countries, and Leonard C. Meeker, who had previously been legal adviser in the Department of State for more than four years.

[32] These include Chile, Cuba, Mexico, and Paraguay.

[33] For Haiti all but one have been careerists since 1914, and only three of twenty-three were noncareerists in the case of Uruguay.

Asia have been assigned to careerists since 1915 should also please the proponents of diplomatic careerism. In the Middle East the percentage of noncareerists is highest for the three countries with which the United States has maintained the longest records of diplomatic relations—Egypt, Iran, and Turkey—and yet in only one of twenty Middle Eastern countries has the number of noncareerists equaled that of the careerists.[34] Not a single noncareerist has been appointed to eleven of these countries, and even in the case of Saudi Arabia and Syria, with whom relations were commenced as early as 1939 and 1942 respectively, only one or two appointments have involved noncareerists. This area, therefore, has clearly become the domain of career American diplomats.

United States chiefs of mission accredited to the new countries of sub-Saharan Africa also have largely been careerists. No noncareerists were sent to thirteen of thirty-three of these countries[35] and, as of 1973, only thirty of 138 (22 percent) appointees to these countries were noncareerists. Career diplomats sent to Ethiopia, with which diplomatic exchanges began in 1909, and South Africa, with which relations were commenced in 1930, also outnumbered noncareerists by two to one. Of all the thirty-six sub-Saharan African countries, the United States has named fewer careerists than noncareerists only to Liberia. Even in this case, however, since 1950 the majority have been Foreign Service Officers. Should this trend continue, and the cumulative quota to 1973 amounted to 73 percent, American representation—as in the Middle East—will be predominantly careerist.

Aside from the countries of Asia and the Western Pacific already mentioned, the United States has generally accredited only a slightly larger number of careerists than noncareerists to such older diplomatic partners as China, New Zealand, and Thailand. However, careerists have been overwhelmingly appointed to Afghanistan, Burma, the Khmer Republic, Korea, Laos, and Malaysia, and, overall, less than one-fourth (23 percent) of more than 100 chiefs of mission accredited to seventeen Asian countries since World War II have been noncareerists. It may be concluded, therefore, that except for a few specific countries, the trend outside of Europe is clearly to appoint careerists as United States chiefs of mission and, for some groups of states, the appointment of noncareerists has become so infrequent as to be exceptional.

34 As of 31 March 1973 the record for Egypt was eight careerists and nine noncareerists, but with the appointment of Hermann F. Eilts later that year, the balance was retrieved.

35 Excluding Ethiopia, Liberia, and South Africa.

It has been said that, because of the politics involved in making diplomatic appointments, normally a new President is initially likely to recruit a higher percentage of noncareerists and subsequently, as posts are vacated and replacements are named, he turns more and more to the careerists. As a matter of fact, however, while there was some validity to this impression, the situation has been changing markedly since World War II. When Franklin D. Roosevelt became President, he named twice as many noncareerists as careerists (twenty-nine to fifteen) to be his initial diplomatic replacements, but he also retained more than a dozen careerists who had been appointed by his predecessor, so that the two groups were equal in number, and as diplomatic relations were launched with new countries, he also named approximately as many careerists as noncareerists.

Presidents Eisenhower, Kennedy, and Nixon—each of whom represented a political change in the White House, at which time the replacement of diplomats is apt to be greatest—named increasing numbers of careerists as their initial appointments. President Eisenhower continued nearly two dozen of President Truman's careerist appointees in their posts,[36] designated more newly appointed careerists than noncareerists,[37] and accredited more than twenty careerists and only one noncareerist to new countries as his initial appointees. President Kennedy retained more than twenty Eisenhower careerists in their posts when he took over, appointed more than forty-five careerists and approximately thirty noncareerists as his initial appointees, and also named more careerists than noncareerists to new countries as diplomatic relations were inaugurated. President Nixon favored careerism even more, continuing some two dozen of his predecessor's careerist appointees in their assignments, designating more than fifty careerists and approximately thirty noncareerists as his initial appointees, and also naming more careerists than noncareerists to new countries. These three Presidents have established a decided precedent, and taken together they appointed or continued at their posts more than twice as many careerists as noncareerists when they commenced their administrations.

As of 1948 there were some two dozen chiefs of mission holding ambassadorial and ministerial posts who had risen within the ranks of the career service. On the average about half of all diplomats were careerists during the Truman administration and, while the same was true early in the Eisenhower administration, the ratio increased to

[36] By this is meant that the incoming President retained an incumbent diplomat for at least fifteen months without change.

[37] This refers to appointments made within fifteen months of inauguration.

two-thirds careerists by the time he left office. In the mid-1960s the figure had risen to approximately 75 percent careerists, and it dropped to roughly 70 percent in 1970 and to 66 percent by 1974.

As a consequence, while fluctuations have occurred in the ratio of careerists, the trend since World War II has clearly been in favor of increasing the quantity of career diplomats, varying from two-thirds to three-fourths. The issue of careerism versus noncareerism appears to be of diminishing importance, and as more and more careerists gain initial appointment as chiefs of mission and are available for transfer from one ambassadorial post to another, future Presidents are likely to be even more prone to retain or reassign them. Moreover, with the complementary designation and reappointment of noncareerist professionals, the current status of, and future prospects for, the professionalization of United States diplomatic representation have become gratifyingly salutary.

6
PRESIDENTIAL ASPIRATIONS AND CONGRESSIONAL SERVICE OF DIPLOMATS

Prior to the establishment of the career diplomatic service, it was natural for political leaders to relate service in the diplomatic corps to that in the secretaryship of state, in Congress, and in the presidency and vice-presidency. The fact of such interrelationship was to be expected, and the ascendancy of several secretaries of state to the presidency is well known. However, the degree to which presidential and vice-presidential candidates possessed prior diplomatic experience, and the number of members of Congress who were appointed to diplomatic assignments, sometimes resigning their legislative seats to serve in them, is far less known.

Diplomats as Presidential and Vice-Presidential Candidates

Through the 1860s, substantial relationship between holding high diplomatic office and candidacy for the presidency and vice-presidency became manifest.[1] Prior to the Civil War, six secretaries of state succeeded to the presidency, as already noted.[2] Nine others—six of them also prior to the Civil War—were unsuccessful candidates in presidential elections.[3] Two Presidents—John Adams and William

[1] "Candidacy" for purposes of this analysis is interpreted, not in such a broad sense as to include all of those with presidential and vice-presidential ambitions, or who competed at nominating conventions, but rather in the restricted sense of those who were formally considered by, and received votes in, the Electoral College.

[2] These included Thomas Jefferson, James Madison, James Monroe, John Quincy Adams, Martin Van Buren, and James M. Buchanan.

[3] These included John Jay, Edward Everett, and Lewis Cass, as presidential candidates; and Henry Clay, John C. Calhoun, Daniel Webster, James G. Blaine, William Jennings Bryan, and Charles Evans Hughes, as vice-presidential candidates. All of these, except Hughes, also had served in Congress (Jay in the Continental Congress), and Jay and Hughes were also appointed chief justice of the United States. Blaine, Bryan, and Hughes were the only post-Civil War candidates.

Henry Harrison—had previous diplomatic experience abroad, although they had not been appointed secretary of state, and Andrew Jackson was nominated as the first United States minister to Mexico in 1823, but he declined the appointment. Moreover, three vice-presidents also were nominated for diplomatic appointments prior to the Civil War, and three additional vice-presidents have held such appointments since 1880.[4] Thus, while fifteen of the sixty-four individuals (approximately 25 percent) who served as President and vice-president during nearly two centuries also received diplomatic appointments, either as secretary of state, or as chiefs of mission abroad, or both,[5] the ratio prior to the Civil War was nearly 58 percent.

In addition, though less well known, is the fact that an additional twenty-four unsuccessful presidential and vice-presidential candidates also were nominated for diplomatic appointments. Two-thirds of these stood for election prior to 1870 and, aside from those who also became secretary of state, they included such political figures as Charles Francis Adams and Rufus King, as well as journalist Horace Greeley and General George B. McClellan. In more recent times, they have included Adlai E. Stevenson and Henry Cabot Lodge.

All told, therefore, since 1778 nearly fifty persons served in top positions in the Department of State or as chiefs of diplomatic missions in the field and subsequently stood for election to the highest executive offices in the United States. This would seem to demonstrate a potent relationship between diplomatic experience and service in the presidency and vice-presidency and, although the affinity was greater in earlier history, it has not entirely disappeared. The diplomatic careerists, because of the nonpolitical traditions of the Foreign Service, are unlikely to have high-level political aspirations. Occasionally, however, noncareerist diplomats, such as W. Averell Harriman, may go into politics.

Although the position of secretary of state is no longer a stepping stone to the presidency, and even though no secretary of state has run for the office since the days of William Jennings Bryan and Charles Evans Hughes, some recent candidates for the presidency and vice-presidency have also been considered as possible appointees to the

[4] Five of these were formally accredited, namely, George M. Dallas (Russia, 1837, and Great Britain, 1856), William R. King (France, 1844), Hannibal Hamlin (Spain, 1881), Levi P. Morton (France, 1881), and Charles G. Dawes (Great Britain, 1929). The sixth, John C. Breckinridge, elected vice-president in 1856, had been named minister to Spain the preceding year, but declined the appointment.

[5] The diplomatic service as chiefs of mission of secretaries of state, in sequential multiple appointments, has been discussed in chapter 3.

secretaryship. This raises the issue as to whether the time is not at hand when the secretary of state, on appointment, should be considered primarily in terms of his qualifications in foreign affairs management and not because of his political importance or constituency—or, to put it another way, whether he should be essentially apolitical rather than a potential candidate for high elective office.

Members of Congress as Diplomats[6]

Paralleling the relationship between diplomatic service and the presidency is the relationship between service in Congress and the diplomatic profession. The number of former members of Congress appointed to high position in the Department of State and as diplomats in the field is surprising. Of the 1,869 individuals appointed as chiefs of mission, ambassadors at large, and ranking members of the Department of State since 1778, 294 (16 percent) were previously members of Congress. More significantly, they accounted for 22 percent of the 1,359 noncareer appointees.[7]

During the early period, a great many diplomats were former members of Congress. Thus, to 1800, thirteen of twenty-seven of the appointments were filled with former senators and congressmen, including nine who had served in the Continental Congress.[8] While the average subsequently declined, the number of such appointments generally exceeded 40 percent (103 of 245) to 1850, and accounted for nearly one-third of all appointees (200 of 639, or 31 percent) during the first century to 1879, but then dropped to an average of approximately 13 to 15 percent between 1870 and 1890. The number has been negligible since 1900, however, generally amounting to five or less congressmen-diplomats per decade, except during the period 1910–1920 and in the 1950s. Overall, the number has averaged only 2 percent since World War I. Table A-15 gives statistics on the diplomatic appointment of former members of Congress. It indicates the number of such appointees, by decades, with percentages, the number of legislators who resigned expressly to accept diplomatic

---

6 For the identification of, and other information concerning, the members of Congress who have been appointed as diplomats, the author had the benefit of the research of John C. Butner, who has under way a comprehensive study of "Congressmen-Diplomats: Executive-Legislative Collaboration in Appointing Active and Former Members of Congress as Diplomatic Emissaries."

7 Grouping all pre-1915 and designated post-1915 noncareer appointees.

8 These included John Adams, William Carmichael, Francis Dana, Benjamin Franklin, John Jay, Thomas Jefferson, Robert R. Livingston, Gouverneur Morris, and Edmund J. Randolph.

appointment, their political affiliations, the legislative chamber in which they served, and the types of diplomatic positions they held.

Whereas most of these 294 members of Congress left the legislature because they were unsuccessful in gaining renomination, were defeated for reelection, or simply decided not to run for legislative office again, sixty-six (22 percent) specifically resigned their legislative seats to accept diplomatic appointment (see column C, Table A-15), and an additional twenty-one were named to diplomatic assignments shortly before the expiration of their congressional terms, so that eighty-seven (30 percent) moved directly from Congress into diplomatic service.

In the case of the remaining 207 (70 percent), the interim periods varied,[9] ranging from less than a month to nearly thirty years. Approximately two dozen were commissioned as diplomats within a year, and about half of the 207 received diplomatic appointments within five years; but roughly one in four experienced delays ranging from ten to thirty years. A few held other intervening governmental positions, including cabinet posts in the Justice, Treasury, and War departments, judgeships, gubernatorial office, and the like.

So far as political party affiliation was concerned, 142 were Democrats, eighty-nine were Republicans, and the remainder included thirty-three Whigs, seven Federalists, some Unionists, and members of other lesser parties. Nine had served in the Continental Congress without such party designations, and for a few, especially in earlier history, party affiliation was difficult to determine. (See column D, Table A-15).

Democrats predominated in the first half of the nineteenth century, Whigs were involved primarily during the period from the 1840s to the 1860s, Republican appointees gained substantially following the Civil War, and since 1900 the party affiliation of congressmen-diplomats has been largely reflective of the party of the incumbent President. Nevertheless, although it might be taken for granted that such appointments invariably mirror the party affiliation of the appointing President, in seventy-four (25 percent) of the 294 cases the party affiliation actually differed. This variation was common in the early years through the 1820s, and reached high peaks in the 1840s (nearly 40 percent) and the politically disturbed 1860s (nearly 60 percent), but has since been of negligible significance.

[9] These intervening periods are timed from the end of the latest congressional service (where an individual served for more than one term) and the first diplomatic appointment (even though the individual held more than one such appointment).

One early appointee was named secretary of foreign affairs,[10] and twenty-two of these congressional members were appointed directly as secretary of state [11]—of which half (eleven) resigned their legislative seats to assume their cabinet posts. Two others functioned as secretary of state ad interim.[12] Thus, twenty-five were named to the secretaryship as their initial or sole appointment. In addition, eight became secretary following service as chief of mission abroad,[13] and one was initially named under secretary and later promoted to the secretaryship.[14] As already noted, two of these secretaries—Blaine and Webster—served as secretary twice. Therefore, aside from those whose service was ad interim, thirty-two (11 percent) of the congressmen-diplomats became secretary of state, and they accounted for nearly two-thirds (60 percent) of American secretaries of state since the 1770s. As a matter of fact, the relationship between service in Congress and appointment as secretary of state was so common that during a period of more than a century (1790–1892) only five of twenty-nine secretaries lacked prior congressional experience, and the combined tenure of the five amounted to only eleven years. In addition, two former members of Congress have been appointed under secretary and five more have been named assistant secretary, but this relationship appears to be less common. For statistics on types of diplomatic appointments, see Table A-15, column G.

The remaining 262 congressmen-diplomats were appointed as chiefs of mission in the field. Four of these were accredited to international organizations,[15] and the rest headed American embassies and

---

[10] Robert R. Livingston was appointed to this post in 1781.

[11] These included Edmund Randolph, John Marshall, James Madison, Henry Clay, Martin Van Buren, Edward Livingston, Daniel Webster, John C. Calhoun, John M. Clayton, William L. Marcy, Lewis Cass, William H. Seward, Elihu B. Washburne, Hamilton Fish, James G. Blaine, Thomas F. Bayard, John Sherman, Philander C. Knox, William Jennings Bryan, Cordell Hull, James F. Byrnes, and John Foster Dulles.

[12] John Marshall, following his tenure as secretary, also functioned ad interim while he was chief justice, which raises some interesting questions respecting the doctrine of the separation of powers.

[13] James M. Buchanan, John Forsyth, Frederick T. Frelinghuysen, John Jay, Thomas Jefferson, Frank B. Kellogg, Louis McLane, and James Monroe. Jay, after serving in Spain, was named secretary of foreign affairs in 1784 and he continued transitionally as secretary of state until Thomas Jefferson took over in 1790.

[14] Christian A. Herter was appointed under secretary in 1957, and succeeded to the secretaryship on the death of John Foster Dulles in 1959.

[15] Warren R. Austin, George H. W. Bush, and Henry Cabot Lodge were named ambassador to the United Nations, and Donald H. Rumsfeld was accredited to represent the United States in the North Atlantic Treaty Organization.

legations abroad, primarily in Europe and Latin America.[16] In recent years, members of Congress appointed as diplomats have occasionally been accredited to such countries as Australia, India, Malagasy, New Zealand, the Philippines, and Sierra Leone. At times they also have represented the United States in Egypt, Iran, Thailand, and Turkey. However, half of these congressmen-diplomats (135) have been accredited to Europe (especially France, Portugal, Russia, Spain, and the United Kingdom), and more than one-third (ninety-two) have been sent to Latin American countries (especially Brazil, Mexico, and Colombia). China has been the most popular post for these appointees outside Europe and the Western Hemisphere. Nearly half of the appointments of these congressmen-diplomats have been made to these nine countries, and the total appointed to Europe and Latin America amounts to 87 percent.

The preceding analysis concerns specifically the initial diplomatic appointments of former members of Congress, but some have served on more than a single diplomatic mission. Multiple diplomatic assignments were held by sixty-three (21 percent) congressmen-diplomats, most of whom were named to two missions, but a few—such as John Quincy Adams, Chester Bowles, Edwin H. Conger, Henry Cabot Lodge, and James Monroe—held three or more missions. Sixteen of these sixty-three also were appointed secretary of state, most of whom served abroad before being appointed as secretary, but several—including Thomas F. Bayard, Edward Livingston, Robert R. Livingston, Martin Van Buren, and Elihu B. Washburne were accredited abroad after serving as secretary, whereas James M. Buchanan held chief of mission assignments in the field both prior to and after being appointed secretary. A few multiple diplomatic appointees also had multiple service in Congress—such as John A. Kasson, William Pinkney, William C. Rives, Robert C. Schenck, and Joseph A. Wright—each of whom received noncontinuous diplomatic assignments, with each appointment preceded by congressional service. These figures, however, do not include special diplomatic missions such as that of John Foster Dulles who, as personal emissary of President Harry S. Truman, negotiated the World War II Japanese Peace Treaty, signed at San Francisco in 1951.

---

[16] Concern at this point is restricted to initial diplomatic appointment. The matter of multiple appointments is dealt with separately in the following paragraph. Occasionally, as in the case of Robert M. McLane, John S. Pendleton, and William W. Phelps, an individual held appointments as chief of mission both before and after serving in Congress, and Frederick T. Freylinghuysen, after election to Congress was nominated as envoy to the United Kingdom but declined it and was then reelected to Congress.

Whereas nine of these 294 gained their legislative experience in the Continental Congress, fifty-five (19 percent) served in the Senate, 184 (63 percent) in the House of Representatives, and forty-six (16 percent) were elected to terms in both chambers. In general, similar ratios apply to the appointments made before and after 1900, evidencing no significant trend toward greater appointment of either congressmen or senators. Only two congressmen-diplomats were women. In 1933 President Franklin D. Roosevelt selected Ruth Bryan Owen, congresswoman from Florida, as envoy extraordinary and minister plenipotentiary to Denmark, and twenty years later President Dwight D. Eisenhower accredited Clare Boothe Luce, congresswoman from Connecticut, as ambassador to Italy. (See columns E and F, Table A-15.)

Another point to be noted is that, for various reasons, thirty-five (12 percent) of the 294 congressmen-diplomats nominated by the President did not actually assume their diplomatic duties. Of these, eleven—including Horace Greeley and Andrew Jackson—declined appointment, six decided not to proceed to their appointed posts or otherwise did not serve, and William T. Barry died en route to his assignment in Spain in 1835. Most exceptional was the appointment of Henry W. Blair in 1891, who took the oath of office but did not proceed to his post because the Chinese government objected to his designation.[17] In addition, four failed to present their credentials, including Francis Dana and John Randolph appointed to Russia, Lewis D. Campbell to Mexico, and William B. Rochester to the Central American Republics. All proceeded to their posts, and Dana actually remained for nearly three years although he was not officially received by the Tsar, whereas the other three proceeded to their posts but returned to the United States without presenting their credentials.

The remaining dozen nominees were never technically appointed because either the nomination was withdrawn by the White House, remained unapproved by the Senate, or in two cases, was rejected by the Senate. One of the two rejections involved Francis P. Blair—who served in Congress for a time in the late 1850s and early 1860s and was nominated as envoy to Austria in 1867. In the 1860s eight nominations to that country were either tabled or rejected by the Senate. John S. Carlile, after serving in both houses of Congress, was also rejected in the 1860s. He was nominated as minister to Sweden and, although he was initially confirmed, his nomination was recon-

---

[17] This antedated the institution of prior *agrément*. This process and the matter of *persona non grata* were discussed in chapter 3.

sidered and then tabled by the Senate while he was already en route to Stockholm.

Some of these congressmen-diplomats are remembered for the roles they played in helping to shape particular developments in the diplomatic history of the United States. Little need be said of the remarkable record of Benjamin Franklin. Francis Dana unsuccessfully sought Russian recognition of American independence and America's affiliation with the Armed Neutrality of Catherine the Great during the American Revolution. Joel R. Poinsett became involved in the revolutionary movement of several Latin American countries and, as first American emissary to Mexico (1825–1829), sought to negotiate a boundary settlement for the Louisiana Territory that was favorable to the United States, but he is best commemorated by the naming of the poinsettia. John A. Kasson, minister to Germany, represented his country at the Berlin Conference of 1884–1885, which was concerned with the Congo and Niger River basins, African slave trade, and the formalization of legal precepts governing the acquisition of sovereign title to African territory. This was the first major European international conclave attended by the United States, presaging its later participation in a series of conferences concerned with important issues of international law and politics. Warren R. Austin resigned his seat in the Senate to become United States representative to the United Nations during its formative years, 1947–1953, and participated in its critical actions taken during the Korean War. Henry Cabot Lodge served as ambassador to Saigon twice and as ambassador at large during the Vietnamese War, and contributed to U.S. policy in Southeast Asia.

Certain other congressmen-diplomats, such as Pierre Soulé and James H. Blount, are remembered for their association with more specific diplomatic situations. Soulé, a naturalized French republican émigré, exacerbated relations with Spain over the Cuban question in the 1850s by issuing an ultimatum to the Spanish government intended to force the cession of the island to the United States. Blount, an avowed anti-imperialist, who was President Grover Cleveland's emissary to Hawaii in the 1890s, helped to implement the President's anti-annexation policy prior to the Spanish-American War.

Nine congressmen-diplomats may be best remembered because they were later elected to the presidency.[18] Except for George Washington, all early Presidents, to the 1840s, had such prior legislative-

[18] These included John Adams, Thomas Jefferson, James Madison, James Monroe, John Quincy Adams, Martin Van Buren, William Henry Harrison, and James Buchanan, together with Andrew Jackson who, as noted, was appointed but declined.

diplomatic experience.[19] John Marshall is less remembered for his diplomatic exploits than for his later achievements as chief justice. Other congressmen-diplomats are listed among well-remembered secretaries of state. Aside from John Quincy Adams, who is generally regarded as one of the great secretaries of state, these include Daniel Webster for the settlement of the northeast boundary issue (Webster-Ashburton Treaty, 1842), William H. Seward for the purchase of Alaska in 1867, James G. Blaine for initiating the first inter-American conference of 1889 which presaged the Organization of American States, William Jennings Bryan for his isolation policy at the time of World War I, Frank B. Kellogg for negotiating the Paris Peace Pact of 1928, Cordell Hull for the trade agreements program of the 1930s and 1940s, and James F. Byrnes for the negotiation of the European Axis satellite peace treaties signed in 1947.

This analysis concerns *former* members of Congress as diplomats and secretaries of state. The very fact that a good many members of Congress gave up their seats to accept diplomatic appointment evidences sensitivity to the constitutional issue of separation of powers. The Constitution specifies that "no person holding any office under the United States shall be a member of either House [of Congress] during his continuance in office."[20] The practice of appointing incumbent members of Congress as special presidential emissaries on ad hoc diplomatic assignments or as members of negotiating delegations to international conferences or to sessions of international organizations, such as the General Assembly of the United Nations, has, at times, generated serious constitutional debate. While this issue is not directly relevant to this analysis, suffice it to say that it came to a head during President McKinley's administration, when an understanding was reached whereby the President, while not specifically promising to refrain from future appointments of this nature, indicated that it might not occur again. However, the practice of appointing sitting members of Congress to diplomatic assignments was revived a quarter century later by President Harding, it was freely employed by President Franklin D. Roosevelt during World War II, and it has since become commonplace.[21]

---

[19] Whereas Washington served in the Continental Congress, he held no diplomatic appointment.

[20] U.S. Constitution, Article 1, Section 6, Clause 2.

[21] For additional comment on this aspect of the appointment of senators and congressmen as diplomats, see Plischke, *Conduct of American Diplomacy*, pp. 404–409.

7
DIPLOMATS AS AUTHORS

Diplomats should be masters of prose for, in the course of their careers, they will be expected to employ that gift almost daily in their official reports. The degree to which they are moved to write for publication, however—either of their diplomatic experiences, or of their personal interests, or of other matters—is less well understood. A survey of the publications of leading American diplomats reveals that they have published as widely as other professional groups except, perhaps, for journalists, academicians, and those others whose careers rely upon writing, and that their literary tastes and interests have been virtually boundless.

Nevertheless, despite the production of a comprehensive library of writings, there are deficiencies in their collective endeavors. This results, in part, from the fact that authors who are appointed as diplomats are rarely selected because of prior literary concern with the diplomatic art. On the other hand, serving career diplomats often are discouraged from writing about their chosen career, and some retired careerists devote their energies to mastering a second profession and discover later that the allurement of serious authorship has evanesced.

A substantial number of authors, historians, poets, essayists, academicians, journalists, dramatists, and other exponents of culture and the literary arts have been called upon to serve in the American diplomatic corps, and have, therefore, become author-diplomats. Prior to the specialization of the diplomatic profession, such widely heralded men of letters as Washington Irving, James Russell Lowell, and Bayard Taylor, as well as other productive writers like John Bigelow, Ephraim G. Squire, and Lewis (Lew) Wallace were accredited as United States emissaries to Britain, France, Germany, Spain, Turkey, and Latin America. David Jayne Hill, president of Bucknell and Rochester universities, the eminent historians George Bancroft and John Lothrop Motley, and other scholar diplomats were similarly appointed to European countries, as were a number of early statesmen-diplomats, including Benjamin Franklin, John Adams, John Quincy Adams, and Thomas Jefferson—all authors of some renown. More recently, in the twentieth century, such well-known academicians and writers as James B. Conant, Maurice Francis Egan, John Kenneth Galbraith, Arthur S. Hardy, Carlton J. H. Hayes, Robert Strausz-Hupé, Meredith Nicholson, Edwin O. Reischauer, Henry van Dyke, and Brand Whitlock have also been commissioned chiefs of United States diplomatic missions. In addition, a good many others, some of whom are far better known for their literary accomplishments than for their diplomatic roles, have held lesser American diplomatic posts.[1]

On the other hand, career diplomats frequently have also turned to authorship during their careers or on retirement, not only to produce their memoirs, but also to write a variety of biographies, histories, commentaries, poems, and other works. Some publications of these diplomat-authors have become widely known, including certain writings of James Rives Childs, Hugh S. Gibson, George F. Kennan, Dana G. Munro, Charles W. Thayer, and (George) Post Wheeler. As a group, they have produced a broad menu of published materials, often more representative of their extraprofessional interests than of the diplomatic process, perhaps evidencing a desire to avoid publications which might inhibit the advancement of their careers.

The degree to which American diplomats have engaged in literary ventures—both the author-diplomats and the diplomat-authors—is surprising. Since 1778, some 345 of the 1,869 (18 percent) chiefs of mission, ambassadors at large, and ranking officers of the Department of State have published a library of materials.[2] Put another way,

---

[1] Although this analysis is concerned solely with chiefs of mission, ambassadors at large, and senior Department of State officers, it may be interesting to note some of the noncareerist appointees who held lesser diplomatic assignments. To mention only a few, these include such men of letters and literary analysts as Hamilton Fish Armstrong, Ray Stannard Baker, Stephen Vincent Benet, James Fennimore Cooper, Francis Brett Harte, Nathaniel Hawthorne, William D. Howells, John Howard Payne, and James G. Thurber. Also to be noted are academicians such as Cyril Edwin Black, Arthur C. Millspaugh, and Graham H. Stuart; historian Herbert Feis; international lawyer Ellery C. Stowell; and missionaries Chester Holcombe, Peter Parker, and Samuel Wells Williams.

[2] This analysis is based largely on the comprehensive and valuable pioneering compilation of Richard Fyfe Boyce and Katherine Randall Boyce, eds., *American Foreign Service Authors: A Bibliography* (Metuchen, N.J.: Scarecrow Press, 1973), supplemented by Elmer Plischke, *American Diplomacy: A Bibliography of Biographies, Autobiographies, and Commentaries* (College Park, Md.: Bureau of Governmental Research, University of Maryland, 1957) and Elmer Plischke, "Bibliography on United States Diplomacy," section entitled "Bibliography of Autobiographies, Biographies, Commentaries, and Memoirs," in *Instruction in*

these 345 represent approximately 12 percent of all (2,926) nominations to such appointments. Collectively, they have produced more than 1,800 publications, not including the mass of official correspondence and reports which they turn out. Nor do they include the profusion of biographies of diplomats by nondiplomat-writers,[3] the writings of diplomats' wives and other members of their families,[4] or the many productions of other diplomats who have served in posts at levels below that of chief of mission. Many diplomat-authors have written only a single volume or two, more than half produced three or more volumes, and at least fifty published ten or more. Maurice Francis Egan, Washington Irving, Meredith Nicholson, Bayard Taylor, and Henry van Dyke are among the most prolific author-diplomats.[5]

It is natural that a good many diplomats should write their memoirs and publish their "papers," or write on the subjects of diplomatic history, foreign policy, and political biography. However,

---

Diplomacy: The Liberal Arts Approach, ed. by Smith Simpson, Monograph No. 13 of the American Academy of Political and Social Science (Philadelphia: American Academy, 1972), pp. 299–342. The last two compilations are restricted to publications by and about American diplomats since 1900.

[3] Bibliographical guidance to such biographical literature may be found in Samuel Flagg Bemis and Grace Gardner Griffin, *Guide to the Diplomatic History of the United States* (Washington, D. C.: Government Printing Office, 1935); Samuel Flagg Bemis, ed., *The American Secretaries of State and Their Diplomacy, 1776–1925* (New York: Knopf, 1927–1929) and subsequent volumes on individual secretaries by different authors under the general editorship of Robert H. Ferrell; Norman A. Graebner, ed., *An Uncertain Tradition: American Secretaries of State in the Twentieth Century* (New York: McGraw-Hill, 1961); and the compilations of this author listed in the preceding footnote. Also see the bibliographies contained in the literature on American diplomatic history, the secretary and the Department of State, and the Foreign Service.

[4] Though less numerous, these publications of the members of diplomats' families also contribute to the total literary output. They include, for example, the publications of Isabel Weld Anderson (wife of Ambassador Larz Anderson), Maude Parker Child (Richard Washburn Child), and Halle Ermine Rives (Post Wheeler), each of whom produced ten or more volumes. Others who also published include Phyllis Penn Kohler (Ambassador Foy D. Kohler), Fannie Davenport MacVeagh (Charles MacVeagh), Lily Constance Morris (Ira Nelson Morris), Elizabeth Reeve Morrow (Dwight W. Morrow), Susan Arnold Wallace (Lew Wallace), and others.

Occasionally, volumes are produced by other members of a diplomat's family, such as Henry Brooks Adams (son of Charles Francis Adams) and Martha Dodd (Ambassador William E. Dodd's daughter). At times others also contribute, such as Emily Bax, secretary in the American embassy in London, and Letitia Baldrige, private secretary to the wife of Ambassador David K. E. Bruce and secretary to Clare Boothe Luce in Rome.

[5] Some of those who have extensive publications lists, but who served at levels below that of chief of mission, are cited in footnotes 1 and 18, to which may be added a good many others with shorter publications lists, such as William P. Blatty, author of the best seller *The Exorcist* (1971); and Alexander Wheelock Thayer, biographer of Beethoven; playwright Donald Hannibal Robinson; and composer William Henry Fry.

the breadth of their literary interests is revealing. Their collective pen has produced poetry; treatises on creative cookery, parliamentary procedure, human freedom, and geographical nomenclature; commentaries on geopolitics, on major international conferences, on the United Nations and the North Atlantic Treaty Organization, and on basic social and other issues, as well as on art, boating, and polo. Included also are collections of fairy tales, essays, sermons, and sonnets, together with analyses of such disparate subjects as ceramics, genealogy, poverty, printing, and prison affairs. The publications of American diplomats include Alvey A. Adee's twenty-two-volume limited edition of commentary on and comparative texts of the plays of William Shakespeare (1888–1906), (George) Post Wheeler's *Hathoo of the Elephants* (1943), Washington Irving's *Legend of Sleepy Hollow* (1864), Benjamin Franklin's *Poor Richard's Almanac* (1732–1757), John Kenneth Galbraith's *The Affluent Society* (1958), William Attwood's *The Decline of the American Male* (co-author, 1958), Henry W. Ellsworth's *The American Swine Breeder* (1840), and Samuel S. Cox's nearly 400 pages on *Why We Laugh* (1876). Other titles should also whet the literary appetite, such as Philip K. Crowe's *Sport Is Where You Find It* (1953) and *The Empty Ark* (1967), John Bartlow Martin's *Butcher's Dozen, and Other Murders* (1950), and Frederick Jesup Stimson's *Jethro Bacon of Sandwich* (1902).

Table A-16 lists figures for the number of American diplomat-authors, by decade, with their career status. The ratio of authors to the total number of diplomatic appointments was relatively high in the early decades, amounting to one-third of all diplomatic nominee-appointees to 1820.[6] The ratio declined somewhat after 1840, and except for one decade (the first of this century), ranged between 11 and 18 percent. Since 1950, because of both the increase in the number of appointees and their recency, the ratio has declined. With the rise in the quota of career diplomats, this may reflect some change in the nature of recent appointees, but in all probability it is due more to the need for the passage of time pending the writing of memoirs and the publication of the official papers of retiring diplomats.

Categories of Diplomat-Authors

Five secretaries of state who were later elected to the presidency—namely, Thomas Jefferson, James Monroe, John Quincy Adams, Martin Van Buren, and James Buchanan—as well as two Presidents

[6] Specifically the figures are twenty of fifty-nine, or 34 percent, during the first four decades.

who had diplomatic experience as chiefs of mission abroad—John Adams and William Henry Harrison—comprise an exclusive group of president-diplomat-authors. Most of their publications, totaling approximately seventy-five volumes and collections, as may be expected, consist of memoirs, compilations of state papers, and other materials related to their own public careers. However, they also produced a mixture of other publications, such as John Adams's *Discourses on Davila* (essays on public issues, 1805), James Monroe's *The People the Sovereigns* (comparing the government of the United States with earlier republics, not published until 1867), and John Quincy Adams's *Lectures on Rhetoric and Oratory* (1810), *Letters on the Masonic Institution* (1847), and *Poems of Religion and Society* (1850).

Approximately half of the secretaries of state since 1778 have authored publications,[7] the majority of them prior to 1900 and they include every secretary of state since the appointment of Henry L. Stimson in 1929 except for William P. Rogers.[8] They have written more than 155 publications, averaging six for each secretary. The products of their literary labor have ranged from a single two-volume memoir—as in the case of Cordell Hull—to the series of volumes published by Dean G. Acheson, John W. Foster, John Hay, and Henry A. Kissinger.

Aside from the large quantity of autobiographies and state papers by secretaries of state (but since World War I including genuine memoirs only by Secretaries Robert Lansing, Cordell Hull, James F. Byrnes, and Dean Acheson), their publications include commentaries on Latin America by Robert Bacon, on American diplomatic history by John W. Foster, on the Big Four leaders at the World War I Peace Conference by Robert Lansing, on American foreign policy in Nicaragua by Henry L. Stimson, and on United States aid to Germany (1870–1871) by Elihu B. Washburne. Other publications constitute reflections on the lend-lease program by Edward R. Stettinius, on peace and war by John Foster Dulles, and *Toward an Atlantic Community* (1963) by Christian A. Herter. In addition, former Secretary Edward Livingston wrote on state and national penal codes and prison reform, Edward Everett produced a *Eulogy of Lafayette* (1834), Dean

---

[7] This total includes the five who became President.

[8] This includes not only nine of the last ten secretaries of state to March 1973—Henry L. Stimson, Cordell Hull, Edward R. Stettinius, James F. Byrnes, George C. Marshall, Dean G. Acheson, John Foster Dulles, Christian A. Herter, and Dean Rusk—but also Henry A. Kissinger, who enjoyed an extensive publication record prior to his appointment as secretary of state, including some half dozen books (for example, *Nuclear Weapons and Foreign Policy*, 1957; *The Necessity for Choice*, 1961; and *The Troubled Partnership*, 1965), and more than forty articles in professional and literary journals.

Acheson outlined *Sketches From Life of Men I Have Known* (1961), and in a lighter vein, Henry L. Stimson contributed a volume entitled *My Vacations* (1949). While John Hay may be best remembered for the Open Door policy, associated directly with his name in American diplomatic chronicles, it is less well known that, among other writings, he authored a biography of Abraham Lincoln, an anonymous satirical attack on labor unions entitled *The Breadwinners* (1884), and several volumes of poetry.

Thirty-five diplomat-authors were former members of Congress [9] and, together, they produced approximately 125 publications. Aside from Benjamin Franklin, who wrote on such subjects as paper currency, education in Pennsylvania, and experiments in electricity, the more active congressman-diplomat-authors included Chester B. Bowles, Samuel S. Cox, and Caleb Cushing, each of whom published more than ten volumes. Supplementing their personal journals, memoirs, and official papers, these former congressmen tended toward biographical writing—such as Jabez L. M. Curry's volume on William Edward Gladstone, Caleb Cashing's short outline of the life of William Henry Harrison, and John H. Eaton's *The Life of Andrew Jackson* (1817). They also produced various historical studies and a number of descriptive and analytical commentaries. The latter, by way of illustration, include studies on admiralty jurisdiction, constitutional government in Spain, farming, and penology. Also included are several volumes on travel and foreign lands, (Joseph R.) *Chandler's Common School Grammar* (1848), and George P. Marsh's *The Origin and History of the English Language, and of the Early Literature it Embodies* (1862), to say nothing of his essay on "The Camel" published in the Smithsonian Institution's *Annual Report* in 1854.

Beginning with the appointment of William Phillips as third assistant secretary of state in 1909 and as envoy extraordinary and minister plenipotentiary to the Netherlands eleven years later, fifty-eight of these 345 diplomat-authors have been careerists (17 percent). More significant is the fact that, since 1910 nearly one in every three has been a career diplomat, with the highest percentages peaking in the 1920s and 1940s. Of the remaining 287, some 161 were pre-1910 appointees, and 126 were post-1910 noncareerists.

In addition to the careerists and those who ventured into the political arena or were professional novelists and poets, American author-diplomats represent a variety of professions. A good many

[9] In addition to those who also became secretary of state and/or President, but not counting those former members of Congress, such as Albert Gallatin, who held lesser diplomatic appointments.

were lawyers, journalists, publishers, and educators, the latter including college administrators, economists, political scientists, and especially historians. Others were bankers, businessmen, financiers, industrialists, and merchants, and a few had previously been clergymen, jurists, military officers, missionaries, or physicians.

Only four of the 345 diplomat-authors were women—Florence Jaffray Harriman, Perle Mesta, Clare Boothe Luce, and Ruth Bryan Owen—all noncareerist diplomats. The literary efforts of the first two were essentially autobiographical. Ruth Bryan Owen also wrote of other matters, including a volume on the *Elements of Public Speaking* (1931), a collection of Scandinavian fairy tales (1939), and a short inspirational presentation of her yearnings for a new world of law and stability entitled *Look Forward, Warrior* (1942). Clare Boothe Luce was an acknowledged journalist (*Vogue* and *Vanity Fair*), novelist (*Stuffed Shirts*, 1931), and playwright (*The Women*—1937, *Kiss the Boys Goodbye*—1939, and others).

Publications of Diplomat-Authors

These 345 author-diplomats and diplomat-authors, as noted, published more than 1,800 volumes, collections, and other works,[10] which may be grouped into several broad categories. Perhaps the most popular was the field of autobiography and the compilation of letters, addresses, and other professional and personal papers. These were produced not only by those who had served in Congress, the secretaryship of state, and the presidency, but also by a considerable number of chiefs of diplomatic mission. One hundred and thirty-one author-diplomats (38 percent) published their autobiographies, memoirs, reminiscences, recollections, diaries, or journals. Of these, 102 produced memoirs and reminiscences, and twenty-nine contributed diaries and journals. Since World War II the memoirs include the contributions of such widely known diplomats as Willard L. Beaulac, Charles E. Bohlen, Claude G. Bowers, Chester Bowles, Spruille Braden, Joseph C. Grew, George F. Kennan, Robert D. Murphy, Walter Bedell Smith, and others.

A second category comprises various types of documentary materials. Thus, the papers and correspondence of seventy-one (21 percent) have been published, usually compiled by a separate editor,

[10] The list of items identified for this survey numbers more than 1,825, but no claim is made that this list is definitive. While other publications might be added, the list is deemed to be sufficiently comprehensive to warrant the analysis which follows.

or deposited in the Library of Congress or some other repository. Moreover, thirty have produced collections of their addresses and speeches. In a few cases, these include series of lectures, such as Charles E. Bohlen's Blaustein Lectures at Columbia University (*The Transformation of American Foreign Policy,* 1969), George F. Kennan's Walgreen Lectures at the University of Chicago (*American Diplomacy, 1900–1950,* published in 1951), Adlai E. Stevenson's Godkin Lectures at Harvard University (*Call to Greatness,* 1954), and Maxwell D. Taylor's Lehigh University Lectures (*Responsibility and Response,* 1967).

While diplomats file a good many official reports—which generally are excluded from this enumeration, except as they may be embodied within collections of communications and public papers—a few reports, presumably of major significance, were published separately and need to be noted. The following are representative of such reports: Edwin de Leon's *The Purchase of Camels* (for the War Department), Henry F. Grady's *A Survey of India's Industrial Production for War Purposes* (1942), Howard H. Tewksbury's analyses of the automotive markets in Argentina, Brazil, and Chile (1929 and 1930), and John Foster Dulles's historical summary of the final negotiations on the World War II Japanese Peace Treaty in 1951.[11] Among the most memorable reports, however, is J. Reuben Clark's 238-page *Memorandum on the Monroe Doctrine* (1930) which, after a century of interpretation, reinterpretation, and confusion, redefined the official meaning of the Monroe Doctrine at the beginning of the very decade during which the United States undertook to commence negotiating its adoption by other countries of the hemisphere, culminating in the Rio Pact.

A third category consists of the biographical writings of more than fifty diplomat-authors. Included were works on the founding fathers, early political and intellectual leaders, and later Presidents and secretaries of state,[12] and also on such foreign political figures as Gustavus Adolphus (by John L. Stevens), Bismarck and Mussolini (by Charles H. Sherrill), Juarez (by W. Wendell Blancké), Mahomet (by Washington Irving), Peter the Great (by historian John Lothrop Motley and also by Eugene Schuyler), and Sforza (by William Wal-

[11] *A Peace Treaty in the Making: Japanese Peace Conference, San Francisco, September 4–8, 1951* (Washington, D. C.: Government Printing Office, 1951).

[12] Such as, merely by way of illustration: Josephus Daniels on Woodrow Wilson, John H. Eaton on Andrew Jackson, Norman Hapgood on both George Washington and Daniel Webster, Carl Schurz on Henry Clay and Abraham Lincoln, and Edward H. Strobel on James G. Blaine. Presidents Washington and Lincoln were especially popular subjects for such biographical works.

dorf Astor), as well as seven volumes on the romantic Giacomo Casanova (by James Rives Childs). Biographies were written on other Americans, including Washington Irving and William Cullen Bryant (by David Jayne Hill), and baseball player Jackie Robinson (by Carl T. Rowan). Worthy of special note, perhaps, are Hugh S. Gibson's publication of *The Ciano Diaries* (1946), Philip C. Jessup's biography of *Elihu Root* (1938), and Edward R. Stettinius's account on *Roosevelt and the Russians: The Yalta Conference* (1949).

In addition to broaching the subject in their own memoirs and reminiscences, a group of these diplomat-authors—nearly fifty—wrote about their travels and the distant lands they visited. They produced a potpourri of travelogues, recounted "adventures," and sketches of or guides to foreign places. Their journeying took them to many corners of the globe at a time when information concerning them was relished. Aside from the contributions to this category by Washington Irving and James Russell Lowell, the following illustrate this extensive body of literature: J. Ross Browne, *A Peep at Washoe* (article in *Harper's*, republished in 1959); William Jennings Bryan, *Under Other Flags* (1904); James Rives Childs, *The Pageant of Persia* (under pseudonym Henry Filmer, 1936); Samuel S. Cox, *Arctic Sunbeams* (1882) and others; Joseph C. Grew, *Sport and Travel in the Far East* (1910); Ruth Bryan Owen, *Caribbean Caravel* (1949) and *Leaves from a Greenland Diary* (1935); and William Woodville Rockhill, *Diary of a Journey Through Mongolia and Thibet* . . . (1894). Bayard Taylor also published a dozen and a half volumes belonging to this category, even including a fifty-year history of nearly a thousand pages on travel and adventure entitled *Cyclopedia of Modern Travel: A Record of Adventure, Exploration, and Discovery* . . . (1856).

Seventy-five—or one of every five—diplomat-authors have devoted some attention to the writing of history. A few were acknowledged historians appointed to diplomatic missions, such as George Bancroft, Claude G. Bowers, and William E. Dodd, who wrote primarily about the United States, and John Lothrop Motley and Carlton J. H. Hayes, who concentrated more on the history of other countries. Some of their writings were well known and widely used, such as Bancroft's ten-volume *History of the United States from the Discovery of the American Continent* (many editions and translations) and Hayes's historical texts on Europe, nationalism, and modern civilization. Others, though less prolific, such as Andrew D. White, first president of the American Historical Association, also belong to this category of historian-diplomats. Far more numerous as a group, however, are those who, serving in a diplomatic capacity, tried their hand at the writing of history. This group includes both noncareerists such as David K. E. Bruce [13] and Jacob G. Schurman,[14] and a variety of careerists, including FSOs Hermann Frederick Eilts, George F. Kennan, Dana G. Munro, and Sumner Welles.[15]

Another substantial category of writings consists of technical handbooks, guides, and textual literature. These have been written by educators, lawyers, military officers, and a few medical practitioners appointed to diplomatic missions. Some thirty, largely noncareerists, engaged in this type of writing. Their subjects have varied, resulting in individual volumes on such matters as agriculture, mineral ores, and Greek pottery, together with a commercial handbook on Yugoslavia, and Admiral Arthur A. Ageton's widely used *The Naval Officer's Guide* (1943). Also included are textbooks and readers on celestial navigation, chemistry, education, geography, government, mathematics, and psychology, as well as Theodore S. Fay's atlases.[16] To these may be added some half dozen diplomat-authors who published volumes on grammar and rhetoric, supplemented with the readers produced by Washington Irving, Meredith Nicholson, and others, as well as John Leighton Stuart's *Greek-Chinese-English Dictionary of the New Testament* (Shanghai, 1918).

More than half of the contributors to this category of publications, however, have written in the field of law and jurisprudence. These include, for example, volumes of cases and materials on corporation finance and business law, Lewis Cass's code of Michigan territorial law, William J. Sebald's five codes of Japanese civil and criminal laws (in English), and Charles E. Magoon's reports on the legal status of the territory and inhabitants of the islands acquired by the United States during the Spanish-American War and on the law of civil government in territory under American military occupation. Understandably, a number have addressed themselves to questions of international and admiralty law, which are closely related to diplomatic and consular functions. Perhaps the best known author-diplomats in this field include Henry Wheaton (chargé d'affaires to

---

[13] *Revolution to Reconstruction* (1939) and *Sixteen American Presidents* (1962).

[14] *Philippine Affairs: A Retrospect and Outlook* (1902) and *The Balkan Wars, 1912–1913* (1914).

[15] In this connection, although an FSO who was not appointed to the rank of chief of mission, mention needs to be made of the dozen penetrating historical accounts of Herbert Feis on World War II and subsequent diplomatic developments.

[16] *Atlas to Fay's Great Outline of Geography for High Schools and Families* (1867) and *Atlas of Universal Geography for Libraries and Families* (1869).

Denmark and minister to Prussia), John Bassett Moore (assistant secretary of state and counselor), Green H. Hackworth (legal adviser in the Department of State), and Philip C. Jessup (ambassador at large). Wheaton contributed more than half a dozen volumes in this field, including *Elements of International Law* (1836) and several legal digests. Moore was remarkably productive, publishing nearly sixty volumes, including a *History and Digest of International Arbitrations . . .* (6 vols., 1898), *International Adjudications . . .* (8 vols., 1929), and his classic *A Digest of International Law* (8 vols., 1906). Hackworth continued the latter as *Digest of International Law,* covering the period from the early twentieth century to World War II (8 vols., 1940–1944). Jessup published some dozen and a half volumes, largely on selected international and transnational law issues. Moore, Hackworth, and Jessup also served as American judges on the World Court.

Several diplomat-authors applied their literary talents to matters of religion, morals, and missionary activities. A few, such as John Leighton Stuart, had a missionary background. In addition to Stuart's *Essential of New Testament Greek* (1916) and *Commentary on the Apocalypse* (1922), both of which were published in Chinese, the following illustrate this category of publications: John Bigelow, *The Bible that Was Lost and Is Found* (1912); Charles Denby, *American Missionaries in China* (1888); George P. Marsh, *Medieval and Modern Saints and Miracles* (1876); Jacob Gould Schurman, *Agnosticism and Religion* (1896); Henry van Dyke, *The Christ Child in Art* (1894), *The Childhood of Jesus Christ* (1905), and others; and Andrew D. White, *A History of the Warfare of Science With Theology in Christendom* (1896). Some diplomats also published their sermons, such as J. Reuben Clark's *Behold the Lamb of God* (1962) and Henry van Dyke's *Sermons to Young Men* (1898).

For want of a more precise designation, the largest category of writings may simply be classified as commentaries. Approximately 40 percent of the diplomat-authors contributed to this field. The subjects cover a broad spectrum of intellectual interests, ranging from serious tomes on economics, international trade, philosophy, population, poverty, and science, to volumes on flying, road races, yachting, and sports in general, together with publications on monuments, art, and other diverse subjects, including Charles H. Sherrill's five volumes on mosaics and stained glass. This category also includes commentaries on Irish orators, the American University Club in Shanghai, the Red Cross, the Townsend Plan, wildlife, conservation, and a great many other matters, as well as John Bigelow's *The Mystery of Sleep* (1897).

This category of commentaries also embraces studies of the diplomatic process, foreign policy, international affairs, and the conduct of American foreign relations, several of which, together with certain memoirs, provide some of the more useful contributions to that literature. These range from such earlier writings as John W. Foster's *A Century of American Diplomacy* (1900) and *The Practice of Diplomacy as Illustrated in the Foreign Relations of the United States* (1906) to a profusion of more recent analyses of American foreign relations prepared by both noncareerists and FSOs. Illustrative of the general literature on the diplomatic service written by careerists are: W. Wendell Blancké, *The Foreign Service of the United States* (1969); Ellis O. Briggs, *Anatomy of Diplomacy: The Origin and Execution of American Foreign Policy* (1968); James Rives Childs, *American Foreign Service (1948);* Hugh S. Gibson, *The Road to Foreign Policy* (1944); Charles W. Thayer, *Diplomat* (1959); Henry S. Villard, *Affairs at State* (1965); and Charles W. Yost, *The Conduct and Misconduct of Foreign Affairs* (1972).[17] More limited in scope are such volumes as Wiley T. Buchanan's *Red Carpet at the White House* (1964), and James W. Symington's *The Stately Game* (1971) which focus on the matter of diplomatic protocol. Concerned specifically with foreign policy making and analysis are: Andrew H. Berding, *The Making of Foreign Policy* (1966), and Robert R. Bowie, *Shaping the Future: Foreign Policy in an Age of Transition* (1964), Thomas K. Finletter, *Power and Policy: United States Foreign Policy and Military Power in the Hydrogen Age* (1954), and a host of more specialized studies, represented by the half dozen volumes published by Sumner Welles and, more recently, those of Henry A. Kissinger. Still other volumes concerned with issues of foreign relations, but more restricted in scope, are Stanley K. Hornbeck's *The Most Favored Nation Clause in Commercial Treaties . . .* (1910), and two volumes contributed by Paul S. Reinsch, appointed minister to China in 1913, namely, *Secret Diplomacy: How Far Can It Be Eliminated?* (1922) and his pioneering and comprehensive survey of international integration entitled *Public International Unions* (1911, revised in 1916). Few of these specialized works have been produced by careerists; of those listed, only Sumner Welles was a careerist for a few years (1915–1922).

---

[17] Literature on this subject written by noncareerists, most of whom did not serve as chiefs of mission, is even more extensive. See, for example, the bibliographies of this author in *Conduct of American Diplomacy*, pp. 625–642, and "Research on the Conduct of United States Foreign Relations," *International Studies Quarterly*, vol. 15 (June 1971), pp. 221–250; and "Research on the Administrative History of the Department of State," in Milton O. Gustafson, ed., *The National Archives and Foreign Relations Research* (Athens, Ohio: Ohio University Press, 1974), pp. 73–102.

Somewhat less expected, perhaps, is the number of diplomat-authors who have written poetry, fiction, and plays. Some twenty-five to thirty have published more than sixty volumes of poetry, verse, sonnets, and songs. In addition to James Russell Lowell, Bayard Taylor, and John Quincy Adams, already mentioned, these consist largely of noncareerist diplomats, including Secretary of State John Hay and such chiefs of mission as Joel Barlow, Maurice Francis Egan, Arthur S. Hardy, and Thomas Nelson Page. A few career officers also have turned their talents to composing verse. Nathaniel P. Davis, G. Lewis Jones, Ralph J. Totten, and (George) Post Wheeler are representative of this literary elite. More than half of these diplomat-poets published their works before the turn of the twentieth century. Occasionally a diplomat has also contributed to poetry analysis, such as James Russell Lowell (*Conversations on Some of the Old Poets,* 1845) and William T. Coggeshall (*The Poets and Poetry of the West,* 1860).

Preferring prose to rhyme, however, about two dozen diplomats have written fiction and short stories. These include an occasional best seller—epitomized by Lew Wallace's *Ben Hur*—and other widely read volumes represented by Henry van Dyke's *The Story of the Other Wise Man* (1896), the short stories of Richard Washburn Child and others, the collection of fairy tales by Ruth Bryan Owen, and the novels of Maurice Francis Egan, Theodore S. Fay, Gideon H. Hollister, Thomas Nelson Page, Charles A. Washburn, and Brand Whitlock—all noncareerists. It appears to have been rare for careerists—such as James Rives Childs—to undertake the writing of fiction. Few of these novels have concerned diplomacy, although John Kenneth Galbraith wrote *The Triumph: A Novel of Modern Diplomacy* (1968), and careerists Charles W. Thayer published *Moscow Interlude* (1962) and *Checkpoint* (1964). A number of diplomats published fiction under pseudonyms, such as Frederic J. Stimson, using the name of J. S. Dale, and John Kenneth Galbraith, writing as Mark Epernay and Julian K. Prescott.[18] Half a dozen diplomat-authors have also been playwrights. In addition to Clare Boothe Luce, these include George H. Boker, Meredith Nicholson, Bayard Taylor, Henry van Dyke, and Lew Wallace, all noncareerists.

---

[18] Although serving in a consular capacity in the 1870s and never appointed as chief of mission, one of the better illustrations of an author-diplomat writing under pseudonyms was John Russell Coryell, who published the Nick Carter detective stories and others under such pseudonyms as Julia Edwards, Geraldine Flemming, and Margaret Grant. John Franklin Carter, who served in United States missions to Rome and Constantinople, published under the pen names of Jay Franklin and "Diplomat."

In retrospect, despite this array of literary competence and production, in some respects the publications of diplomat-authors are disappointing. As a group, diplomats ought to be willing and able to describe and evaluate their functions and their profession. A good many statesmen, publicists, and scholars—most of whom have not had the benefit of personal diplomatic experience—have produced a plethora of books and monographs concerning the foreign relations of the United States. A substantial quantity of these quite properly deal with the matter of substantive foreign policy. Unfortunately, on the other hand, diplomat-authors in general, and careerists in particular, seem to be surprisingly unconcerned literarily with the nature and problems of diplomatic method. Many, if they publish at all, devote their attention to personal memoirs, and although some of these are excellent, informative contributions, occasionally they are primarily public relations accounts motivated by visions of immortality in the best seller lists, or they degenerate into the "I-Was-There-When" species of reminiscences. Other diplomat-authors concentrate on producing policy studies, including thoughtful commentaries, or assessments of the place of the United States in world affairs or of its manner of coping with particular international events. Some of these literary efforts are of historical value and constitute commendable additions to the publications in the field.

It is somewhat disappointing to the serious student of American public affairs, however, to discover that, unlike diplomatists of other countries, so few American practitioners who have devoted their lives to diplomacy regard it as sufficiently important or challenging to write critically about the great issues of the administration of United States foreign relations, or to scrutinize and evaluate their chosen profession in an objective, impersonal fashion. This survey suggests that additional comprehensive and analytical reflections are needed and that their authors ought to devote greater attention to the essentials and operational techniques of diplomacy. Even if this goal is not achieved, however, hopefully such noncareerists as David K. E. Bruce, Ellsworth Bunker, Averell Harriman, George C. McGhee, and Dean Rusk, as well as experienced careerists, including Loy W. Henderson, U. Alexis Johnson, Foy D. Kohler, H. Freeman Matthews, Livingston T. Merchant, Frances E. Willis, Robert F. Woodward, Charles W. Yost, and others, in retirement, will add their contributions and will, by their example, inspire future generations of United States envoys. Students of American foreign relations will owe them a debt of gratitude.

8
RETROSPECT AND OUTLOOK

Although diplomats play a vital role in the conduct of United States foreign relations, they, and the nature of their missions, are frequently misunderstood or misjudged. One reason for this is that more than 1,800 of them have labored in the diplomatic vineyard on nearly 3,000 appointments for approximately 200 years, and they have come to represent a variety of personal backgrounds, qualities, assignments, achievements, and fame or notoriety, which makes it difficult to generalize systematically in regard to them. At the same time, differing images of the diplomat—equally unscientifically contrived—have come to be held by groups such as political leaders, scholars, and journalists, by the practitioners themselves, and by the man in the street. Both types of adjudgments have been founded on misty preconceptions, isolated circumstances, or nebulous impressions rather than on explicit and comprehensive analysis.

The simplest way to characterize the diplomat, using the dictionary definition, is to regard him as one who employs or is skilled in international diplomacy. This has the obvious weakness of requiring a definition of diplomacy; and to maintain simplistically that it is the art or business of the diplomat resorts to sterile circumlocution. To argue whether the diplomat engages primarily in an art, a science, a practice, a process, or a profession adds little but confusion. To dispute the value of certain general or specialized categories of emissaries and their functions merely augments misunderstanding.

Diplomats themselves have contributed to the confusion. Frequently they disagree not only on the essentials of success in the diplomatic arena, but also on the very nature of their craft. As a matter of fact, few are anxious to expose their conceptualizations in cold print. Other analysts appear to be more willing to cope with the essence of diplomacy—as a field of human knowledge, as a segment of academic and research programming, or as a pragmatic matter of state practice—but they also produce a confounding array of interpretations.

Some assessments raise the specter of dishonesty and deception. For example, when the French emissary Francois de Callières is quoted as propounding that the diplomat has two principal functions—to conduct the business of his master and to discover the business of others [1] —while he may be entirely correct, he invites misinterpretation. The distinguished British diplomatist Sir Henry Wotton contributed one of the most frequently quoted aphorisms, when early in the seventeenth century, on his way to his post in Venice, he inscribed in a guest book in Augsburg that: "An ambassador is an honest man sent to lie abroad for the good of his country." Although presumably intended as a witticism, it so embarrassed King James I that he dismissed the envoy, but the epigram lives on in the standard textbooks and usually evokes a gleeful chuckle. Wotton, it is believed, was characterizing the Machiavellian brand of diplomacy in which emissaries, serving as agents of competitive national self-interest, are presumed to engage in chicanery and deception. Or as Charles W. Thayer puts it, in some American circles diplomats are ranked with cardsharps.[2]

A second major perception of the diplomat, also engendered largely by practitioners, flows from attempts to prescribe those personal qualities regarded as desirable for a diplomatic emissary. Contradicting Wotton's depiction, many analysts have stressed the requisite of honesty. For example, Ambassador Clare Boothe Luce has said that "it takes just one good lie, found out, to destroy confidence." [3] However, the story is told that Earl Stanhope, another British emissary, claimed that he usually confounded other diplomats by telling them the naked truth. Since they did not believe that the envoy of a major power would speak truthfully, they usually reported the opposite to their governments. Some would conclude that this practice, if deliberate, regardless of intent, also may result in deception.

Others have expounded more comprehensive prescriptions. Benjamin Franklin stressed sleepless tact, unmovable calmness, and such patience that all folly, provocation, and blunder would be obviated. Sir Ernest Satow regarded the diplomat as requiring intelligence, tact, and sound judgment. Callières expanded the list to include friendliness, dignity, alert observation, reliable judgment, unlimited patience, presence of mind, fertile wit, birth and breeding, charm, and noble appearance, and he added that a diplomat should lose at cards if that

1 Quoted in Charles W. Thayer, *Diplomat* (New York: Harper, 1959), p. 161.

2 Ibid., p. 45.

3 U.S. Department of State, *The American Ambassador* (Washington, D. C.: Government Printing Office, 1957), p. 3.

will help him to make friends. Sir Harold Nicolson emphasized truth, accuracy, calm, patience, good temper, modesty, and loyalty as constituting the characteristics of the ideal diplomat; if his readers objected that he had overlooked intelligence, knowledge, discernment, prudence, hospitality, charm, industry, courage, and tact, he responded that these were simply taken for granted.[4]

In a pamphlet entitled *Career Opportunities in the Foreign Service* (1958), the Department of State, quoting a deputy under secretary, asserted that it was seeking the following qualities in its diplomatic recruits:

> They should have friendly, attractive personalities; they should possess a sensitiveness which renders them quick to understand the views, the prejudices, and the problems of people of different national, racial, or occupational backgrounds; their faces and their bearings should reflect an eagerness to learn and a lively intellectual curiosity—the Foreign Service is no place for dull, unimaginative persons. They should be interested in the manners, customs, languages and history of peoples of other times and places. . . . In their studies and work they should be thorough without being pedantic. They should have a healthy sense of humor. They should not shrink from tasks requiring a high degree of intellectual concentration. They should be complete masters of English grammar and should have a feeling for the structure of the English language. . . . Natural brilliance is a great asset in the Service; but brilliance in itself is not enough; it is likely to burn itself out quickly unless it is accompanied by integrity, steadiness, sincerity and real modesty.[5]

One may well wonder how many of these seraphic paragons have ever served the cause of diplomacy. This and similar grandiose prescriptions, if made seriously, evoke a questioning if not an unbelieving reaction, thereby compounding confusion respecting diplomats. Nor is this condition apt to be ameliorated for the skeptic when the Department of State confesses, in *The American Ambassador:*

> To meet the demands of his assignment, our American ambassador has to be extraordinary in more ways than are implied by his title. His interests, his knowledge, his culture,

---

[4] Spaulding, *Ambassadors Ordinary and Extraordinary*, p. 282; Sir Ernest M. Satow, *A Guide to Diplomatic Practice*, ed. Sir Neville Bland, 2nd ed. (London: Longmans Green, 1957), p. 1; Harold Nicolson, *Diplomacy* (London: Butterworth, 1939), p. 126; and U.S. Department of State, *The American Ambassador*, p. 22.

[5] U.S. Department of State, *Career Opportunities in the Foreign Service* (Washington, D. C.: Government Printing Office, 1958), p. 6.

> his humanity must be extraordinarily broad and deep. It has been said that the practice of diplomacy today calls for the exercise of so many mental and spiritual qualities that the portrait of "the ideal diplomat" cannot be painted, but only sketched or suggested.[6]

A third conception of the diplomat is schizophrenic—regarding him as both essential as the vanguard of American relations with foreign governments and international organizations, and as routine and unnecessary for major negotiations. On the one hand, he is viewed merely as the eyes, the ears, and the mouth of the government abroad—simply a messenger, who is bypassed on most important matters and exercises little if any influence on policy making, possesses minimum opportunity for applying initiative, and discovers that others in Washington claim credit if American ventures succeed, whereas he is blamed if they fail. This view has been widely publicized by careerists.

On the other hand, the diplomat also is depicted as the indispensable official abroad—not only a "Jack of all trades," but also a master of them all. Traditionally, according to the Department of State, he had four major responsibilities—protection of his country's interests abroad, reporting to his government on conditions in the country of his assignment, negotiating treaties and agreements, and ceremonial representation. Since World War II these have been expanded to encompass an infinite array of duties, undreamed of before. Now he is expected also to administer an extensive complex of operational programs in foreign lands, handle relations respecting a host of commercial, economic, financial, legal, scientific, technical, and other matters, and serve as the primary agent through whom the network of American policies and practice are conveyed to the foreign world. In this regard, the diplomat is crucial to the conduct of foreign relations. This attitude is propounded by the Department of State and, in certain respects, by a good many American emissaries. The antitheticality of these two views of the contemporary diplomat tends to negate both, and thereby augment the confusion.

A fourth major notion—actually a disdainful misconception—of the diplomat is more vague and less flattering than that of most other public officials and the members of many other professional and career groups. Often he is regarded as a member of an effete white-spat brigade devoted chiefly to the afternoon tea and cocktail circuit, to the calling-card routine, to luncheon and reception buffet gossip, and to bickering over matters of protocol and the social graces—a

[6] U.S. Department of State, *The American Ambassador*, p. 21.

shining knight in ostentatious cummerbund, beneficiary of duty-free liquor, a punctilious Beau Brummell, and devotee of the *aide memoir.* Hugh S. Gibson, while ambassador to Belgium, denied before a congressional committee that career diplomats are rich, good-for-nothing, idle playboys and "cookie-pushers." The very defensive nature of his statement is revealing. The inauspicious designation "cookie-pusher" was pounced upon with great glee by critics and has become one of the most contemptuous epithets applied to American diplomats. As a consequence, in the popular view, many are regarded as affable but indecisive, sociable but ineffectual, often proforeign to the point of being un-American, and sometimes inutile, who should be replaced by more "shirt-sleeve diplomats"—by real Americans.

Such unfortunate impressions can only be allayed by carefully examining the facts. This study concentrates on surveying some of the more readily available and arbitrarily measurable, though admittedly more prosaic, factors. From such analysis, certain conclusions respecting the American experience, the current status of United States diplomats, and future trends may be discerned.

When the United States was emerging into the diplomatic arena in the late eighteenth century, the President appointed only a handful of officers to conduct the foreign affairs of the United States— a secretary of state and half a dozen or so emissaries, possessing somewhat inferior ranks and titles, accredited to a few of the leading European powers. The President, the secretary, and the envoys were well known to one another. Today the President commissions a team of some twenty deputy secretaries, under secretaries, assistant secretaries, and other ranking departmental officers to assist the secretary, and he appoints several ambassadors at large and a corps of chiefs of mission to approximately 135 foreign governments and ten international organizations—totaling nearly 175 top-level officers. Adding replacements and reassignments, the total may average 200 every four years. Quantitatively, by the 1970s presidential appointments amounted to nearly twenty-five times the number commissioned in the late eighteenth and early nineteenth centuries. The President's task of selection and appointment, therefore, has become more demanding, while the opportunity of the expectant diplomat has been enhanced, but the degree of acquaintance, friendship, and intimacy among the participants has doubtless suffered considerably.

The newly appointed American diplomat has a 16 percent chance of serving at high levels in the Department of State, approximately a 77 percent certainty of designation as chief of mission to some foreign government, and only a minor possibility of accreditation to an international organization or commissioning as ambassador at large. This general distribution is not apt to change extensively, although the number of missions to both foreign governments and international organizations could increase by as much as 15 to 20 percent in the next decade or two. As in the past, future diplomats must realize that the preponderant share of top-level appointment opportunity lies in the field where, in any case, most of them prefer to practice their profession.

Whereas for decades early American emissaries were assigned solely to European or Latin American countries, the diplomatic community has not only expanded numerically, but has also changed in basic geographic composition. Today's American diplomat has only a one in five chance of being assigned to either Europe or the Western Hemisphere, and the odds that he will be sent to one of the Asian or western Pacific countries are nearly as great; it is less probable that he will go to the Middle East, and considerably greater that he will be accredited to a sub-Saharan African state. If the United States should add two dozen more countries to its diplomatic roster, as suggested in chapter 1, by the beginning of the twenty-first century, the chances of a diplomat being assigned to either Europe or Latin America will decrease. On the other hand, one in ten will be accredited to the Middle East, more than two to Asia and the Pacific, and nearly three of every ten will serve in Africa south of the Sahara.

This basic ratio of assignments is unlikely to change materially in the decades that follow. However, the fact that 60 to 70 percent of all emissaries will be destined for appointment to the Middle East, Africa, and Asia is bound to affect future diplomatic recruitment, particularly so far as language competence is concerned, and especially among bilingual FSOs who aspire to ambassadorships. It also will mean that competition for appointment to what are sometimes regarded as preferred posts will increase. The emergent careerist who covets the crowning achievement of ambassadorial appointment will be well advised, therefore, to plan his career development to take account of these changes in the representational pattern of the United States.

During the two centuries since the 1770s, nearly 70 percent of American diplomats have been named to single appointments. Conversely, almost one-third have been accorded multiple assignments, which means that every emissary, once commissioned at this level, has better than a 30 percent chance of reappointment. The preponderant majority of such multiple appointments have been and will be sequential rather than simultaneous. More than half of the reappointees, according to past experience, will be given two assignments, while one of every five may aspire to three, and one in every four may be designated to four or more such posts. As a matter of fact, a high level of reappointment—that is, to five or more missions—seems to be somewhat on the increase. Simultaneous multiple appointments have served a variety of useful purposes, but they tend to be exceptional and may very well decline if not disappear in American practice, except for emergency situations and for the temporary handling of representation to some of the smaller, newer countries as they emerge into the diplomatic arena. Reappointment of a single emissary to the same country has become quite rare.

Overall, four of every ten multiple appointees have been careerists; since World War I the figure has risen to two of every three. If this later ratio continues—and the logic and pressures favoring a high degree of reappointment of careerists is not apt to change—Foreign Service Officers who gain admission to this inner circle of ranking emissaries in the field and senior departmental officers, enjoy a reasonable if not a substantial possibility of reappointment. If anything, in view of the recent trend toward naming careerists to such posts at a relatively young age, such reappointment is bound to increase. Of approximately sixty careerists designated to African countries within a decade (1963 to 1973), for example, nearly 85 percent were under fifty-five years of age when first appointed, and several were in their late thirties and early forties. Discounting those still in their posts at the end of the decade, six of every ten received more than a single appointment. The current ratio, favorable to careerist multiple appointees, is likely to continue. However, it could be affected by lengthening the average period of mission tenure, by increasing the number of potential career appointees, by raising or lowering the retirement age of careerists, or by altering the existing balance between careerists and noncareerists.

If overall past experience were a reliable guide to the future, one in every ten nominations for appointment as chiefs of mission to foreign governments would fail to be consummated. However, since 1910 this ratio has declined to less than one of every twenty-five, so that the contemporary diplomatic nominee has a far greater certainty of appointment than was the case with earlier candidates. Employing the yardstick of the past, approximately one-third of the nonconsummations of appointment will be due to Senate inaction or rejection of the nomination, more than one of every five will be occasioned by the nominee declining appointment, and one of every twenty, though confirmed, will die before his commissioning and reception are fully consummated.

Prior to the 1890s, those diplomats who were appointed, accredited, and officially received, were accorded inferior ranks and titles. However, currently American diplomats almost universally bear the rank of ambassador extraordinary and plenipotentiary—the highest of the regular diplomatic titles. Consequently, contemporary and future United States emissaries, even if accredited to minor countries in remote corners of the globe, no longer need to suffer the stigma of inferior diplomatic status. The only exceptions are chargés d'affaires ad interim, serving temporarily while a chief of mission is absent from his post, or pending the arrival of a newly appointed envoy. Most chiefs of mission to international organizations also are commissioned as ambassadors, although a few, accredited to United Nations specialized agencies, still hold the rank of minister, but in the years to come these may very well be elevated to the ambassadorial level. A major exception to the current norm is the ambassador at large, but this lofty title is relatively new and sparsely used. Although at present it does not signify an added supergrade internationally, if it is employed freely by the White House in the future and also is adopted by other countries, it could eventually come to denominate such a superior diplomatic rank.

More than half of the diplomats of the United States have hailed from the Atlantic seaboard states, ranging from Maine to Virginia. Since 1940, however, one of every two chiefs of mission has come from the following six states—New York, California, Illinois, Maryland, Pennsylvania, and Connecticut, plus the District of Columbia—and the pattern is roughly the same for careerists. New York has been the state of residence of the largest number of American emissaries—approximately 15 percent, but in the 1960s the quota appointed from the District of Columbia rose to equal that of New York. On the other hand, no emissaries have been recruited from several states, and, except for California, only small numbers have been chosen from fourteen of the West-South-Central, Mountain, and Pacific states.

This factor of geographic origin need not seriously concern future diplomats, however, because American practice evidences little consciousness of, or emphasis upon, areal distribution in the selection process, nor does the geographic origin of Presidents seem to have any distinct bearing on the matter. Yet, because of the political sensitivities of members of Congress, it is not without the realm of possibility that some determined effort may be launched—overtly or indirectly by pressures behind the scenes—to redress major discrepancies in order to achieve a greater geographic spread of appointments, at least so far as noncareerists are concerned. The geographic origin of ranking diplomats has little if any logical relevancy to their service—especially in view of the large proportion of careerists currently being appointed as chiefs of mission—and certainly an arbitrary program of proportional distribution could be detrimental to the quality and flexibility of American diplomatic practice. Nevertheless, the injection of politics into the selection process to eliminate discrimination and achieve a broader geographic spread is not inconceivable, and the President and his advisers ought to forestall a development in which the cure could be worse than the apparent malady, by consciously rectifying gross inequities.

It is no surprise that historically more than seven of every ten American diplomats have been in middle age at the time of their appointment, with the largest numbers ranging between the ages of forty-seven and fifty-three. Although some have been as young as their twenties when first commissioned, these appointments have been rare, and no such youthful appointees have been named since the 1920s. Moreover, even though a few may still be accredited in their thirties to serve on an interim basis, as American mission staffs increase in size, this practice may disappear, except in the most unusual circumstances.

During the post-World War II expansion of the American diplomatic community, careerists generally were designated to ranking diplomatic positions while in their fifties—often the lower fifties—and in the 1960s there appeared to be some trend toward earlier appointment. On the other hand, most of the diplomats who were in their sixties when first appointed, and certainly those in their seventies, have been noncareerists. While careerists remain in their diplomatic careers only until they reach mandatory retirement age in their early sixties, and rarely exceed sixty-five, some noncareerists may continue into their late sixties, with a number of them even surviving into the seventies and early eighties. The younger diplomats, both careerists and noncareerists, naturally, enjoy a greater opportunity than do their older colleagues for sequential multiple appointment. However, such reappointment is by no means guaranteed, even for careerists, and some noncareerists are reappointed at an advanced age, in exceptional cases even in their late seventies and early eighties.

No significant trend is discernible in these developments, and existing averages and ratios are not likely to change unless the law should be modified respecting careerist retirement age, the ratio of careerists to noncareerists should be altered, or a particular presidential administration should develop a preference for either younger or older diplomats. Consequently, some careerists will leave active service disgruntled that they could not continue at the highest levels of diplomacy for longer periods, while their continuance probably would be opposed by younger career officers who are standing by vying to achieve ambassadorial status.

The age and reappointment factors relate directly to the duration of diplomatic missions which, in isolated cases, may vary from only a few days to more than twenty years. On the average, American diplomatic missions last approximately three years, with turnover least frequent in the countries of Europe and most rapid in sub-Saharan Africa. At present, because of the short time span involved, the situation in Africa may be unique and in the future the general turnover rate for this area probably will approximate the overall norm. So far as individual appointees are concerned, approximately 55 percent of American emissaries serve in a given post for less than three years, of which one of every five remains for less than a year. On the other hand, nearly 20 percent have continued at their posts from three to four years, and more than 25 percent have served tenures of four years or longer.

There appears to be little demonstrable interrelation between the duration of missions and their geographic distribution, and much the same may be said respecting historical timing, except for an apparent tendency to reduce the quantity and frequency of prolonged tenure in a given mission. This doubtless is attributable in large measure to the increasing number of careerists seeking such appointment as chiefs of mission and their continuance for short periods. Augmenting the level of careerism, therefore, does not necessarily result in extending tenure averages. As a matter of fact, careerists account for 80 percent of the very short appointments (amounting to six months or less) since World War I, which demonstrates the relationship of short tenure to turnover chain reaction among careerists. As a result, unless firm action is taken to control the matter, the problem and consequences of brief tenure and multiple reassignment will not only continue, but intensify.

Prior to the Franklin D. Roosevelt administration, no women were appointed as diplomats, and in forty years only fifteen were named to nineteen missions, as of March 1973. There is evidence of some trend, however, both to increase the number of women diplomats and to expand the types of positions to which they are commissioned and the range of countries to which they are sent. To some extent, but only in part, the restriction on the number of women diplomats has reflected the status of their appointment to the career Foreign Service, but in recent decades, this has been in the process of liberalization in their favor. Although the modification of attitudes both in the United States and abroad has been slow, progress is being made, and certain recently emergent pressures are bound to compel the naming of more women to diplomatic posts in the future.

American diplomats have been drawn from a variety of backgrounds and professions—statesmen, politicians, bureaucrats, lawyers, businessmen, historians, educators, men of letters, publishers, journalists, a few missionaries, and others—and for decades political patronage influenced the selection of a good many nominees. This spoils system, wrote E. Wilder Spaulding, "provided a rich fund of enticing awards for political hacks and lame ducks as well as genuinely worthy statesmen—awards that can be dispensed by the President with honorable mention going to the United States Senators who must approve the nomination and to the party in power." [7]

Some of these diplomatic appointees—at one time amounting to a substantial proportion—who benefited from the spoils system were former members of Congress. To 1870, the quantity of diplomats who possessed previous congressional experience ranged from 25 percent to as high as 70 percent per decade. However, since 1920, this ratio has dropped to only five to twelve individuals (amounting to less than 1 to 3 percent of the total number of diplomatic appointees) per decade—and averaging only 2 percent during more than half a century. This also represents a very small percentage of the total membership of Congress, so that prior congressional service has become a negligible precondition to diplomatic appointment, and while the practice has not entirely disappeared, the number of such appointments has become minute.

Although occasional vestiges of the spoils system remain, they have been substantially offset by the institution of the career service. Since the introduction of the careerist designation, beginning during the World War I period, careerists have been the recipients of approximately 55 percent of American diplomatic appointments. This overall quota has been influenced somewhat by the relatively large number of noncareerists appointed to the limited number of ranking positions in the Department of State—approximately 70 percent since 1915, but declining to 60 percent since 1940. On the other hand, some 60 percent of American chiefs of mission accredited to foreign governments since 1920 have been careerists, and this average has risen to more than 65 percent since 1950. In other words, the proportion of careerists has been gaining both within the Department of State and the field. Especially high has been the quantity of careerists accredited to

---

[7] Spaulding, *Ambassadors Ordinary and Extraordinary*, p. 8.

the East European Communist countries (approximately 85 percent since World War II), and to the Middle East, Africa, Asia, and in the Pacific (in each case ranging between 73 and 78 percent). While the general averages for Europe and Latin America have been somewhat lower, the era of large-scale sanctuaries for political rewardees and other noncareerists has diminished markedly, whereas conversely, extensive preserves for careerists appear to have become entrenched in American diplomatic practice.

By and large, the upward ascent of the ratio of careerist appointees seems to be leveling off at between 65 and 75 percent. This average may fluctuate, but given the American tradition and political system, the level of careerism is unlikely to achieve 100 percent, and there are many who question whether it should. Certain categories of diplomatic officials—such as some of the senior departmental appointees, ambassadors at large, and even particular chiefs of mission—will continue to be recruited from outside the career service. Every President is persuaded to exercise his authority to designate some of his ambassadors from outside the Foreign Service. In this connection account needs to be taken of the fact that a nucleus of noncareerists evolves into genuine professional diplomats who, added to the FSOs, provide a preponderance of senior American diplomats. In view of the high level of careerism already achieved, it seems logical to conclude that the problem with the appointment of noncareerists is no longer a matter of basic principle—as it once was—but rather a question of judgment respecting the specific individuals selected—and this applies to careerists no less than to noncareerists.

Diplomatic missions to foreign governments and international organizations are terminated on the determination of the White House and the Department of State. The reasons ascribed in most cases—such as recall presentation, relinquishing charge of the mission, supersession of the appointee, and leaving the post or the country of assignment—fail to reveal the real causes of mission termination. The latter consist rather of the wishes of an incoming President to name his own ambassadors (sometimes by shifting individual emissaries to new assignments), the desire of the White House or the Department of State to accredit a different individual to a particular country for specific reasons, the request of the noncareerist to leave the diplomatic service, the compulsory retirement of the careerist, the desire of the envoy to change his post, and the like. More than 93 percent of diplomatic appointments and missions in the field have been terminated for such reasons, which are quite normal in diplomatic practice. While ultimately the government makes the final decision respecting such termination, the individual diplomat exercises some influence in the matter, especially with respect to the retirement of the non-careerist and, if it can be maneuvered, the change of assignment of the careerist.

Only in a small number of cases, on the other hand, is there coalescence of publicly acknowledged and genuine reasons for diplomatic mission termination. These include recall of the emissary at the request of the host government or dismissal by it, temporary interruption or formal severance of diplomatic relations, military occupation or change in the legal status of the country to which the envoy is accredited, and the death of the emissary. The probability that the individual diplomat is likely to have his mission terminated for any of these reasons is not very great. If careerists increase in quantity and are given multiple appointments until they reach retirement age, the rate of those who die in service may increase, but this would be no more abnormal than it is for other professions. Certainly it would not justify the lowering of the mandatory retirement age, increasing the number of younger appointees as chiefs of mission, or restricting opportunity for sequential reappointment. Such action is not apt to be taken, but if it were, there ought to be more compelling reasons for doing so.

If future American diplomats emulate their predecessors, approximately one in every five will try his hand at authorship, each of whom will publish one or more—in exceptional cases as many as fifty—volumes of recollections, biography, commentary, fiction, and poetry. Some of these will be authors who are temporarily recruited as diplomats, but most will be diplomats who became authors. While not surprising, but nevertheless significant, more than half of them will produce autobiographies, memoirs, diaries, state papers, and other compilations of documentary materials. Two of every five will author commentaries on a broad range of subjects, three of every ten will write biographies and travelogues, and nearly one of every ten will prepare a variety of manuals, guides, and textbooks. Approximately 15 percent will devote themselves to writing poetry and fiction. A good many will contribute to several of these categories of publications, and a few will be contributing to most of them.

Because of greater central control of policy making, the increased quota of careerists, and regulations governing the management and possession of official documentation, the future diplomat will probably publish fewer collections of state papers. These will become available primarily in the publications and archives of the Department of State and other official documentary services. On the other hand, the high ratio of memoirs, commentaries, histories, and biographies—the preferred categories of publication of diplomat-authors—will probably continue, but the spectrum of literary and publishing interests is likely to remain as diverse as it has been in the past.

In the early decades a good many American diplomats not only had prior congressional experience, but also possessed presidential and vice-presidential aspirations. During the first century the relationship between diplomatic office, including the secretaryship of state, and candidacy for the presidency and vice-presidency was clearly evident. To the time of the Civil War nearly 60 percent of those who were elected President and vice-president had previous diplomatic experience, and prior to 1870 approximately two-thirds of those who stood for election to these offices, but were defeated, had also been nominated for some diplomatic appointment. While this relationship has not disappeared entirely, the ratio has declined considerably during the past century, so that in recent years it has become unique.

On leaving their appointments, American diplomats in the past often returned to their former professions—politics, academia, banking, business, journalism—and others passed gracefully into retirement. With the increase in the number of careerists who are required to retire by the time they reach sixty-five, or earlier, a much higher percentage may proceed from active service directly into retirement. Nevertheless, imbued with a compulsion to remain active, to continue in the limelight, or simply to remain on a payroll, some have been undertaking a second career. Inasmuch as politics and the federal bureaucracy are closed to them, they have turned rather to academic, research, corporation management, and other types of appointments. The second career objective is also prevalent among a quantity of FSOs who fail to achieve appointments as chiefs of mission, and their choices are similar. As long as careerists are retired in their early and mid-sixties and attractive opportunities are made available to early retirees, this trend toward a subsidiary career is bound to continue.[8]

A variety of serious-minded analysts, including distinguished diplomats, have sought to define the ideal diplomat and, as the United States approaches the commencement of its third century, it would be a stimulating challenge to attempt such delineation and to design a plan for inculcating and molding in American emissaries those qualities that are deemed to be most desirable. However, because of the

---

[8] The problem of a second profession is even more acute for the career officer who never achieves ambassadorial appointment, particularly if he is in a given rank or career class for a fixed period of time without being promoted and is therefore "retired" from the Foreign Service by the "selection out" process. See Foreign Service Act of 1946, as amended, sec. 633.

constraints of practical politics and the realities of diplomatic bureaucracy and practice, it may be more useful to concentrate on the demonstrable facts of past experience in order to define those areas which warrant improvement. The foregoing analysis may help to set forth some of the basic characteristics of the average—as well as the atypical—American diplomat and his mission, and suggest a number of opportunities for change in pursuing the projection of a more realistic image of the ideal diplomat.

APPENDIX TABLES

Except as otherwise noted in Tables A-2, A-3, A-15, and A-16, all statistics were compiled by the author based on information derived from Richardson Dougall and Mary Patricia Chapman, *United States Chiefs of Mission, 1778–1973* (Washington, D. C.: Historical Office, Department of State, 1973). Unless otherwise noted, statistics cover the period to 31 March 1973.

Table A-1

U.S. REPRESENTATION TO FOREIGN GOVERNMENTS, THEIR MEMBERSHIP IN THE LEAGUE OF NATIONS AND THE UNITED NATIONS

A Country	B Commencement of Diplomatic Relations[a]	C United States Representation[b]											D League of Nations	E United Nations (Jan. 1975)
		1800	1850	1900	1910	1920	1930	1940	1950	1960	1970	1973		
Afghanistan	4 May 1935							X	X	X	X	X	X	X
Albania (1922–1939)[c]	4 Dec. 1922						X	—	—	—	—	—	X	X
Algeria	17 Dec. 1962										d	d		X
Argentina	27 Dec. 1823		X	X	X	X	X	X	X	X	X	X	X	X
Australia	17 July 1940								X	X	X	X	X	X
Austria	7 Nov. 1838		X	X	X	X	X	X	X	X	X	X	X	X
Bahrain	17 Feb. 1972											X		X
Bangladesh	11 Sep. 1973[e]											X		X
Barbados	27 Nov. 1967										X	X		X
Belgium	25 Sep. 1832		X	X	X	X	X	X	X	X	X	X	X	X
Bolivia	3 Jan. 1849		X	X	X	X	X	X	X	X	X	X	X	X
Botswana (Bechuanaland)	14 Sep. 1971											X		X
Brazil	29 Oct. 1825		X	X	X	X	X	X	X	X	X	X	X	X
Bulgaria	19 Sep. 1903				X	X	X	X	X	X	X	X	X	X
Burma	3 Mar. 1948								X	X	X	X		X
Burundi	17 Jan. 1963										X	X		X

Cameroon	9 June 1960									X	X		X
Canada	1 June 1927						X	X	X	X	X	X	X	X
Central African Republic	6 Jan. 1961										X	X		X
Chad	9 Jan. 1961										X	X		X
Chile	23 Apr. 1824		X	X	X	X	X	X	X	X	X	X	X	X
China[f]	12 June 1844		X	X	X	X	X	X	X	X	X	X	X	X
Colombia	16 Dec. 1823		X	X	X	X	X	X	X	X	X	X	X	X
Congo (Brazzaville)	23 Dec. 1960										d	d		X
Costa Rica	14 Sep. 1858			X	X	X	X	X	X	X	X	X	X	X
Cuba	27 May 1902				X	X	X	X	X	X	d	d	X	X
Cyprus	19 Sep. 1960										X	X		X
Czechoslovakia	11 June 1919					X	X	X	X	X	X	X	X	X
Dahomey	26 Nov. 1960										X	X		X
Denmark	20 Sep. 1827		X	X	X	X	X	X	X	X	X	X	X	X
Dominican Republic	26 Mar. 1884			X	X	X	X	X	X	X	X	X	X	X
Ecuador	12 Aug. 1848		X	X	X	X	X	X	X	X	X	X	X	X
Egypt	17 Mar. 1849		X	X	X	X	X	X	X	X	d	d	X	X
El Salvador	15 June 1863			X	X	X	X	X	X	X	X	X	X	X
Equatorial Guinea	21 Nov. 1968										X	X		X
Estonia (1922–1940)[c]	20 Nov. 1922						X	X	—	—	—	—	X	
Ethiopia	6 July 1909				X	X	X	X	X	X	X	X	X	X
Fiji	22 May 1972											X		X
Finland	19 Mar. 1920						X	X	X	X	X	X	X	X
France	23 Mar. 1779	X	X	X	X	X	X	X	X	X	X	X	X	X
Gabon	13 Jan. 1961										X	X		X
Gambia	9 Aug. 1965										X	X		X

Table A-1 (Continued)

A Country	B Commencement of Diplomatic Relations[a]	C United States Representation[b] 1800	1850	1900	1910	1920	1930	1940	1950	1960	1970	1973	D League of Nations	E United Nations (Jan. 1975)
Germany (Prussia)	5 Dec. 1797	X	X	X	X	X	X	X	X	X	X	X	X	X
Ghana	12 Mar. 1957									X	X	X		X
Greece	16 June 1868			X	X	X	X	X	X	X	X	X	X	X
Guatemala	3 May 1826		X	X	X	X	X	X	X	X	X	X	X	X
Guinea	30 July 1959									X	X	X		X
Guyana	17 Aug. 1966										X	X		X
Haiti	1 Oct. 1862			X	X	X	X	X	X	X	X	X	X	X
Hawaii (1853–1898)[c]	20 Dec. 1853													
Honduras	10 Aug. 1858			X	X	X	X	X	X	X	X	X	X	X
Hungary	24 Jan. 1922						X	X	X	X	X	X	X	X
Iceland	30 Sep. 1941								X	X	X	X		X
India	1 July 1947								X	X	X	X	X	X
Indonesia	30 Dec. 1949								X	X	X	X		X
Iran (Persia)	11 June 1883			X	X	X	X	X	X	X	X	X	X	X
Iraq	18 June 1931							X	X	X	d	d	X	X
Ireland	27 July 1927						X	X	X	X	X	X	X	X
Israel	28 Mar. 1949								X	X	X	X		X
Italy	15 Sep. 1840		X	X	X	X	X	X	X	X	X	X	X	X
Ivory Coast	20 Nov. 1960										X	X		X

Jamaica	26 Nov. 1962									X	X		X
Japan	5 Nov. 1859		X	X	X	X	X	X	X	X	X	X	X
Jordan	24 Feb. 1950								X	X	X		X
Kenya	2 Mar. 1964									X	X		X
Khmer Republic (Cambodia)	11 July 1950								X	X	X		X
Korea (1883–1905; 1949–)	20 May 1883/ 20 Apr. 1949		X	—	—	—	—	X	X	X	X		
Kuwait	18 Oct. 1961									X	X		X
Laos	29 Dec. 1950								X	X	X		X
Latvia (1922–1940) [c]	13 Nov. 1922					X	X	—	—	—	—	X	
Lebanon	19 Nov. 1942							X	X	X	X		X
Lesotho	23 Sep. 1971										X		X
Liberia	23 Feb. 1864		X	X	X	X	X	X	X	X	X	X	X
Libya	6 Mar. 1952								X	X	X		X
Lithuania (1922–1940) [c]	5 Dec. 1922					X	X	—	—	—	—	X	
Luxembourg	17 July 1903			X	X	X	X	X	X	X	X	X	X
Madagascar (Malagasy)	5 Oct. 1960									X	X		X
Malawi	8 July 1964									X	X		X
Malaysia	4 Sep. 1957								X	X	X		X
Maldives	9 Apr. 1966									X	X		X
Mali	17 Jan. 1961									X	X		X
Malta	5 Oct. 1965									X	X		X
Mauritania	28 Nov. 1960									X	X		X
Mauritius	29 July 1968									X	X		X
Mexico	1 June 1825	X	X	X	X	X	X	X	X	X	X	X	X

Table A-1 (Continued)

A Country	B Commencement of Diplomatic Relations[a]	C United States Representation[b]											D League of Nations	E United Nations (Jan. 1975)
		1800	1850	1900	1910	1920	1930	1940	1950	1960	1970	1973		
Montenegro (1905–1918)[c]	30 Oct. 1905				X	—	—	—	—	—	—	—		
Morocco	29 Sep. 1906				X	X	X	X	X	X	X	X		X
Nepal	3 May 1948								X	X	X	X		X
Netherlands	19 Apr. 1782	X	X	X	X	X	X	X	X	X	X	X	X	X
New Zealand	24 Apr. 1942								X	X	X	X	X	X
Nicaragua	18 Feb. 1852			X	X	X	X	X	X	X	X	X	X	X
Niger	23 Nov. 1960										X	X		X
Nigeria	4 Oct. 1960										X	X		X
Norway	31 May 1905				X	X	X	X	X	X	X	X	X	X
Oman	17 Apr. 1972											X		X
Pakistan	26 Feb. 1948								X	X	X	X		X
Panama	17 Dec. 1903[e]				X	X	X	X	X	X	X	X	X	X
Paraguay	26 Nov. 1861			X	X	X	X	X	X	X	X	X	X	X
Peru	21 May 1827		X	X	X	X	X	X	X	X	X	X	X	X
Philippines	4 July 1946								X	X	X	X		X
Poland	2 May 1919					X	X	X	X	X	X	X	X	X
Portugal	13 May 1791	X	X	X	X	X	X	X	X	X	X	X	X	X
Qatar	19 Mar. 1972											X		X
Romania	25 Jan. 1881			X	X	X	X	X	X	X	X	X	X	X
Rwanda	19 Apr. 1963										X	X		X

Saudi Arabia	4 Feb. 1940								X	X	X	X		X
Senegal	31 Oct. 1960										X	X		X
Sierra Leone	9 June 1961										X	X		X
Singapore	8 Dec. 1966										X	X		X
Somalia	11 July 1960										X	X		X
South Africa	18 Feb. 1930							X	X	X	X	X	X	X
Soviet Union (Russia)	19 Dec. 1780[e]	X	X	X	X	X	X	X	X	X	X	X	X	X
Spain	28 Sep. 1779[e]	X	X	X	X	X	X	X	X	X	X	X	X	X
Sri Lanka (Ceylon)	3 Aug. 1948								X	X	X	X		X
Sudan	17 Mar. 1956									X	X	X		X
Swaziland	3 Nov. 1971											X		X
Sweden	29 Apr. 1814		X	X	X	X	X	X	X	X	X	X	X	X
Switzerland	29 June 1853			X	X	X	X	X	X	X	X	X	X	
Syria	30 Nov. 1942								X	X	d	d		X
Tanzania	3 Oct. 1962										X	X		X
Texas (1837–1845)[c]	23–27 Oct. 1837													
Thailand (Siam)	23 Oct. 1882			X	X	X	X	X	X	X	X	X	X	X
Togo	22 Aug. 1960										X	X		X
Tonga	6 Nov. 1972											X		
Trinidad and Tobago	1 Dec. 1962										X	X		X
Tunisia	6 June 1956									X	X	X		X
Turkey	13 Sep. 1831		X	X	X	X	X	X	X	X	X	X	X	X
Two Sicilies (1832–1860)[c]	25 Jan. 1832		X											
Uganda	14 Jan. 1963										X	X		X

Table A-1 (Continued)

A Country	B Commencement of Diplomatic Relations[a]	C United States Representation[b]											D League of Nations	E United Nations (Jan. 1975)
		1800	1850	1900	1910	1920	1930	1940	1950	1960	1970	1973		
United Arab Emirates	20 Mar. 1972											X		X
United Kingdom	1 June 1785	X	X	X	X	X	X	X	X	X	X	X	X	X
Upper Volta	6 Dec. 1960										X	X		X
Uruguay	2 Oct. 1867			X	X	X	X	X	X	X	X	X	X	X
Vatican City (1848–1867; 1941–1944)[c]	19 Aug. 1848		X											
Venezuela	30 June 1835		X	X	X	X	X	X	X	X	X	X	X	X
Vietnam	22 Oct. 1950									X	X	X		
Western Samoa	14 July 1971											X		
Yemen Arab Republic	30 Sep. 1946								X	X	X	X		X
Yugoslavia (Serbia)	10 Nov. 1882			X	X	X	X	X	X	X	X	X	X	X
Zaire (Congo/ Leopoldville)	25 July 1960										X	X		X
Zambia	24 Mar. 1965										X	X		X
141 countries Total		7	27	42	49	50	58	60	73	83	121	132	63	128[g]

[a] Dates are those of first presentation of diplomatic credentials.

[b] Representation as of 1 January of year indicated, except for 1973 (31 March).

[c] Diplomatic representation discontinued.

[d] Diplomatic relations suspended, but country counted in totals.

[e] Date given is for nomination/appointment of first emissary—diplomat not formally received, date of reception not known, or appointment pending as of March 1973.

[f] The United States maintains relations with the Republic of China, while the Democratic People's Republic is represented in the United Nations, and liaison missions were exchanged in 1973.

[g] In addition to this total, the following countries are members of the United Nations: Bahamas, Bhutan, Byelorussia, Germany (East-DRG), Grenada, Guinea-Bissau, Mongolia, Ukraine and Yemen (Aden). Total United Nations membership as of January 1975 (including the United States) is 138. The United States commenced diplomatic relations with the Bahamas in 1973, subsequent to 31 March and with East Germany, Grenada, and Guinea-Bissau in 1974.

Table A-2

COMMENCEMENT, DURATION, AND LENGTH OF U.S. DIPLOMATIC REPRESENTATION BY GEOGRAPHIC AREA

A Country	B Area (square miles in thousands)	C Population, 1970 (millions)	D Commencement of Diplomatic Relations [a]	E Suspension and Termination of Diplomatic Relations	F Duration of Diplomatic Relations (full years)		G Number of Chiefs of Mission		H Average Length of Service (years) [f]
					Total [b]	Net [c]	Nom [d]	Ser [e]	
Western Hemisphere									
Argentina	1,072	24.1	27 Dec. 1823		149		50	43	3.47
Barbados	0.2	(260,000)	27 Nov. 1967		5		2	2	2.50
Bolivia	424	4.7	3 Jan. 1849		124		50	45	2.76
Brazil	3,286	91.9	29 Oct. 1825		147		40	38	3.87
Canada	3,800	22.0	1 June 1927		45		18	18	2.50
Chile	292	9.3	23 Apr. 1824		148		43	40	3.70
Colombia	440	21.1	16 Dec. 1823		149		54	51	2.92
Costa Rica	20	1.7	14 Sep. 1858		114		40	34	3.35
Cuba	44	8.4	27 May 1902	(Jan. 1961—) [g]	70	(58)	20	20	2.90
Dominican Republic	19	4.1	26 Mar. 1884		89		30	29	3.07
Ecuador	109	6.1	12 Aug. 1848		124		40	31	4.00
El Salvador	83	3.4	15 June 1863		109		38	35	3.11
Guatemala	42	5.3	3 May 1826		146		53	40	3.65
Guyana	83	(760,000)	17 Aug. 1966		6		2	2	3.00
Haiti	11	4.9	1 Oct. 1862		110		31	29	3.79
Honduras	4.3	2.7	10 Aug. 1858		114		41	32	3.56
Jamaica	4	2.0	26 Nov. 1962		10		4	4	2.50
Mexico	762	50.1	1 June 1825	(Mar.–Nov. 1845) [g]	147		49	42	3.50

Nicaragua	50	1.9	18 Feb. 1852		121		40	36	3.36
Panama	29	1.4	17 Dec. 1903 [i]		69		27	26	2.65
Paraguay	157	2.4	26 Nov. 1861		111		33	30	3.70
Peru	496	13.6	21 May 1827		145		42	39	3.72
Texas	—	—	23–27 Oct. 1837	5 Aug. 1845 [h]	8		6	6	1.33
Trinidad and Tobago	2	1.0	1 Dec. 1962		10		4	4	2.50
Uruguay	72	2.9	2 Oct. 1867		105		39	34	3.09
Venezuela	352	10.4	30 June 1835		137		45	41	3.34
Total					2,512	(2,500)	841	751	3.33
			Europe						
Albania	11	2.1	4 Dec. 1922	27 Sep. 1939 [h]	16		5	5	3.20
Austria	32	7.4	7 Nov. 1838	(1917–21; 1938–46) [g]	134	(121)	50	40	3.03
Belgium	12	9.7	25 Sep. 1832		140		46	43	3.26
Bulgaria	43	8.5	19 Sep. 1903	(1941–47; 1950–60) [g]	69	(53)	20	16	3.31
Cyprus	4	(600,000)	19 Sep. 1960		12		3	3	4.00
Czechoslovakia	49	14.5	11 June 1919		53		20	19	2.79
Denmark	17	4.9	20 Sep. 1827		145		45	40	3.63
Estonia	—	—	20 Nov. 1922	5 Sep. 1940 [h]	17		6	5	3.40
Finland	130	4.7	19 Mar. 1920	(1944–46) [g]	52	(50)	18	17	2.94
France	211	50.8	23 Mar. 1779	(1942–44) [g]	194	(192)	58	53	3.62
Germany (Prussia)	96	61.7	5 Dec. 1797	(1917–21; 1941–55) [g]	175	(123) [j]	38	37	3.32
Greece	51	8.9	16 June 1868	(1801–35) [g]	104	(70)	36	33	2.12
Hungary	36	10.3	24 Jan. 1922	(1941–46) [g]	50	(46)	13	12	3.83
Iceland	40	(200,000)	30 Sep. 1941		31		11	11	2.82
Ireland	27	2.9	27 July 1927		45		14	14	3.21
Italy	116	54.5	15 Sep. 1840	(1941–45) [g]	132	(128)	38	34	3.76

Table A-2 (Continued)

A Country	B Area (square miles in thousands)	C Population, 1970 (millions)	D Commencement of Diplomatic Relations [a]	E Suspension and Termination of Diplomatic Relations	F Duration of Diplomatic Relations (full years)		G Number of Chiefs of Mission		H Average Length of Service (years) [f]
					Total [b]	Net [c]	Nom [d]	Ser [e]	
			Europe (Continued)						
Latvia	—	—	13 Nov. 1922	5 Sep. 1940 [h]	17		6	5	3.40
Lithuania	—	—	5 Dec. 1922	5 Sep. 1940 [h]	17		5	5	3.40
Luxembourg	1	(300,000)	17 July 1903		69		31	29	2.38
Malta	0.12	(300,000)	5 Oct. 1965		7		4	4	1.75
Montenegro	—	—	30 Oct. 1905	4 Dec. 1918 [h]	13		7	6	2.17
Netherlands	16	13.0	19 Apr. 1782		190		50	46	4.13
Norway	125	3.9	31 May 1905		67		16	16	4.19
Poland	121	32.5	2 May 1919		53		19	17	3.12
Portugal	36	9.6	13 May 1791		181		54	49	3.69
Romania	92	20.3	25 Jan. 1881	(1941–47) [g]	92	(87)	30	27	3.22
Spain	195	33.3	28 Sep. 1779 [i]	(1898–99) [g]	193	(192)	65	56	3.43
Sweden	174	8.1	29 Apr. 1814		158		40	36	4.39
Switzerland	16	6.3	29 June 1853		119		33	31	3.84
Two Sicilies	—	—	25 Jan. 1832	2–6 Nov. 1860 [h]	28		10	8	3.50
United Kingdom	94	55.7	1 June 1785	(1812–15) [g]	187	(184)	57	52	3.54
USSR (Russia)	8,649	242.8	19 Dec. 1780 [i]	(1917–33) [g]	192	(150) [j]	65	54	2.78
Vatican City	—	—	19 Aug. 1848 24 Dec. 1941	17 Aug. 1867 8 July 1944 [h]	21		10	7	3.00
Yugoslavia	99	20.5	10 Nov. 1882		90		32	28	3.21
Total					3,063	(2,885)	955	858	3.36

Middle East and North Africa									
Algeria	920	13.8	17 Dec. 1962	(6 June 1967) [g]	4		2	2	2.00
Bahrain	0.23	(215,000)	17 Feb. 1972		1		1	1	1.00
Egypt	387	34.2	17 Mar. 1849	(6 June 1967) [g]	118		37	36	3.28
Iran (Persia)	636	29.5	11 June 1883		89		35	31	2.87
Iraq	168	9.8	18 June 1931	(6 June 1967) [g]	36		11	10	3.60
Israel	8	3.0	28 Mar. 1949		24		5	5	4.80
Jordan	38	2.4	24 Feb. 1950		23		10	9	2.56
Kuwait	6	(770,000)	18 Oct. 1961		11		5	5	2.20
Lebanon	4	2.9	19 Nov. 1942		30		9	9	3.33
Libya	679	1.9	6 Mar. 1952		21		6	6	3.50
Morocco	172	15.8	29 Sep. 1906		66		19	18	3.67
Oman	82	(660,000)	17 Apr. 1972		1		1	1	1.00
Qatar	8	(79,000)	19 Mar. 1972		1		1	1	1.00
Saudi Arabia	830	5.5	4 Feb. 1940		33		12	11	3.00
Sudan	967	15.8	17 Mar. 1956	(1967–72) [g]	17	(12)	6	6	2.00
Syria	71	6.3	30 Nov. 1942	(1958–62; 6 June 1967) [g]	24	(20)	8	7	2.86
Tunisia	63	5.2	6 June 1956		16		6	6	2.67
Turkey	301	35.2	13 Sep. 1831	(1917–27) [g]	141	(131)	41	38	3.45
United Arab Emirates	32	(193,000)	20 Mar. 1972		1		1	1	1.00
Yemen Arab Republic	75	5.9	30 Sep. 1946	(1967–72) [g]	26	(21)	8	7	3.00
Total					683	(659)	224	210	3.14
Sub-Saharan Africa									
Botswana (Bechuanaland)	232	(620,000)	14 Sep. 1971		1		1	1	1.00
Burundi	11	3.6	17 Jan. 1963		10		4	4	2.50
Cameroon	183	5.8	9 June 1960		12		4	4	3.00
Central African Republic	241	1.5	6 Jan. 1961		12		5	5	2.40
Chad	496	3.7	9 Jan. 1961		12		6	6	2.00
Congo (Brazzaville)	132	(940,000)	23 Dec. 1960	15 Aug. 1965 [g]	4		2	2	2.00

Table A-2 (Continued)

A Country	B Area (square miles in thousands)	C Population, 1970 (millions)	D Commencement of Diplomatic Relations [a]	E Suspension and Termination of Diplomatic Relations	F Duration of Diplomatic Relations (full years)		G Number of Chiefs of Mission		H Average Length of Service (years) [f]
					Total [b]	Net [c]	Nom [d]	Ser [e]	
Sub-Saharan Africa (Continued)									
Dahomey	43	2.5	26 Nov. 1960		12		5	5	2.40
Equatorial Guinea	11	(280,000)	21 Nov. 1968		4		3	3	1.33
Ethiopia	472	25.3	6 July 1909	(1937–43) [g]	63	(45)	13	13	3.46
Gabon	103	(490,000)	13 Jan. 1961		12		5	5	2.40
Gambia	4	(360,000)	9 Aug. 1965		7		4	4	1.75
Ghana	92	9.0	12 Mar. 1957		16		8	8	2.00
Guinea	95	3.9	30 July 1959		13		6	6	2.17
Ivory Coast	125	4.2	20 Nov. 1960		12		4	4	3.00
Kenya	225	11.2	2 Mar. 1964		9		3	3	3.00
Lesotho	12	1.0	23 Sep. 1971		1		1	1	1.00
Liberia	43	1.5	23 Feb. 1864		109		38	32	3.41
Madagascar (Malagasy)	227	7.3	5 Oct. 1960		12		5	5	2.40
Malawi	45	4.4	8 July 1964		8		3	3	2.67
Mali	479	5.1	17 Jan. 1961		12		6	5	2.40
Mauritania	398	1.2	28 Nov. 1960	(1967–71) [g]	12	(8)	4	4	2.00
Mauritius	0.72	(840,000)	29 July 1968		4		2	2	2.00
Niger	489	3.8	23 Nov. 1960		12		5	5	2.40
Nigeria	357	55.1	4 Oct. 1960		12		4	4	3.00
Rwanda	10	3.6	19 Apr. 1963		9		3	3	3.00
Senegal	76	3.9	31 Oct. 1960		12		6	6	2.00
Sierra Leone	28	2.6	9 June 1961		11		5	4	2.75

Somalia	246	2.8	11 July 1960		12		5	5	2.40
South Africa	471 [k]	21.5 [k]	18 Feb. 1930		43		13	13	3.31
Swaziland	7	(420,000)	3 Nov. 1971		1		1	1	1.00
Tanzania	363	13.3	3 Oct. 1962		10		4	4	2.50
Togo	22	1.9	22 Aug. 1960		12		5	5	2.40
Uganda	91	9.8	14 Jan. 1963		10		4	4	2.50
Upper Volta	106	5.1	6 Dec. 1960		12		5	5	2.40
Zaire (Congo/Leopoldville)	906	17.8	25 July 1960		12		5	5	2.40
Zambia	291	4.2	24 Mar. 1965		8		3	3	2.67
Total					533	(511)	200	192	2.66
			Asia and Pacific						
Afghanistan	250	17.4	4 May 1935		37		11	11	3.36
Australia	3,000	12.6	17 July 1940		32		14	13	2.46
Bangladesh	55	74.0	11 Sep. 1973 [i]		—		1	0	—
Burma	262	28.0	3 Mar. 1948		25		10	10	2.50
China	14 [l]	14.6 [l]	12 June 1844		128		40	32	4.00
Fiji	7	(520,000)	22 May 1972		1		1	1	1.00
Hawaii	—	—	20 Dec. 1853	12 Aug. 1898 [h]	44		15	13	3.38
India	1,262	547.0	1 July 1947		25		10	10	2.50
Indonesia	736	120.0	30 Dec. 1949		23		6	6	3.83
Japan	143	103.5	5 Nov. 1859	(1941–52) [g]	113	(102)	32	31	3.29
Khmer Republic (Cambodia)	70	7.0	11 July 1950		22		7	6	3.67
Korea	38	31.8	20 May 1883 20 Apr. 1949	17 Nov. 1905 [h]	45		17	16	2.81
Laos	91	3.0	29 Dec. 1950		22		8	8	2.75
Malaysia	128	11.0	4 Sep. 1957		15		5	5	3.00
Maldives	0.12	(111,000)	9 Apr. 1966		6		4	4	1.50
Nepal	54	11.3	3 May 1948		24		8	8	3.00
New Zealand	104	2.8	24 Apr. 1942		30		12	11	2.73
Pakistan	310	60.0	26 Feb. 1948		25		11	9	2.78

Table A-2 (Continued)

A Country	B Area (square miles in thou-sands)	C Population, 1970 (millions)	D Commencement of Diplomatic Relations [a]	E Suspension and Termination of Diplomatic Relations	F Duration of Diplomatic Relations (full years)		G Number of Chiefs of Mission		H Average Length of Service (years) [f]
					Total [b]	Net [c]	Nom [d]	Ser [e]	
			Asia and Pacific (Continued)						
Philippines	116	38.0	4 July 1946		26		12	12	2.17
Singapore	0.23	2.0	8 Dec. 1966		6		3	3	2.00
Sri Lanka (Ceylon)	25	12.8	3 Aug. 1948		24		11	11	2.18
Thailand (Siam)	198	36.0	23 Oct. 1882	(1941–46) [g]	90	(86)	29	26	3.31
Tonga	0.27	(87,000)	6 Nov. 1972		—		1	1	—
Vietnam	67	18.0	22 Oct. 1950		22		8	8	2.75
Western Samoa	1	(146,000)	14 July 1971		1		1	1	1.00
Total					786	(771)	277	256	3.01

[a] Dates are those of first presentation of diplomatic credentials.

[b] Total number of years since commencement of United States diplomatic relations (to March 1973).

[c] Net number of years during which United States maintained diplomatic relations.

[d] Nominated for diplomatic appointment.

[e] Net number of appointees who actually served in diplomatic appointments.

[f] Computation based on number of diplomats who actually served during net number of years of diplomatic relations as given in parentheses.

[g] Dates in parentheses indicate temporary suspension of diplomatic relations or withdrawal of mission as of 30 March 1973. By 1975, relations were revived with Algeria, Egypt, and Syria, and the United States mission to Uganda was closed in November 1973.

[h] Dates indicate termination of diplomatic relations.

[i] Date given is for nomination/appointment of first emissary—diplomat not formally received, date of reception not known, or appointment pending as of March 1973.

[j] Also no emissary sent to Prussia 1801–1835 or to Russia 1783–1809.

[k] Includes Southwest Africa.

[l] Figures for area and population are for Nationalist China (Taiwan).

Source: Area and population figures are from U.S., Department of State, *World Data Handbook—Issues* (1972).

Table A-3

POTENTIAL ADDITIONS TO THE U.S. DIPLOMATIC COMMUNITY

A Country	B Area (square miles in thousands)	C Population 1970 (millions)	D Dependency of (where pertinent)
Members of United Nations [a]			
Bahamas [b]	4	(145,000)	
Bhutan	18	(870,000)	
Byelorussia	80	8.8	U S S R
China (People's Republic) [c]	3,700	800.0	
Germany (East—DRG) [d]	42	17.1	
Mongolia	604	1.3	
Ukraine	232	46.4	U S S R
Yemen (Aden)	111	1.3	
Others			
Western Hemisphere			
British Honduras (Belize)	9	(120,000)	United Kingdom
French Guiana	35	(51,000)	France
Puerto Rico	3.5	2.8	United States
Surinam (Dutch Guiana)	63	(400,000)	Netherlands
Virgin Islands	0.1	(60,000)	United States
Europe			
Andorra	0.2	(19,500)	
Liechtenstein	0.06	(21,000)	
Monaco	0.4	(23,000)	
San Marino	0.02	(19,000)	
Vatican City	0.1	(1,000)	
Sub-Saharan Africa			
Afars and Issas	9	(130,000)	France
Angola [e]	481	5.7	Portugal
Camoro Islands	0.84	(270,000)	France
Cape Verde Islands	1.6	(272,000)	Portugal
Mozambique [e]	302	7.7	Portugal
Namibia/Southwest Africa	318	(750,000)	South Africa
Portuguese Guinea (Bissau) [e]	14	(550,000)	Portugal
Reunion	1	(460,000)	France
Rhodesia [f]	150	5.3	
Seychelles	0.16	(50,000)	United Kingdom
Spanish Sahara	103	(60,000)	Spain

Table A-3 (Continued)

A Country	B Area (square miles in thousands)	C Population 1970 (millions)	D Dependency of (where pertinent)
Asia			
Brunei (Borneo)	2.2	(100,000)	United Kingdom
Hong Kong	0.4	3.9	United Kingdom
Korea (North)	47	14.5	
Sikkim	2.7	(179,000)	India
Vietnam (North)	61	20.0	
Pacific			
American Samoa	0.08	(30,000)	United States
Cook Islands	0.09	(20,000)	New Zealand
French Polynesia	1.5	(98,000)	France
Gilbert and Ellis	0.3	(55,000)	United Kingdom
Guam	0.2	(85,000)	United States
Micronesia	0.7	(102,000)	United States
Nauru [g]	0.008	(7,000)	Australia
New Caledonia	8.5	(107,000)	France
New Hebrides	5.7	(84,000)	United Kingdom
Niue	0.1	(6,000)	New Zealand
Papua/New Guinea	183.5	2.4	Australia
Pitcairn	0.02	(124)	United Kingdom
Solomon Islands	11.5	(161,000)	United Kingdom
Tokelau	0.004	(2,000)	New Zealand
Wallis Futuna	0.09	(9,000)	France

[a] The United States had not established normal diplomatic relations by March 1973.

[b] The United States established diplomatic relations in 1973, after 31 March.

[c] A special "liaison" mission was established in Peking in 1973.

[d] The United States established diplomatic relations in 1974.

[e] Independence granted or promised in 1974 subsequent to March 1973.

[f] Southern Rhodesia declared its independence in November 1965.

[g] Nauru became independent in 1968, but U.S. relations handled by embassy in Australia.

Source: U.S., Department of State, *World Data Handbook—Issues* (1972).

Table A-4

SENIOR DEPARTMENT OF STATE OFFICERS AND CHIEFS OF DIPLOMATIC MISSIONS[a] BY CATEGORIES OF APPOINTMENT AND WITH CAREER STATUS

	A Department of State[b]				B Chiefs of Mission to Foreign Governments[c]			
Decade	No.	U[f]	C[g]	NC[h]	No.	U	C	NC
1778–79					2	2		
1780–89	1	1			5	5		
1790–99	2	2			17	17		
1800–09	3	3			10	10		
1810–19	2	2			17	17		
1820–29	2	2			40	40		
1830–39	3	3			46	46		
1840–49	5	5			90	90		
1850–59	8	8			107	107		
1860–69	8	8			169	169		
1870–79	9	9			93	93		
1880–89	15	15			164	164		
1890–99	17	17			149	149		
1900–09	11	10	1		150	150		
1910–19	12	7	1	4	123	51	11	61
1920–29	25		12	13	143		64	79
1930–39	21		6	15	176		82	94
1940–49	47		14	33	233		149	84
1950–59	72		35	37	279		190	89
1960–69	88		32	56	388		249	139
1970–73	13		7	6	96		65	31
Total	364	92	108	164	2,497	1,110	810	577
Percent		25.27	29.67	45.06		44.45	32.44	23.11
Overall Percent	12.44				85.34			

[a] Statistics represent number of nominations/appointments, not individual appointees.

[b] See Table A–6 for detailed breakdown.

[c] See Table A–5 for breakdown by country to which appointed.

[d] Begun with President Truman; none appointed by President Eisenhower.

[e] Also see Table A–5 for countries to which women were appointed.

C Chiefs of Mission to International Organizations			D Ambassadors at Large[d]			E	F Career Status			G Sex[e]	
No.	C	NC	No.	C	NC	Total	U	C	NC	M[i]	F[j]
						2	2			2	
						6	6			6	
						19	19			19	
						13	13			13	
						19	19			19	
						42	42			42	
						49	49			49	
						95	95			95	
						115	115			115	
						177	177			177	
						102	102			102	
						179	179			179	
						166	166			166	
						161	160	1		161	
						135	58	12	65	135	
						168		76	92	168	
						197		88	109	195	2
6	2	4	1		1	287		165	122	285	2
11	1	10				362		226	136	358	4
31	11	20	7	1	6	514		293	221	506	8
7	1	6	2	1	1	118		74	44	115	3
55	15	40	10	2	8	2,926	1,202	935	789	2,907	19
	27.27	72.73		20.00	80.00						
.88			00.34			100.00	41.08	31.95	26.97	99.35	00.65

f Pre–1915 Undesignated Appointees.

g Careerists.

h Noncareerists (post–1915).

i Male.

j Female.

Table A-5

APPOINTMENT OF U.S. CHIEFS OF MISSION TO FOREIGN GOVERNMENTS, BY DECADES

A Country	B First Appointment[a]	C Decades											
		1778–79	1780–89	1790–99	1800–09	1810–19	1820–29	1830–39	1840–49	1850–59	1860–69	1870–79	1880–89
Afghanistan	4 May 1935												
Albania (1922–1939)[b]	4 Dec. 1922												
Algeria	17 Dec. 1962												
Argentina	27 Dec. 1823						2	3	2	6	5	3	2
Australia	17 July 1940												
Austria	7 Nov. 1838							1	3	4	12	3	6
Bahrain	17 Feb. 1972												
Bangladesh	11 Sep. 1973[c]												
Barbados	27 Nov. 1967												
Belgium	25 Sep. 1832							3	2	3	2	4	5
Bolivia	3 Jan. 1849								2	4	5	3	7
Botswana (Bechuanaland)	14 Sep. 1971												
Brazil	29 Oct. 1825						2	2	3	3	3	2	3
Bulgaria	19 Sep. 1903												
Burma	3 Mar. 1948												
Burundi	17 Jan. 1963												
Cameroon	9 June 1960												
Canada	1 June 1927												
Central African Republic	6 Jan. 1961												
Chad	9 Jan. 1961												
Chile	23 Apr. 1824						2	2	4	3	2	4	4
China	12 June 1844								4	8	4	2	3
Colombia	16 Dec. 1823						4	2	3	5	5	2	5
Congo (Brazzaville)	23 Dec. 1960												
Costa Rica	14 Sep. 1858									4	4	3	2
Cuba	27 May 1902												
Cyprus	19 Sep. 1960												
Czechoslovakia	11 June 1919												
Dahomey	26 Nov. 1960												
Denmark	20 Sep. 1827						1	1	4	4	4	1	7
Dominican Republic	26 Mar. 1884												3
Ecuador	12 Aug. 1848								2	3	8	3	0
Egypt	17 Mar. 1849								1	2	1	4	4
El Salvador	15 June 1863[d]									2	4	3	2
Equatorial Guinea	21 Nov. 1968												
Estonia (1922–1940)[b]	20 Nov. 1922												
Ethiopia	6 July 1909												
Fiji	22 May 1972												

C Decades									D Career Status			E	F
1890–99	1900–09	1910–19	1920–29	1930–39	1940–49	1950–59	1960–69	1970–73	Pre-1915	Career	Non-career	Women	Total
				1	4	4	2	0		9	2		11
			2	3	—	—	—	—		2	3		5
							2	0		2			2
2	5	3	3	2	4	3	5	0	32	11	7		50
					6	3	4	1		4	10		14
3	4	1	2	4	1	3	3	0	36	8	6		50
								1		1			1
								1		1			1
							2	0		1	1	1	2
3	2	3	3	3	5	4	3	1	26	7	13		46
4	2	3	3	5	4	4	4	0	28	13	9		50
								1			1		1
4	3	1	0	2	3	5	3	1	25	10	5	1	40
	6	2	2	3	2	1	3	1	7	9	4	1	20
					1	5	3	1		9	1		10
							3	1		3	1		4
							3	1		3	1		4
			1	5	4	4	4	0		9	9		18
							4	1		5			5
							5	1		6			6
3	4	1	2	4	0	3	4	1	27	7	9		43
3	3	1	4	0	3	2	3	0	27	6	7		40
2	5	3	2	3	3	5	4	1	34	12	8		54
							2	0		2			2
4	0	2	2	4	7	4	2	2	18	11	11		40
	3	3	3	3	4	4	—	—	4	7	9		20
							3	0		3			3
		1	1	5	4	3	5	1		13	7		20
							4	1		5			5
2	2	1	3	5	3	2	4	1	25	5	15	3	45
3	3	3	2	2	6	3	5	0	10	15	5		30
4	2	3	1	4	2	3	4	1	24	10	6		40
5	3	2	3	2	4	2	4	0	20	8	9		37
4	2	1	4	3	4	5	3	1	17	13	8		38
							2	1		3			3
			1	5	—	—	—	—		5	1		6
	1	0	1	1	3	3	3	1	1	9	3		13
								1			1		1

Table A-5 (Continued)

APPOINTMENT OF U.S. CHIEFS OF MISSION TO FOREIGN GOVERNMENT, BY DECADES

A Country	B First Appointment[a]	C Decades											
		1778–79	1780–89	1790–99	1800–09	1810–19	1820–29	1830–39	1840–49	1850–59	1860–69	1870–79	1880–89
Finland	19 Mar. 1920												
France	23 Mar. 1779	1	1	5	3	4	2	3	5	1	5	1	3
Gabon	13 Jan. 1961												
Gambia	9 Aug. 1965												
Germany (Prussia)	5 Dec. 1797			1	0	0	0	1	2	3	3	3	5
Ghana	12 Mar. 1957												
Greece	16 June 1868										2	2	3
Guatemala	3 May 1826						4	3	2	6	5	2	2
Guinea	30 July 1959												
Guyana	17 Aug. 1966												
Haiti	1 Oct. 1862										5	1	3
Hawaii (1853–1898)[b]	20 Dec. 1853									2	6	1	3
Honduras	10 Aug. 1858									3	7	2	2
Hungary	24 Jan. 1922												
Iceland	30 Sep. 1941												
India	1 July 1947												
Indonesia	30 Dec. 1949												
Iran (Persia)	11 June 1883												5
Iraq	18 June 1931												
Ireland	27 July 1927												
Israel	28 Mar. 1949												
Italy	15 Sep. 1840								4	3	1	0	4
Ivory Coast	20 Nov. 1960												
Jamaica	26 Nov. 1962												
Japan	5 Nov. 1859									1	4	1	2
Jordan	24 Feb. 1950												
Kenya	2 Mar. 1964												
Khmer Republic (Cambodia)	11 July 1950												
Korea (1883–1905; 1949—)	20 May 1883 20 Apr. 1949												4
Kuwait	18 Oct. 1961												
Laos	29 Dec. 1950												
Latvia (1922–1940)[b]	13 Nov. 1922												
Lebanon	19 Nov. 1942												
Lesotho	23 Sep. 1971												
Liberia	23 Feb. 1864										5	3	5
Libya	6 Mar. 1952												
Lithuania (1922–1940)[b]	5 Dec. 1922												
Luxembourg	17 July 1903												
Madagascar (Malagasy)	5 Oct. 1960												

C Decades									D Career Status			E	F
1890–99	1900–09	1910–19	1920–29	1930–39	1940–49	1950–59	1960–69	1970–73	Pre-1915	Career	Non-career	Women	Total
			4	3	2	4	4	1		9	9		18
3	3	3	2	2	3	3	3	2	41	3	14		58
							4	1		4	1		5
							3	1		2	2		4
3	2	2	3	3	0	3	3	1	24	3	11		38
						3	4	1		6	2	e	8
4	5	3	3	2	4	5	3	0	18	9	9		36
4	4	3	3	2	3	6	3	1	33	12	8		53
						1	3	2		3	3		6
							2	0		2			2
3	1	2	0	4	4	3	5	0	14	16	1		31
3	—	—	—	—	—	—	—	—	15				15
4	6	3	3	2	2	3	3	1	25	9	7		41
			3	2	4	2	2	0		9	4		13
					5	1	4	1		8	3		11
					2	4	3	1		2	8		10
					1	3	2	0		6			6
6	4	1	3	2	4	5	3	2	15	13	7		35
				2	5	3	1	—		11			11
			1	3	2	3	5	0		1	13		14
					1	3	1	0		3	2		5
4	5	2	4	2	2	3	3	1	22	7	9	1	38
							4	0		3	1		4
							4	0		1	3		4
3	3	4	5	2	0	3	3	1	16	6	10		32
						5	4	1		8	2		10
							3	0		1	2		3
						4	2	1		7			7
3	1	—	—	—	1	4	3	1	8	8	1		17
							4	1		5			5
						4	4	0		8			8
			1	5	—	—	—	—		5	1		6
					2	4	2	1		9			9
								1			1		1
4	2	5	3	2	2	3	3	1	21	5	12		38
						3	3	0		5	1		6
			1	4	—	—	—	—		3	2		5
	3	3	5	3	8	2	6	1	4	10	17	3	31
							4	1		3	2		5

Table A-5 (Continued)

APPOINTMENT OF U.S. CHIEFS OF MISSION TO FOREIGN GOVERNMENT, BY DECADES

A Country	B First Appointment[a]	C Decades 1778–79	1780–89	1790–99	1800–09	1810–19	1820–29	1830–39	1840–49	1850–59	1860–69	1870–79	1880–89
Malawi	8 July 1964												
Malaysia	4 Sep. 1957												
Maldives	9 Apr. 1966												
Mali	17 Jan. 1961												
Malta	5 Oct. 1965												
Mauritania	28 Nov. 1960												
Mauritius	29 July 1968												
Mexico	1 June 1825						4	1	5	4	8	1	5
Montenegro (1905–1918)[b]	30 Oct. 1905												
Morocco	29 Sep. 1906												
Nepal	3 May 1948												
Netherlands	19 Apr. 1782		1	3	0	2	2	2	2	3	5	4	4
New Zealand	24 Apr. 1942												
Nicaragua	18 Feb. 1852									7	5	2	2
Niger	23 Nov. 1960												
Nigeria	4 Oct. 1960												
Norway	31 May 1905												
Oman	17 Apr. 1972												
Pakistan	26 Feb. 1948												
Panama	17 Dec. 1903[c]												
Paraguay	26 Nov. 1861										2	2	5
Peru	21 May 1827						4	3	3	0	2	4	5
Philippines	4 July 1946												
Poland	2 May 1919												
Portugal	13 May 1791			3	1	1	3	1	4	3	2	3	4
Qatar	19 Mar. 1972												
Romania	25 Jan. 1881												3
Rwanda	19 Apr. 1963												
Saudi Arabia	4 Feb. 1940[d]												
Senegal	31 Oct. 1960												
Sierra Leone	9 June 1961												
Singapore	8 Dec. 1966												
Somalia	11 July 1960												
South Africa	18 Feb. 1930[d]												
Soviet Union (Russia)	19 Dec. 1780[c]		1	0	2	3	1	6	4	3	7	4	8
Spain	28 Sep. 1779[c]	1	0	3	2	2	3	2	4	4	7	2	6
Sri Lanka (Ceylon)	3 Aug. 1948												
Sudan	17 Mar. 1956												
Swaziland	3 Nov. 1971												
Sweden	29 Apr. 1814[d]		1	0	0	2	2	1	3	1	6	1	3
Switzerland	29 June 1853									1	3	2	3

C Decades 1890–99	1900–09	1910–19	1920–29	1930–39	1940–49	1950–59	1960–69	1970–73	D Career Status Pre-1915	Career	Non-career	E Women	F Total
							2	1		3			3
						2	3	0		5			5
							2	2		3	1		4
							5	1		6			6
							3	1		1	3		4
							3	1		3	1		4
							1	1		1	1		2
3	3	2	3	2	2	3	3	0	34	7	8		49
	3	3	1	—	—	—	—	—	5		2		7
	2	2	2	0	3	5	4	1	3	13	3		19
					2	5	1	0		4	4	1	8
2	2	3	3	3	4	2	3	0	33	6	11		50
					6	2	4	0		5	7		12
4	2	3	3	3	5	1	2	1	24	10	6		40
							4	1		3	2		5
							3	1		4			4
	2	2	1	3	3	2	3	0	3	5	8	3	16
								1		1			1
					3	4	4	0		6	5		11
	5	3	2	4	5	3	4	1	7	11	9		27
2	2	2	3	3	3	5	3	1	14	9	10		33
2	1	3	2	2	5	2	4	0	25	9	8		42
					3	5	4	0		4	8		12
		1	2	6	3	3	3	1		10	9		19
5	3	5	2	2	5	4	3	0	37	8	9		54
								1		1			1
4	8	2	3	3	1	3	3	0	16	9	5		30
							2	1		3			3
				1	4	3	3	1		10	2		12
							5	1		3	3		6
							3	2		4	1		5
							2	1		3			3
							4	1		5			5
			1	1	3	5	2	1		9	4		13
5	4	4	0	3	4	3	3	0	50	6	9		65
5	3	1	4	2	2	4	7	1	44	6	15		65
					2	4	3	2		8	3	1	11
						3	2	1		6			6
								1			1		1
2	1	1	2	4	3	4	2	1	23	12	5		40
4	5	2	4	1	1	3	4	0	19	6	8	1	33

Table A-5 (Continued)

APPOINTMENT OF U.S. CHIEFS OF MISSION TO FOREIGN GOVERNMENTS, BY DECADES

A Country	B First Appointment[a]	C Decades 1778–79	1780–89	1790–99	1800–09	1810–19	1820–29	1830–39	1840–49	1850–59	1860–69	1870–79	1880–89
Syria	30 Nov. 1942												
Tanzania	3 Oct. 1962												
Texas (1837–1845)[b]	23–27 Oct. 1837							1	5	—	—	—	—
Thailand (Siam)	23 Oct. 1882												2
Togo	22 Aug. 1960												
Tonga	6 Nov. 1972												
Trinidad and Tobago	1 Dec. 1962												
Tunisia	6 June 1956												
Turkey	13 Sep. 1831							2	2	2	2	4	5
Two Sicilies (1832–1860)[b]	25 Jan. 1832							2	5	3	—	—	—
Uganda	14 Jan. 1963												
United Arab Emirates	20 Mar. 1972												
United Kingdom	1 June 1785		1	2	2	3	4	3	4	3	4	6	3
Upper Volta	6 Dec. 1960												
Uruguay	2 Oct. 1867										3	2	5
Vatican City (1848–1867; 1941–1944)[b]	19 Aug. 1848								2	1	5	—	—
Venezuela	30 June 1835							1	4	2	6	3	4
Vietnam	22 Oct. 1950												
Western Samoa	14 July 1971												
Yemen Arab Republic	30 Sep. 1946												
Yugoslavia (Serbia)	10 Nov. 1882												3
Zaire (Congo/ Leopoldville)	25 July 1960												
Zambia	24 Mar. 1965												
Total		2	5	17	10	17	40	46	90	107	169	93	164
Percentage		00.08	00.20	00.68	00.40	00.68	01.60	01.84	03.60	04.29	06.77	03.72	06.57

[a] Dates are those of first presentation of diplomatic credentials.

[b] Diplomatic representation discontinued.

[c] Date given is for nomination/appointment of first emissary—diplomat not formally received, date of reception not known, or appointment pending as of March 1973.

C Decades									D Career Status			E	F
1890–99	1900–09	1910–19	1920–29	1930–39	1940–49	1950–59	1960–69	1970–73	Pre-1915	Career	Non-career	Women	Total
					3	3	2	0		7	1		8
							3	1		4			4
—	—	—	—	—	—	—	—	—	6				6
4	0	4	5	3	4	4	3	0	8	10	11	e	29
							4	1		5			5
								1			1		1
							3	1		1	3		4
						3	2	1		6			6
4	2	3	1	3	3	3	4	1	24	10	7		41
—	—	—	—	—	—	—	—	—	10				10
							2	2		2	2		4
								1		1			1
3	1	2	4	3	4	3	2	0	39		18		57
							4	1		4	1		5
2	2	3	3	5	5	4	5	0	16	20	3		39
—	—	—	—	—	1	1	—	—	8	1	1		10
4	2	4	2	3	1	4	4	1	29	8	8		45
						3	4	1		5	3		8
								1			1		1
					1	4	2	1		8			8
4	8	3	1	2	5	2	3	1	16	11	5		32
							5	0		5			5
							2	1		2	1	1	3
149	150	123	143	176	233	279	388	96	1,110	810	577	17	2,497
05.97	06.01	04.93	05.73	07.05	09.33	11.17	15.54	03.84	44.45	32.44	23.11		

[d] Discrepancy between date of first appointment (presentation of credentials, column B) and date of initial nomination/appointment (column C) is due to nonconsummation of earliest appointment, nonpresentation of credentials, or time lapse between appointment and presentation of credentials.

[e] Women ambassadors appointed after 30 March 1973.

TABLE A-6

SENIOR OFFICERS OF THE DEPARTMENT OF STATE CATEGORIES OF APPOINTMENT

(As of 31 March 1973)

	A Secretary of State[a]				B Deputy Secretary				C Under Secretary				D Under Secretary (functional)[b]			
Decade	U	C	NC	Tot.	U	C	NC	Tot.	U	C	NC	Tot.	U	C	NC	Tot.
1780–89	1			1												
1790–99	2			2												
1800–09	3			3												
1810–19	2			2												
1820–29	2			2												
1830–39	3			3												
1840–49	5			5												
1850–59	4			4												
1860–69	4			4												
1870–79	1			1												
1880–89	4			4												
1890–99	6			6												
1900–09	3			3												
1910–19	1		1	2							1	1				
1920–29			4	4						3	4	7				
1930–39			1	1						1	2	3				
1940–49			4	4						1	4	5			1	1
1950–59			2	2							5	5		2	3	5
1960–69			2	2							4	4		2	4	6
1970–73				n			2	2			1	1		1	2	3
Total	41	0	14	55	0	0	2	2	0	5	21	26	0	5	10	15
Percentage				15.11				00.55				07.14				04.12

E Deputy Under Secretary[c]				F Assistant Secretary (1853–1924)[d]				G Second Assistant Secretary[e]				H Third Assistant Secretary[e]				I Assistant Secretary (1924–1944)[f]			
U	C	NC	Tot.	U	C	NC	Tot.	U	C	NC	Tot.	U	C	NC	Tot.	U	C	NC	Tot.
				4			4												
				3			3	1[l]			1								
				5			5					3			3				
				7			7	1[l]			1	3			3				
				6			6					5			5				
				4			4					3	1		4				
				1	1		2					2		1	3				
					2		2						2	1	3		5	4	9
																	5	10	15
	1	1	2														1	2	3
	6	4	10																
	7	4	11																
0	14	9	23	30	3	0	33	2	0	0	2	16	3	2	21	0	11	16	27
			06.32				09.07				00.55				05.77				07.42

TABLE A-6 (Continued)

SENIOR OFFICERS OF THE DEPARTMENT OF STATE
CATEGORIES OF APPOINTMENT
(As of 31 March 1973)

	J Assistant Secretary (1944—) (functional)[g]				K Counselor				L Legal Adviser			
Decade	U	C	NC	Tot.	U	C	NC	Tot.	U	C	NC	Tot.
1780–89												
1790–99												
1800–09												
1810–19												
1820–29												
1830–39												
1840–49												
1850–59												
1860–69												
1870–79												
1880–89												
1890–99												
1900–09												
1910–19					3		1	4				
1920–29												
1930–39							1	1			1	1
1940–49		8	17	25		2	1	3			3	3
1950–59		22	19	41		3		3			3	3
1960–69		22	27	49		1	4	5			3	3
1970–73		6	1	7								
Total	0	58	64	122[o]	3	6	7	16	0	0	10	10
Percentage				33.52				04.40				02.75

[a] Not including Robert R. Livingston and John Jay, appointed as secretaries of foreign affairs by Continental Congress, before Constitution went into effect.

[b] Political, economic, and administrative affairs, and security assistance.

[c] Political, economic, and administrative affairs.

[d] Only one assistant secretary appointed at a time.

[e] Office of second assistant established in 1866 and of third assistant in 1874.

[f] Several assistant secretaries served simultaneously.

[g] As many as ten to twelve such assistant secretaries may serve simultaneously, heading the geographic and functional bureaus.

[h] Director of Bureau of German Affairs in early 1950s and administrator of Bureau of Security and Security and Consular Affairs in 1960s.

M Chief of Protocol				N Others[h]				O Totals				P
U	C	NC	Tot.	U	C	NC	Tot.	U[i]	C[j]	NC[k]	Total	Percentage
								1			1	00.28
								2			2	00.55
								3			3	00.82
								2			2	00.55
								2			2	00.55
								3			3	00.82
								5			5	01.37
								8			8	02.20
								8			8	02.20
								9			9	02.47
								15			15	04.12
								17			17	04.67
								10	1		11	03.02
								7	1	4	12	03.30
									12	13	25	06.87
									6	15	21	05.77
	1		1						14	33	47	12.91
	1	1	2		1		1		35	37	72	19.78
		6	6			2	2[m]		32	56	88	24.18
									7	6	13	03.57
0	2	7	9	0	1	2	3	92	108	164	364	
			02.47				00.82	25.27	29.67	45.06	100.00	100.00

[i] Pre-1915 undesignated appointees.

[j] Careerists.

[k] Noncareerists (post-1915).

[l] William Hunter served from 1866 to 1886 and Alvey A. Adee served from 1886 to 1924, when title changed to assistant secretary of state.

[m] First woman appointed to ranking Department of State office—Barbara Watson (administrator of Bureau of Security and Consular Affairs).

[n] Henry A. Kissinger appointed secretary of state after 31 March 1973.

[o] First woman assistant secretary appointed after 31 March 1973—Carol C. Laise (Public Affairs).

Table A-7

MULTIPLE DIPLOMATIC APPOINTMENTS

Part 1: Total Multiple Appointments, Sequential and Simultaneous

Category	Number of Multiple Appointments														
	2	3	4	5	6	7	8	9	10	11	12	13	14	15	Total
A Total multiple appointments[a]	334	124	58	41	28	15	5	2	2	2	1	0	1	1	614
B Multiple appointments as chief of mission[b]	296	100	62	30	14	12	3	1	2	1	1	0	1	1	524
C Net multiple appointments[c]	270	90	62	28	9	11	3	1	0	1	1	0	0	0	476

Part 2: Simultaneous Multiple Appointments

Category					Total
D Number of appointees (with simultaneous appointments)	69	24	3	5	84[d]
E Number of simultaneous appointments					101[d]
F Number of countries to which appointed	2	3	4	5	

Part 3: Summary—Total Appointees and Multiple Appointments

Category	Quantity		Career Status						Sex			
	No.	%	Pre-1915	%	Career	%	Non-Career	%	Male	%	Female[e]	%
G Total diplomatic appointees[f]	1,869	—	851	45.53	510	27.29	508	27.18	1,854	99.20	15	00.80
H Total multiple appointments (A above)	614	32.85	226	36.81	248	40.39	140	22.80	611	99.51	3	00.49
I Multiple appointment of chiefs of mission (B above)	524	28.04	198	37.79	227	43.32	99	18.89	521	99.43	3	00.57
J Net multiple appointments (C above)	476	25.47	169	35.50	216	45.38	91	19.12	473	99.37	3	00.63
K Simultaneous appointees (D above)	84	04.49	42	50.00	28	33.33	14	16.67	84	100.00	0	00.00

[a] Includes chiefs of mission, ambassadors at large, and senior Department of State officers.

[b] Includes chiefs of mission to foreign governments only.

[c] Includes chiefs of mission to foreign governments only, but excludes continuing appointments to same country and reappointments with changed rank.

[d] Difference is due to more than one simultaneous, multiple appointment of a given diplomat.

[e] To 31 March 1973; Ambassador Carol C. Laise was appointed assistant secretary of state after this date.

[f] Total number of appointees—single and multiple appointments—including chiefs of mission to foreign governments and international organizations, ambassadors at large, and senior members of Department of State.

Table A-8

REASONS FOR NONCONSUMMATION OF DIPLOMATIC APPOINTMENTS[a]

	Reasons for Not Serving in Appointment	Chiefs of Mission	Percentage
1	Nomination withdrawn from Senate	29	12.78
2	Nomination rejected by Senate	20	08.81
3	Nomination tabled by Senate	7	03.08
4	Nomination not confirmed by Senate	17	07.49
5	Nominee not commissioned	3	01.32
6	Letter of credence cancelled	1	00.44
7	Did not serve under appointment	18	07.93
8	Did not proceed to post	47	20.70
9	Did not present credentials	18	07.93
10	Appointee not acceptable *(non grata)*[b]	3	01.32
11	Appointment declined by nominee	50	22.03
12	Appointee died[c]	12	05.29
13	Others	2	00.88
	Total	227	100.00[d]

[a] Includes chiefs of missions to foreign governments only.

[b] Appointee not acceptable to receiving government and therefore did not commence service; distinguished from those who were declared *persona non grata* or whose recall was requested after they were serving as chiefs of mission.

[c] Appointee died before he presented his credentials and served; distinguished from those appointees who died in service.

[d] Constitutes 09.09 percent of all nominations/appointments.

Table A-9

NONCONSUMMATION OF DIPLOMATIC APPOINTMENTS BY DECADE

Period	Number	Period	Number
1778–79	0	1880–89	19
1780–89	1	1890–99	9
1790–99	3	1900–09	18
1800–09	3	1910–19	8
1810–19	1	1920–29	10
1820–29	9	1930–39	8
1830–39	9	1940–49	9
1840–49	8	1950–59	7
1850–59	23	1960–69	9
1860–69	56	1970–73	1
1870–79	16		
		Total	227

Table A-10

DURATION OF DIPLOMATIC MISSIONS TO FOREIGN GOVERNMENTS

Part 1 Years of Service			Part 2 Months of Service		
Years	Diplomats	Percentage	Months	Diplomats	Percentage
1	457	23.65	1	3	01.35
2	499	25.83	2	10	04.50
3	409	21.17	3	11	04.96
4	276	14.29	4	15	06.76
5	105	05.44	5	16	07.21
6	54	02.80	6	19	08.56
7	62	03.21	7	17	07.66
8	32	01.66	8	26	11.71
9	14	00.73	9	28	12.61
10	8	00.41	10	32	14.41
11	7	00.36	11	45	20.27
12	2	00.10	Total	222	100.00
13	2	00.10			
14	2	00.10			
15	1	00.05			
More than 15	2[a]	00.10			
Total	1,932	100.00			

Part 3
Summary Totals

Duration	Number	Percentage of All Nominees	Number	Percentage of Nominees Who Actually Served
Less than 1 year	222	08.89	222	10.31
More than 1 year	1,932	77.37	1,932	89.69
Still serving (31 March 1973)	113	04.53		
Nominees who did not serve	227	09.09		
Special cases	3	00.12		
Total	2,497	100.00	2,154	100.00

[a] These were for twenty-one years.

Table A-11

REASONS FOR TERMINATION OF DIPLOMATIC APPOINTMENT

	Reasons for Terminating Appointment	Chiefs of Mission	Percentage
1	Left post	1,191	55.27
2	Left country or capital	198	09.19
3	Presented recall or farewell audience[a]	446	20.69
4	Requested passports	1	00.05
5	Notified government of departure	2	00.09
6	Relinquished charge	86	03.99
7	Superseded	51	02.37
8	Notified government successor appointed	1	00.05
9	Appointment terminated	19	00.88
10	Mission terminated	2	00.09
11	Relieved of functions	3	00.14
12	Resigned	5	00.23
13	*Persona non grata* (dismissed)	5	00.23
14	Recall requested	9	00.42
15	Diplomatic relations interrupted[b]	16	00.74
16	Diplomatic relations severed[b]	13	00.60
17	Countries occupied by foreign powers[b]	9	00.42
18	Governments transferred location (governments in exile—World War II)[b]	6	00.28
19	Status of country changed[b]	9	00.42
20	Died	76	03.53
21	Assassinated	2	00.09
22	Others	5	00.23
	Total	2,155	100.00[c]
	Still serving on 31 March 1973	113	
	Total	2,268	

Note: In addition, Francis Dana (Russia) and John Jay (Spain) served abroad for several years, although they were not officially received; they simply returned to the United States.

[a] Recall presented personally or by written communication, had farewell audience, or was received in final interview.

[b] Figures do not reflect the total number of states to which these designations pertain, but only indicate those cases in which these reasons applied for the termination of diplomatic service.

[c] Percentage of all appointments is 86.30 percent. Those serving 31 March 1973 make up 04.53 percent of all appointments.

Table A-12

STATES OF ORIGIN OF U.S. DIPLOMATS

A State	B Year of Statehood	C Decades[a] 1778–79	1780–89	1790–99	1800–09	1810–19	1820–29	1830–39	1840–49	1850–59	1860–69	1870–79	1880–89
Alabama	1819								4	3		1	2
Alaska	1959												
Arizona	1912												
Arkansas	1836									5	2	1	1
California	1850									1	4	4	9
Colorado	1876									1			1
Connecticut	1788			2					1	3	3	1	
Delaware	1787				1	1	2			1	2		
Florida	1845							1		1		1	1
Georgia	1788					2			2	6	2	2	6
Hawaii	1959												
Idaho	1890												
Illinois	1818						1	1		2	9	9	9
Indiana	1816								5	4	6	5	12
Iowa	1846									2	4	2	1
Kansas	1861										2	4	3
Kentucky	1792						2	2	7	5	9	3	5
Louisiana	1812						1	2	4	7	2	5	10
Maine	1820						1	1	3	2	2	5	4
Maryland	1788			2	1	2	1	2	5	6	5	3	2
Massachusetts	1788		3	3	2	4	6	2	4	3	8	3	5
Michigan	1837								1		6	5	4
Minnesota	1858										2		1
Mississippi	1817						1	1	2	3		1	
Missouri	1821								1	1	7	2	2
Montana	1889												
Nebraska	1867												1
Nevada	1864										3		2
New Hampshire	1788							1		1	3		1
New Jersey	1787							2		3	2	1	6
New Mexico	1912												
New York	1788	1		2	2		4	4	10	11	28	9	27
North Carolina	1789						1	2	3	2	1	2	4
North Dakota	1889												
Ohio	1803						3	3	5	3	18	4	6
Oklahoma	1907												

C Decades[a]												
1890–99	1900–09	1910–19	1920–29	1930–39	1940–49	1950–59	1960–69	1970–73	D Total	E %	F Female	G Career
1				1	2	2	2		18	00.72		4
									0	00.00		0
1			1		6		4	1	13	00.52		7
3		1			1	3			17	00.68		4
15	2	4	5	6	14	17	31	11	123	04.93	3	68
		1	1		6	4	3		17	00.68		11
1		1	1	2	13	10	13	3	54	02.16	2	13
2	5	1		2	5				22	00.88		5
2				6	6	1	10	4	33	01.32	2	17
4		1	1		3	3	3	1	36	01.44		9
									0	00.00		0
									0	00.00		0
3	21	14	8	7	7	6	27	5	129	05.17		36
3	2	3		6	4	5	4	1	60	02.40	1	13
6	4	1	2	1	2	8	2		35	01.40		12
4	2	1	5	2	1	9	3		36	01.44		15
4	4	2	3	2	3	4	3		58	02.32		7
1		3	4	3		1	1		44	01.76		12
2			2	1	4	9	11		47	01.88	1	25
1	7	6	2	6	9	12	23	5	100	04.01		44
3	9	8	11	4	1	10	16	1	106	04.25	1	26
5	4	1	3	3	5	6	6		49	01.96		14
6	8	1	6	6	5	3	8		46	01.84	2	11
	2	1				1			12	00.48		1
4	2	5	5	3	6	3	6	2	49	01.96		16
2		1		2			3		8	00.32		3
	3			1		3	4		12	00.48		4
							4		9	00.36		4
7	4		2	1	4	11	7		42	01.68		14
5	10	7	12	5	8	7	11	7	86	03.44	1	29
		2		2	3		3		10	00.40		2
17	26	18	17	34	42	42	51	8	353	14.14	1	88
5	3			1	5	6	2	1	38	01.52		10
						1			1	00.04		0
5	2	5	7	13	8	4	4	4	94	03.77		26
		1	3		2	1	3		10	00.40		6

Table A-12 (Continued)

STATES OF ORIGIN OF U.S. DIPLOMATS

A State	B Year of Statehood	C Decades[a] 1778–79	1780–89	1790–99	1800–09	1810–19	1820–29	1830–39	1840–49	1850–59	1860–69	1870–79	1880–89
Oregon	1859										3		1
Pennsylvania	1787	1	1			2	2	6	9	10	13	9	5
Rhode Island	1790					2	2	1	1		2		2
South Carolina	1788			3	2		3	1	1	3		1	2
South Dakota	1889												
Tennessee	1796					1	2	1	4	6	6	2	4
Texas	1845									3	2	1	3
Utah	1896												
Vermont	1791						2		2		1		1
Virginia	1788		1	4	2		5	3	9	6	1	2	4
Washington	1889												
West Virginia	1863										2		
Wisconsin	1848									1	7	1	6
Wyoming	1890												
District of Columbia						1			1	1		2	6
Others				1		2	1	10	6	1	2	2	5
Totals		2	5	17	10	17	40	46	90	107	169	93	164

[a] Statistics are for chiefs of mission to foreign governments.

C Decades[a]												
1890–99	1900–09	1910–19	1920–29	1930–39	1940–49	1950–59	1960–69	1970–73	D Total	E %	F Female	G Career
4	3	2	1	1		3	2		20	00.80		4
13	8	8	16	13	14	6	21	7	164	06.57		39
1	3	1	3	1	6	6	1	2	34	01.36	1	16
		4		2	3	4	1		30	01.20		7
1		1	3	2			3		10	00.40		5
2	1	2	2	3	3	2	3		44	01.76		5
1		2	2	10	7	7	10	6	54	02.16		19
		1		4	1	4	2	2	14	00.56		7
2	1					2	1		12	00.48		0
3		2	1	3	4	6	17	6	79	03.16		27
2	5	1	3	1		3	2	2	19	00.76		9
2	1	3	1	1		3	4	1	18	00.72		5
2	1	2	1	2	3	1	1		28	01.12		2
			1	4		1		1	7	00.28		5
4	7	5	7	9	12	38	50	14	157	06.29	2	102
			1		5	1	2	1	40	01.60		2
149	150	123	143	176	233	279	388	96	2,497	99.97	17	810

Note: Original thirteen states are printed in italics.

Table A-13

AGE ON APPOINTMENT OF U.S. DIPLOMATS

Age[a]	Number of Appointees	Subtotal	Age	Number of Appointees	Subtotal
20	0		50	80	
21	0		51	92	
22	0		52	82	
23	0		53	78	
24	3	3	54	66	398
25	1		55	64	
26	4		56	52	
27	4		57	54	
28	7		58	39	
29	4	20	59	46	255
30	10		60	45	
31	19		61	37	
32	15		62	26	
33	14		63	20	
34	20	78	64	22	150
35	25		65	21	
36	37		66	17	
37	43		67	16	
38	28		68	11	
39	34	167	69	4	69
40	43		70	7	
41	58		71	5	
42	48		72	8	
43	53		73	2	
44	64	266	74	4	26
45	56		75	3	
46	64		76	0	
47	84		77	1	
48	84		78	1	
49	80	368	79	0	5
				Total	1,805

Summary Totals

Age Group	Number	Percentage
20s	23	01.27
30s	245	13.57
40s	634	35.13
50s	653	36.18
60s	219	12.13
70s	31	01.72
Total	1,805	100.00
Date of Birth Not Available	64	
Total	1,869	

[a] Age computed as of first nomination/appointment.

Table A-14

RANKS AND CAREER STATUS OF U.S. DIPLOMATS

A	B	C Diplomatic Ranks							D Career Status			E
Country	First Appointment[a]	Com.[b]	Chg.[c]	MP[d]	MR[e]	EE/MP[f]	AE/P[g]	O[h]	Pre-1915	Ca-reer	Non-career	Total
Afghanistan	4 May 1935					4	7			9	2	11
Albania (1922–1939)[i]	4 Dec. 1922					5				2	3	5
Algeria	17 Dec. 1962						2			2		2
Argentina	27 Dec. 1823		9	1	12	10	18		32	11	7	50
Australia	17 July 1940					3	11			4	10	14
Austria	7 Nov. 1838		6		1	34	9		36	8	6	50
Bahrain	17 Feb. 1972						1			1		1
Bangladesh	11 Sep. 1973[j]						1			1		1
Barbados	27 Nov. 1967						2			1	1	2
Belgium	25 Sep. 1832		7		10	10	19		26	7	13	46
Bolivia	3 Jan. 1849		5		16	17	12		28	13	9	50
Botswana (Bechuanaland)	14 Sep. 1971						1				1	1
Brazil	29 Oct. 1825		4			19	17		25	10	5	40
Bulgaria	19 Sep. 1903					13	1	6	7	9	4	20
Burma	3 Mar. 1948						10			9	1	10
Burundi	17 Jan. 1963					1	3			3	1	4
Cameroon	9 June 1960						4			3	1	4
Canada	1 June 1927					9	9			9	9	18
Central African Republic	6 Jan. 1961						5			5		5
Chad	9 Jan. 1961						6			6		6
Chile	23 Apr. 1824		6	1		21	15		27	7	9	43

China	12 June 1844	9				23	8		27	6	7	40
Colombia	16 Dec. 1823		9	1	11	20	13		34	12	8	54
Congo (Brazzaville)	23 Dec. 1960						2			2		2
Costa Rica	14 Sep. 1858				10	17	13		18	11	11	40
Cuba	27 May 1902					6	14		4	7	9	20
Cyprus	19 Sep. 1960						3			3		3
Czechoslovakia	11 June 1919					8	12			13	7	20
Dahomey	26 Nov. 1960						5			5		5
Denmark	20 Sep. 1827		12		10	15	8		25	5	15	45
Dominican Republic	26 Mar. 1884		6		4	8	12		10	15	5	30
Ecuador	12 Aug. 1848		4		12	14	10		24	10	6	40
Egypt	17 Mar. 1849					5	8	24	20	8	9	37
El Salvador	15 June 1863				8	18	12		17	13	8	38
Equatorial Guinea	21 Nov. 1968						3			3		3
Estonia (1922–1940) [i]	20 Nov. 1922					6				5	1	6
Ethiopia	6 July 1909				4	2	7		1	9	3	13
Fiji	22 May 1972						1				1	1
Finland	19 Mar. 1920		1			10	7			9	9	18
France	23 Mar. 1779		3	11		22	22		41	3	14	58
Gabon	13 Jan. 1961						5			4	1	5
Gambia	9 Aug. 1965						4			2	2	4
Germany (Prussia)	5 Dec. 1797		2	1		17	18		24	3	11	38
Ghana	12 Mar. 1957		2				6			6	2	8
Greece	16 June 1868				7	18	11		18	9	9	36
Guatemala	3 May 1826		10		11	19	13		33	12	8	53
Guinea	30 July 1959						6			3	3	6
Guyana	17 Aug. 1966						2			2		2
Haiti	1 Oct. 1862	2			9	9	11		14	16	1	31
Hawaii (1853–1898) [i]	20 Dec. 1853	3			9	3			15			15
Honduras	10 Aug. 1858				11	21	9		25	9	7	41
Hungary	24 Jan. 1922		1			10	2			9	4	13

Table A-14 (Continued)

A Country	B First Appointment[a]	C Diplomatic Ranks Com.[b]	Chg.[c]	MP[d]	MR[e]	EE/MP[f]	AE/P[g]	O[h]	D Career Status Pre-1915	Ca-reer	Non-career	E Total
Iceland	30 Sep. 1941					6	5			8	3	11
India	1 July 1947						10			2	8	10
Indonesia	30 Dec. 1949						6			6		6
Iran (Persia)	11 June 1883		2		8	11	14		15	13	7	35
Iraq	18 June 1931		1		2	2	6			11		11
Ireland	27 July 1927					6	8			1	13	14
Israel	28 Mar. 1949						5			3	2	5
Italy	15 Sep. 1840		7			6	25		22	7	9	38
Ivory Coast	20 Nov. 1960						4			3	1	4
Jamaica	26 Nov. 1962						4			1	3	4
Japan	5 Nov. 1859				5	7	20		16	6	10	32
Jordan	24 Feb. 1950					2	8			8	2	10
Kenya	2 Mar. 1964						3			1	2	3
Khmer Republic (Cambodia)	11 July 1950					1	6			7		7
Korea (1883–1905; 1949—)	20 May 1883/ 20 Apr. 1949				6	2	9		8	8	1	17
Kuwait	18 Oct. 1961		1				4			5		5
Laos	29 Dec. 1950					2	6			8		8
Latvia (1922–1940)[i]	13 Nov. 1922					6				5	1	6
Lebanon	19 Nov. 1942					2	6	1		9		9
Lesotho	23 Sep. 1971						1				1	1
Liberia	23 Feb. 1864	2			26	3	7		21	5	12	38

Libya	6 Mar. 1952					1	5			5	1	6
Lithuania (1922–1940) [i]	5 Dec. 1922						5			3	2	5
Luxembourg	17 July 1903		1			22	8		4	10	17	31
Madagascar (Malagasy)	5 Oct. 1960						5			3	2	5
Malawi	8 July 1964						3			3		3
Malaysia	4 Sep. 1957		1				4			5		5
Maldives	9 Apr. 1966						4			3	1	4
Mali	17 Jan. 1961						6			6		6
Malta	5 Oct. 1965						4			1	3	4
Mauritania	28 Nov. 1960						4			3	1	4
Mauritius	29 July 1968						2			1	1	2
Mexico	1 June 1825		2			29	18		34	7	8	49
Montenegro (1905–1918) [i]	30 Oct. 1905					7			5		2	7
Morocco	29 Sep. 1906		3				7	9	3	13	3	19
Nepal	3 May 1948					2	6			4	4	8
Netherlands	19 Apr. 1782		9	1	15	17	8		33	6	11	50
New Zealand	24 Apr. 1942					6	6			5	7	12
Nicaragua	18 Feb. 1852		2		10	21	7		24	10	6	40
Niger	23 Nov. 1960						5			3	2	5
Nigeria	4 Oct. 1960						4			4		4
Norway	31 May 1905					9	7		3	5	8	16
Oman	17 Apr. 1972						1			1		1
Pakistan	26 Feb. 1948						11			6	5	11
Panama	17 Dec. 1903 [j]					13	14		7	11	9	27
Paraguay	26 Nov. 1861	1	4		4	13	11		14	9	10	33
Peru	21 May 1827		10			16	16		25	9	8	42
Philippines	4 July 1946						12			4	8	12
Poland	2 May 1919					3	16			10	9	19
Portugal	13 May 1791		10	4	12	18	10		37	8	9	54
Qatar	19 Mar. 1972						1			1		1
Romania	25 Jan. 1881				2	25	2	1	16	9	5	30

Table A-14 (Continued)

A Country	B First Appointment[a]	C Diplomatic Ranks Com.[b]	Chg.[c]	MP[d]	MR[e]	EE/MP[f]	AE/P[g]	O[h]	D Career Status Pre-1915	Ca-reer	Non-career	E Total
Rwanda	19 Apr. 1963						3			3		3
Saudi Arabia	4 Feb. 1940				1	4	7			10	2	12
Senegal	31 Oct. 1960						6			3	3	6
Sierra Leone	9 June 1961						5			4	1	5
Singapore	8 Dec. 1966						3			3		3
Somalia	11 July 1960						5			5		5
South Africa	18 Feb. 1930				1	4	8			9	4	13
Soviet Union (Russia)	19 Dec. 1780[j]		1	2		39	22	1	50	6	9	65
Spain	28 Sep. 1779[j]		2	7	1	35	20		44	6	15	65
Sri Lanka (Ceylon)	3 Aug. 1948						11			8	3	11
Sudan	17 Mar. 1956		1				5			6		6
Swaziland	3 Nov. 1971						1				1	1
Sweden	29 Apr. 1814		7	2	10	14	7		23	12	5	40
Switzerland	29 June 1853		3		6	18	6		19	6	8	33
Syria	30 Nov. 1942					4	3	1		7	1	8
Tanzania	3 Oct. 1962						4			4		4
Texas (1837–1845)[i]	23–27 Oct. 1837		6						6			6
Thailand (Siam)	23 Oct. 1882		1		6	15	7		8	10	11	29
Togo	22 Aug. 1960						5			5		5
Tonga	6 Nov. 1972						1				1	1
Trinidad and Tobago	1 Dec. 1962						4			1	3	4
Tunisia	6 June 1956		1				5			6		6
Turkey	13 Sep. 1831		2		12	8	19		24	10	7	41

Two Sicilies (1832–1860) [i]	25 Jan. 1832		9		1				10			10
Uganda	14 Jan. 1963						4			2	2	4
United Arab Emirates	20 Mar. 1972						1			1		1
United Kingdom	1 June 1785		2	5		28	22		39		18	57
Upper Volta	6 Dec. 1960						5			4	1	5
Uruguay	2 Oct. 1867		4		6	15	14		16	20	3	39
Vatican City (1848–1867; 1941–1944) [i]	19 Aug. 1848		4		5		1		8	1	1	10
Venezuela	30 June 1835		6		13	15	11		29	8	8	45
Vietnam	22 Oct. 1950					1	7			5	3	8
Western Samoa	14 July 1971						1				1	1
Yemen Arab Republic	30 Sep. 1946					7	1			8		8
Yugoslavia (Serbia)	10 Nov. 1882				3	19	10		16	11	5	32
Zaire (Congo/Leopoldville)	25 July 1960						5			5		5
Zambia	24 Mar. 1965						3			2	1	3
Total		17	189	36	300	901	1,011	43	1,110	810	577	2,497
Percentage		00.68	07.57	01.44	12.02	36.08	40.49	01.72	44.45	32.44	23.11	100.00

[a] Dates are those of first presentation of diplomatic credentials.

[b] Commissioner.

[c] Chargé.

[d] Minister plenipotentiary.

[e] Minister resident.

[f] Envoy extraordinary and minister plenipotentiary.

[g] Ambassador extraordinary and plenipotentiary.

[h] Others—including diplomatic agents.

[i] Diplomatic representation discontinued.

[j] Date given is for nomination/appointment of first emissary. Diplomat not formally received, date of reception not known, or appointment pending as of March 1973.

Table A-15

MEMBERS OF CONGRESS AS DIPLOMATS[a]

Decade	A Total No. of Diplomatic Appointments[b] No.	Pre-1915	Career-ists	Non-careerists	B No. With Previous Congressional Service No.	Percentage of Total Appointees/Nominees	Percentage of Noncareer Appointees/Nominees	C No. Resigned From Congress For Diplomatic Appointment
1778–79	2	2			2	100.00	100.00	1
1780–89	6	6			4	66.67	66.67	1
1790–99	19	19			7	36.84	36.84	3
1800–09	13	13			9	69.23	69.23	4
1810–19	19	19			5	26.32	26.32	4
1820–29	42	42			19	45.24	45.24	10
1830–39	49	49			19	38.78	38.78	3
1840–49	95	95			38	40.00	40.00	6
1850–59	115	115			38	33.04	33.04	8
1860–69	177	177			45	25.42	25.42	6
1870–79	102	102			14	13.73	13.73	1
1880–89	179	179			23	12.85	12.85	6
1890–99	166	166			24	14.46	14.46	4
1900–09	161	160	1		2	01.24	01.25	1
1910–19	135	58	12	65	10	07.41	08.13	2
1920–29	168		76	92	5	02.98	05.43	1
1930–39	197		88	109	5	02.54	04.59	1
1940–49	287		165	122	5	01.74	04.10	1
1950–59	362		226	136	12	03.31	08.82	1
1960–69	514		293	221	5	00.97	02.26	
1970–73	118		74	44	3	02.54	06.82	2
Totals	2,926	1,202	935	789	294			66
Percentage		41.08	31.95	26.97				22.45

[a] Includes chiefs of mission to foreign governments and international organizations, ambassadors at large, and senior officers of the Department of State.

[b] From Table A-4, columns E and F.

[c] In cases of multiple appointments, only the initial appointment is represented in these figures.

[d] Chiefs of mission.

D Political Affiliation				E Congressional Chamber				F Sex		G Posts to Which Appointed[c]				
Dem.	Rep.	Whig	Other	Sen.	House	Both Houses	Cont. Cong.	Male	Female	COM[d]	SS[e]	US[f]	AS[g]	Others[h]
			2				2	2		2				
			4				4	4		3	1			
	1		6	2	2		3	7		6	1			
5	1		3	2	3	4		9		6	3			
5				2	1	2		5		5				
14	1	1	3	5	8	6		19		17	2			
15	1		3	6	8	5		19		18	1			
21	4	12	1	2	29	7		38		34	4			
23		11	4	8	26	4		38		35	2		1	
15	18	8	4	9	30	6		45		42	3			
2	11	1		3	11			14		14				
11	12			2	17	4		23		21	2			
10	14			5	17	2		24		23	1			
	2			1	1			2		1	1			
8	2				10			10		8	1		1	
	5			3	1	1		5		5				
5					4	1		4	1	3	1		1	
4	1			1	3	1		5		3	1			1
	12			4	6	2		11	1	8	1	1	1	1
4	1				4	1		5		3		1	1	
	3				3			3		1				2
142	89	33	30	55	184	46	9	292	2	258	25	2	5	4
48.30	30.27	11.23	10.20	18.71	62.59	15.65	03.06	99.32	00.68	87.76	08.50	00.68	01.70	01.36

[e] Secretaries of state.

[f] Under secretaries of state.

[g] Assistant secretaries of state.

[h] Chiefs of mission to international organizations.

Source: Identification of congressmen-diplomats and political information from John C. Butner (see chapter 6, note 6).

Table A-16

U.S. DIPLOMATS AS AUTHORS [a]

Decade	A Total Nominees/ Appointees [b]	B Authors, Poets, Dramatists, and Composers		C Sex		D Career Status		
		Number	Percentage	Male	Female	Pre-1915	Career	Non-career
1778–79	2	1	50.00	1		1		
1780–89	6	5	83.33	5		5		
1790–99	19	8	42.11	8		8		
1800–09	13	3	23.08	3		3		
1810–19	19	3	15.79	3		3		
1820–29	42	9	21.43	9		9		
1830–39	49	10	20.41	10		10		
1840–49	95	12	12.63	12		12		
1850–59	115	18	15.65	18		18		
1860–69	177	22	12.43	22		22		
1870–79	102	17	16.67	17		17		
1880–89	179	21	11.73	21		21		
1890–99	166	19	11.45	19		19		
1900–09	161	14	08.70	14		13	1	
1910–19	135	24	17.78	24			2	22
1920–29	168	19	11.31	19			7	12

1930–39	197	24	12.18	22	2		4	20
1940–49	287	44	15.33	43	1		20	24
1950–59	362	33	09.12	32	1		14	19
1960–69	514	36	07.00	36			9	27
1970–73	118	3	02.54	3			1	2
Total	2,926	345		341	4	161	58	126
Percentage (overall)		11.79						
Percentage (of authors)				98.84	01.16	46.67	16.81	36.52
Percentage (since 1910)							31.52	68.48

[a] Includes chiefs of mission to foreign governments and international organizations, ambassadors at large, and senior officers of Department of State. Authors counted only for decade of first appointment.

[b] From Table A-4, column E.

Source: Diplomat-authors identified from Richard Fyfe Boyce and Katherine Randall Boyce, *American Foreign Service Authors: A Bibliography* (Metuchen, N.J.: Scarecrow Press, 1973) and Elmer Plischke, "Bibliography on United States Diplomacy" section entitled "Bibliography of Autobiographies, Biographies, Commentaries, and Memoirs," in *Instruction in Diplomacy: The Liberal Arts Approach,* ed. by Smith Simpson, Monograph No. 13 of American Academy of Political and Social Science (Philadelphia: American Academy, 1972), pp. 299–342.